UNDERSTANDING LIFE-STYLE

The Psycho-Clarity Process

BY THE SAME AUTHORS

An Adlerian Lexicon: Fifty-nine Terms Associated with the Individual Psychology of Alfred Adler

The Individual Psychology Client Workbook

UNDERSTANDING LIFE-STYLE

The Psycho-Clarity Process

Robert L. Powers
Jane Griffith

Foreword by Kurt A. Adler, Ph.D., M.D.

THE AMERICAS INSTITUTE OF ADLERIAN STUDIES, LTD.
PUBLISHER

CHICAGO, ILLINOIS

Printed in the United States of America

First Printing, 1987

Library of Congress Cataloging-in-Publication Data

Powers, Robert L., 1929-
Understanding life-style

Bibliography: p.
Includes index.
1. Personality assessment. 2. Life style.
I. Griffith, Jane, 1934- . II. Title.
[DNLM: 1. Life Style. 2. Personality Assessment--methods.
3. Psychology, Clinical--methods. WM 105 P888u]
BF698.4.P64 1987 155,2'8 87-13146
ISBN 0-918287-02-2 (hardcover)
ISBN 0-918287-03-0 (paperback)

DEDICATION

Joseph Immanuel Meiers

1894 - 1985

Because life is hard we must struggle hard to overcome its difficulties.

One of Adler's earliest students, he was a model for the Adlerian practice of psychiatric medicine. As compassionate in his regard for an overburdened soul as he was unmoved by the alibis of a hesitant one, he knew how to spur both to further effort.

ACKNOWLEDGMENTS

We are grateful to our clients, who extended to us the privilege of entering their lives.

We are grateful to our students and our teachers, all of whom have taught us about life and life-style.

We are grateful to Heinz L. Ansbacher, the dean of Adlerian studies, who graciously reviewed and commented on the theoretical sections in Part I, who saved us from the embarrassment of numerous errors, and who encouraged us, not least by endorsing our neologism.

We are grateful to our other readers: Norman N. Silverman, of the faculties of Loyola University and the Alfred Adler Institute of Chicago, who gave careful reading to large parts of the text, and made many contributions to our thinking; our friend and fellow writer, Michael J. Vitali, student and *amateur* of Individual Psychology, who read everything, and helped us from start to finish; Daniel Knight, who lent us his skills for a final cleansing of the text, reading as only a professional copy editor could, and as only an affectionate friend would; and Cheryl H. Wergin, our associate in AIAS, Ltd., who read much of the text in its first drafts, and never gave up on us. Of course there were points at which we persisted against our protectors and did things our way; only we are responsible for the consequences, which include all the remaining errors both of omission and commission.

We are especially grateful: To the estate of Joseph I. Meiers for a bequest supporting our production of the manuscript; to the Ragdale Foundation of Lake Forest, Illinois, for sanctuary given to us during a crucial period of writing; and to the others, who know who they are, who sustained us by their interest, confidence, and enthusiasm.

Finally, we are grateful to each other, without whom neither of us would have, or could have, done this.

PREFACE

Our plan was to produce a small manual for users of *The Individual Psychology Client Workbook (IPCW)* (1986). We soon recognized that we were writing a book. The further we went the more the book seemed to require and the more it grew, until we finished (or, stopped) with the text you now have in hand. It is much more detailed and extensive than we pictured it to be in our original vision; however, it remains a text to accompany the *IPCW*, which is included here as an appendix.

Our book did not grow into a text on how to do psychotherapy; we assume that our readers are already competent for this work, or are otherwise preparing for it. We also assume a general understanding of Individual Psychology and its clinical applications. Now that we can see what we have written however, we believe that we have produced a useful and instructive introduction to Adlerian theory and practice for people trained in other schools of thought. If this belief turns out to be justified, and if our work inspires further study of Individual Psychology, all the better.

Adler wrote and taught during more than a third of this century; his ideas went on developing as he worked. Our references to his writings almost always cite one of the trilogy of works collected and edited by Heinz L. and Rowena R. Ansbacher. These books have made the full range of Adler's thought accessible to students; researchers will also find in them any information they may require concerning the original writings.

We offer *The Psycho-Clarity Process* as a method not only for *Understanding Life-Style* but also for encouraging people. It is a way for clinicians to rediscover with their clients a sense Adlerians call social interest, the sense of our being responsible for shaping the world we share.

Robert L. Powers
Jane Griffith

Chicago, Illinois

UNDERSTANDING LIFE-STYLE: THE PSYCHO-CLARITY PROCESS

Table of Contents

FOREWORD

> *Whoever has grasped and understood the concept of the unity of the personality will know that he must treat the individual's style of life, and not his symptoms.*
>
> *Alfred Adler (1963, p.viii)*

This text is a comprehensive study of a technique and method for personality assessment. It is designed to enable clinicians to understand individual uniqueness and to teach and inform them how to convey this understanding to their clients or patients.

Following a thorough in-depth explanation of the theoretical concepts of Alfred Adler's Individual Psychology, the authors apply these concepts to the practice of psychotherapy, specifically to the task of understanding the individual style of life.

Detailed case histories, enriched by frequent verbatim dialogues, are used to guide the reader through the assessment process. These histories are most elucidating to the reader, even as they were to the individuals whose cases were being discussed. In each instance the life-style of the person emerges with full clarity.

Moreover, the reports are instructive for demonstrating how concepts are actually applied in therapy, as well as how to use the process the authors present in the text.

For a full understanding of a person's life-style and personality that is consistent with the theoretical concepts of Individual Psychology, this book is of extreme value.

Kurt A. Adler, Ph.D., M.D.

March, 1987
New York, New York

UNDERSTANDING LIFE-STYLE

The Psycho-Clarity Process

A SPECIAL NOTE

Unless otherwise noted in the text, the citations of Alfred Adler refer to pages in THE INDIVIDUAL PSYCHOLOGY OF ALFRED ADLER, edited and annotated by Heinz L. Ansbacher, Ph.D. and Rowena R. Ansbacher, Ph.D. Harper and Row, Publishers, Inc., 1964.

PART I: ORIENTATION

The uncovering of the...style of life for the patient is the most important component in therapy.

Alfred Adler (p. 334)

Chapter 1: THE UNIQUE STYLE OF LIVING

This book comes out of the history of Alfred Adler's Individual Psychology, sometimes regarded as a division or subsection of "depth psychology." The history of depth psychology, in turn, has its place against a background of what Henri F. Ellenberger (1970) called *The Discovery of the Unconscious: The History and Evolution of Dynamic Psychiatry* in the title of his monumental study of the subject.

The modern chapter of this history lay in nineteenth-century medical experiments with hypnosis, which supported the hypothesis of an unconscious dimension of human experience and thought limiting, perhaps dictating, the forms of conscious processes. This idea became central in the search for a "cure" for a variety of peculiar patterns of behavior, then coming to be understood as "illnesses," even though examination of their sufferers did not yield relevant findings of physical disease.

Adler, Sigmund Freud, and Carl Jung were pioneers in the effort to carry medical diagnosis and treatment into the depth of this assumed unconscious dimension. The spatial metaphor of depth was meant to suggest a hidden spiritual (psychic) reality lying not only beneath the surface of observable behavior, but also beneath even our subjective, or conscious, experience of ourselves. If that hidden reality could be uncovered, discerned, and understood, it might yield the reason for (perhaps even the cause of) all the irrational, bizarre, and otherwise inexplicable actions human beings occasionally exhibit. Even more challenging was the thought that this hidden realm might be entered through some access into its secret dynamic, and that correctives could be applied to its disorders.

The language at hand for discussing the scope of this pioneering task was that of western religious and philosophical thought, a language of soul and body, mind and matter. It carried with it a variety of associations, Biblical, Platonic, Aristotelian, Newtonian, and Cartesian. Adapted to the frame of reference of the new discipline and profession of scientific medicine, especially of its newest branch, psychiatry (in which the cure of souls [Gr., *psyche*] was becoming a province of the physician [Gr., *iatros*]), it was a language rich with connotation, and therefore imprecise.

As pioneers, Adler, Freud, and Jung had also to incorporate the new Darwinian assumptions of a continuity between "nature" (already an ambiguous term) and "human nature" (an even more ambiguous one), and to do this against the dualism implied by much of their language. Further (and the importance of this is still far too little appreciated), they were working in a time of mounting democratic critiques of venerable institutions and hierarchical structures hitherto revered as inherent in the requirements of social order. Traditional ideas about the individual's place in society were being called into radical question, especially ideas of "high" and "low," "superior" and "inferior.."

They took on an enormous task, challenging all their considerable powers of intellect and creativity, appealing to their not inconsiderable personal ambitions, and drawing upon their often unexamined values and biases. It cannot be any wonder that they came to disagree.

Doctors Disagree

The major disagreements arose first between Adler and Freud; soon after, between Freud and Jung. Adler's writings do not record his disagreements with Jung's Analytic Psychology in any substantial detail. In his later writings Jung recorded his respect for Adler's work (while remaining critical of certain elements in it), and included a recommendation to his own students that they also study Adler.

The disagreements that interest us here, therefore, are those that ended the collaboration between Adler and Freud, and that led to the creation of Adler's Individual Psychology as a theoretical system distinct from Freud's Psychoanalysis.

In a rather rough abstraction from the ways in which their lives and their careers connected, impinged on one another, and diverged, we can locate these disagreements in three major areas: the field of inquiry; the framework for understanding; and the purpose, desired outcome, and method of corrective intervention.

Field of inquiry. For Freud it was physiological, instinctual, and internal. He wanted to identify universal structural determinants that could be seen as governing personal development in any society.

For Adler it was biological, cultural, and transactional. He was more interested in the varying historical circumstances that could be seen as limiting personal participation in social development.

Framework for understanding. Freud postulated instinctual forces that drive the person into inescapable conflict with the requirements of social living. This conflict is experienced internally as a tension between hungers for gratification and needs for security.

Adler assumed that the person, having evolved in the context and matrix of social living, which provides the distinctive ecological niche for human adaptation, is suited only to the life that social living requires.

Adler also recognized that social requirements, being symbolically transmitted and apprehended, are susceptible to misunderstandings and errors, both in their transmission and in their apprehension. He was unambiguous in arguing that the forms of social living, being subject to cultural variation and evolution, also require further development. To be well adapted to the requirements of social life is also, consequently, to be able to participate in this social development.

In spite of this, critics of Adler persist in reducing his description of the requirements for successful social adaptation to the level of a shallow prescription of conformity. These critics were and they remain unwilling, perhaps unable, to appreciate a perception of individual and society in ecological terms. (Seeing the relationship between individual and society in adversarial terms does not, however, seem philosophically questionable to them.)

Purpose, desired outcome, and method of corrective intervention. For Freud, troubled persons must gain the strength to accept a tragic demand, namely to sacrifice the largest part of gratification to security. The desired outcome of therapy is insight and resignation. The method of intervention involves a "transference" onto the physician of the patient's conflicting desires for gratification on the one hand and "dependency needs" on the other, all of which were originally focused on the parents. The conflicts are then "worked through" in the transference.

For Adler, troubled persons must gain clarity in their awareness of being participants, equally active with others in shaping the community to which they belong. The desired outcome is a liberated sense of engagement. The method of intervention provides an experience of collaboration with the physician, in which the patient discovers and rehearses what parents and other educators had failed adequately to cultivate, namely a clearer sense of choosing (therefore sometimes refusing) equally with others among the many opportunities for making useful contributions, and consequently for enjoying the satisfactions of effectiveness and participation.

In line with his positions in these three areas, Adler was suspicious of the metaphor of depth, which he used sparingly and ironically, and even then chiefly as a reference to *context* (*Zusammenhang*). By this he meant first, the particular context of the individual's unique style of living, providing the indivisible pattern of consistency connecting every movement of the person; and second, the larger context of the social or ecological situation in which the person's movement is indivisibly embedded. In this ecological emphasis he acknowledged his affinity to the Gestalt psychologists and their experiments in the perceptions of figure and ground.

The Assessment of Uniqueness

The ability to assess and understand an individual's unique style of living was therefore of central importance to Adler. It retained this importance for those who originally studied with him, and it is still central to those who are building upon and continuing to develop the implications and applications of his approach.

The question was always, How is this assessment to be done? Those who witnessed or experienced Adler's work, and whose reports we have, all included some admission to astonishment in their accounts of it. Rudolf Dreikurs, in an interview filmed long after the event (Allen, 1969), still sounded breathless as he recalled his skepticism on hearing Adler claim that all the information necessary for understanding a person could be obtained in one hour. Many of Dreikurs's students can recall, in a similar way, their first experience of seeing him prove that it could sometimes be learned in less than an hour.

The assessment of uniqueness was and still remains a difficult thing to teach. Adler called Individual Psychology a "science for the understanding of persons" (*Menschenkenntnis*). Because students find it so difficult to see how this understanding can identify the pattern of a person's movement, they often refer to its practice as "magic" when they first encounter it.

To consider a parallel, there is no one way to score the pattern of movement in dance. Although choreographers may employ their own systems of notation, none of these systems approaches the universality of a language, such as a language of musical notation. A musician reads a score, as an actor reads a script. In contrast to this, the dancer *follows* the movement of the choreographer. By analogy to psychotherapy, the client is at first the choreographer. The therapist is the dancer, following the pattern of movement, and sensing its logic and rhythm. As this is taking place their change of roles has already begun, as the client learns, even from the therapist's following the logic of the steps, how patterns of personal movement can come into harmony with larger circles of social movement.

But of course movement in the individual's unique style of living is not art for art's sake. Rather, "Human life...expresses itself in movement and direction toward [successful solutions]" (Adler, p. 163). The movement of a life is in the direction of a personally defined goal of success; any step in that movement is intelligible only as it is seen as serving to maintain the individual's line of direction toward that goal.

In an assessment of uniqueness one must therefore be prepared to see that "everything is in anything" (Powers, 1979) in a holistic rather than a linear apprehension. It defies the ordinary uses of language to speak of such a task. Since we must speak of it in order to teach it, we risk using artistic metaphor to avoid the greater risk of reducing the holistic to the linear.

We therefore sum up our difficulty by borrowing a classic exclamation and question from William Butler Yeats (Untermeyer, 1942, p. 128):

> O body swayed to music, O brightening glance,
> How can we know the dancer from the dance?

We must avoid thinking in terms of the life-style of a person apart from the person. A person does not *have* a life-style, in the sense of its being attached like a possession, a piece of clothing, or a shadow. It is closer to the sense of one's having an accent of speech, which may reveal something of the context in which one learned to talk. To understand life-style is to think in terms of movement and pattern. It is to recognize an indivisible person moving in a characteristic style in every situation, and to know how to identify every thought, feeling, and action of that person as having its place in coherence with this unmistakably unique pattern.

In fact, we perceive pattern and movement without being aware of it in our everyday identification of one another. Walking on the street we may recognize someone familiar to us long before we are able to distinguish the details of facial or other features. It may be someone whom we have not seen in years. Yet there is already something in gait, posture, and pace that we recognize. As we draw closer each newly revealed detail fits in the overall impression to confirm recognition: "Well, there's old Bob Taylor! I'd know him anywhere."

We also rely on our ability to perceive pattern and movement for a sense of predictability in our dealings with others. We are aware of certain probabilities as to how a person known to us will think, feel, and act in a given situation: "If George thinks you're loafing he'll be furious, and he'll fire you in a minute." We are also aware of how life-style shapes responses to the social world, independent of reality: "She's the sort of woman who could start a fight in an empty house" (Irish saying).

The Law of Movement

What psychologists do in the assessment of uniqueness is a refinement of the commonplace mode of perception and discrimination described above. Through the mastery of a set of skills and the practice of an imaginative empathy we seek to "get the sense" of an individual's "law of movement." When we understand this, we can see that in this person's situation (as this person experiences it) any behavior that seemed puzzling or even alien until now is in fact (given the "private sense" of this one human being) intelligent.

We define the key to an individual's law of movement by reference to belief and attitude, words connoting evaluation and predisposition. We want to evoke the image of a person's basic preparation for social living laid down in infancy, before language was available to express thought, before feelings were rehearsed out of sensation, and before action was independent of the random movements of trial and error. In that time before *a* time could be distinguished, we were already in a world of social being, already beginning to sense the extent of our being welcome or unwelcome in it in our striving. We were learning how to move in it wherever we had or could enlist the assent and support of others. We were alert to the extent to which we were unimpeded by opposition or reproach. We were moving within a genetically given range of possibilities, including a greater or lesser degree of activity that marked our efforts to make a place for ourselves among the others. We had a sense of what was possible, what was invited, what we might do to proceed. "Once upon a time," *in illo tempore* (Eliade, 1959, p. 21), we were sizing up our world, ourselves, and our prospects. We were beginning to shape our movement in harmony with evaluations we would later argue for in language and support by feelings. Our attitude (to borrow an image from sculpture) was displayed in our posture, that is, our readiness to move -- toward, away from, or against others.

In this movement of our early childhood each of us formed the prototype of a unique style of living. We were already inclined (another postural image) to see things in a particular way, and to appraise our opportunities on the basis of our expectations of what would unfold. As we developed out of infancy our experiences were more and more subject to these expectations, and our perceptions were more and more selected and shaped to conform with them. We were reaching the point where a particular impression of a single event could be chosen to illustrate and confirm the validity of the general principles on which we were basing our efforts. Adler therefore looked to the person's earliest recollections from childhood to locate the first notes of a melody that is by now fully developed and well rehearsed, in which a person continues to express an attitude toward all the experiences of life (p. 175). He attended to what was presented: The practiced tune (and tone), not only in its parts, but in the whole, and in its resonance of meanings.

Our way of persisting in these meanings, in efforts to make sense of the world, is revealed most clearly in exaggeration, and recognized most unmistakably by laughter. Not long ago the *New York Times* ran a photograph showing a man standing beside his expensive new car in an upper level of a parking garage. The rear end of the car was tilted up; the front end had broken a protective barrier, and had gone through an open space to rest on the roof of an adjoining structure just below. "My whole life has been like this," the man was quoted as saying. Common sense tells us that his whole life could not have been like this extraordinary incident, but his belief is independent of common sense. Understanding life-style depends on an ability to recognize the personal symbolism and attendant meanings that an individual can believe to be illustrated in a single, and sometimes exceptional, event.

The Unique Orientation

A child gives meaning to circumstances, and the meaning of life that is first a child's creation, serves as the starting point for a system of *orientation*. Such a system is the primary, inescapable, and essential basis for progress through the human world of symbols, values, and the uncertainties of choice, risk, and experimentation. Being the work of a child, it was at first narrowly conceived and only partly subject to the corrections of a larger world of social experience. "The truth emerges more readily from error than from confusion," said Francis Bacon at the dawn of the modern era. He was alluding to the intellectual situation of the experimental scientist; he could just as well have been reflecting on the existential situation of every child.

Adler recognized that the situation of any child was inherently different from the situation of any other: "It is a common fallacy to imagine that children of the same family are formed in the same environment" (p. 376). Not only are no two children born into the same environment, but no two are born into the same family. Each child coming into the world alters it by entering. It is not enough to ask how or to what extent parents and siblings share an influence on the child's development. By virtue of being born into the family a child has already changed the lives of both its parents and siblings. The first born changes the social status of the parents, ordaining husband and wife to the irrevocable social roles of mother and father. The second born dethrones the first from the eminence of onliness, and enters not only as a child but as one of the children (perhaps, if there are no others, as the one to be known as "the baby" forever after). And so on. Even in multiple births there is an ordinal position, and a meaning attached to it. (In the course of a public lecture, a famous physician and author reflected on her position as the second born of triplets, and on her experience of herself as squeezed between her older sister's claim to a position of prerogative and her younger sister's assignment to a position of indulgence.)

The law of movement is therefore applicable only to the single case, to the unique creation of an individual who works it out in a situation that is unlike any other. Where the situation supports efforts to move toward success, offers opportunities for participation, and conveys respect for the ways in which the child is able to make contributions, we expect the person's law of movement to tend toward the useful side of life in response to the encouragement. The child is likely to give a meaning to life that is generally useful in that it enables cooperative and respectful movement among others, and so provides the basis for an effective and satisfying adult development. To the extent that a person's basic convictions reflect this meaning, there is little or no reason to inquire into them, to examine their content, or to ask how or for what purpose they were formed.

Even in such a case a challenge requiring greater courage and a greater capacity for cooperation than the person's law of movement has encompassed may still present itself. Life-Style Assessment and psychotherapy may be useful for the recovery of equilibrium in such a crisis. In the absence of the shock of such a challenge to the style, people are free to go through life with biases intact, and with the happy ability to make friends, make a living, and make love.

There are, however, many childhood situations that can be seen only as "overburdened" (Adler, p. 367). A crushing sense of organ weakness or other disadvantage may be unrelieved by the presence of an ally, or by the inspiration to see what could be done to overcome it. A pattern of pampering may limit a child's sense of competence to a hazy awareness of how victories are gained by displays of suffering, weakness, accusation, or complaint. Any form of parental hatred or neglect may thwart efforts directed toward success in socially useful behavior, leaving only a negative sense of how triumphs can be won through maneuvers of conflict, revenge, or avoidance. We cannot expect a child's law of movement, if it was devised and rehearsed in adaptation to situations such as these, to rest on meanings other than those that are mostly safeguarding, private, and useless for a socially effective and satisfying life.

The basic discouragement of such a beginning enters into the person's development, which it then partly directs. A dread of further loss constricts the capacity to share the common sense of participation in the give and take of life, and fosters a private sense in its place. Possible difficulties appear as threatened defeats in a life-style which deviates more and more, by means of a variety of cautionary warnings and arguments, from the promise, the value, or even the possibility of cooperation and contribution.

Whatever probabilities may suggest themselves, it is important to resist an intimation of determinism. Any individual who comes to a counselor out of an overburdened and discouragenic background draws upon remnants of courage retained in hope (even if the hope is often disguised by expressions of suspicion and disdain). Such a move proceeds on the basis of some glimmer of an awareness, however reluctant, of having created a law of movement with a meaning that will not work.

There are myriad variations in the ways different individuals prepare themselves for life. Each of these is bound to incorporate some element of error. As children, none of us could have devised an encompassing and balanced view of life's meaning, or could have prepared ourselves for any and every contingency we might encounter in meeting life's challenges. A discrepancy between our practiced style of living and some demand for a creative solution to a novel and unexpected problem will present a crisis. A "good" childhood cannot prevent that; a "bad" childhood does not produce it. Whenever such a discrepancy occurs it reveals a failure to understand the extent to which all the problems of life, being social problems, require cooperation for their solution. Whether it is in a sudden shock of betrayed confidence, or the final culmination of despair over a chronic pattern of misfittedness, life does not yield; it is the life-style that is called into question.

The problem remains: How are we to derive an understanding of the unique style, and how are we to convey a useful awareness of its distortions to the person who resorts to us for the task of correcting errors and reconsidering goals through the processes of psychotherapy or other counseling? How, to quote "an English author" (whom Adler cited, but did not name), can we learn the way "to see with the eyes of another, to hear with the ears of another, to feel with the heart of another"(p. 135)?

Conclusion

In this chapter we have presented a brief review of Adler's concepts concerning life-style development, and an exposition to the ways in which the creative child gains an orientation in the world. At the same time, we have offered an orientation to the reader by which to approach the task of assessing life-style with an attitude of discovery and of enhanced respect for what the client has achieved out of the numberless possibilities open in the childhood situation.

In the first part of Chapter 2 we discuss the process we employ in the assessment of a life-style with the help of an illustrative case example. In the second part of Chapter 2 we review various instruments of assessment suggested by Adler and others. We then introduce the format on which the present text is based, namely, *The Individual Psychology Client Workbook*, or *IPCW*, written by us and published as a separate volume by AIAS, Ltd., in 1986. Because the *IPCW* provides the outline for the organization of the present book, there will be many quotations from it and references to it in the pages that follow; for this reason it is included here in its entirety as an appendix.

Chapter 2: PSYCHO-CLARITY AND THE PSYCHO-CLARITY PROCESS

In 1982 we coined and registered a new word: Psycho-Clarity. Like any other prospect for employment, it requires an introduction and a recommendation. After that, if it proves useful, it will speak for itself.

Neologisms appear whenever familiar terms are no longer equal to the tasks we set for them. The familiar term in this case, psychotherapy, is a word that we do not expect our new word to replace. Our hope is, rather, to enhance its meaning and to support a clearer use of it.

According to the *Oxford English Dictionary*, the term psychotherapy is itself a neologism, first used in 1904 as a simpler form for psychotherapeutics (meaning, in its original usage, the medical treatment of physical illnesses by psychological means). Subsequently psychotherapy came to refer to the process in which one person seeks the guidance of another in quest of relief from any of a variety of painful, often troublesome, feelings, thoughts, or actions.

The usefulness of this term remains limited, however, by its association to medical procedures, at least where these continue to be understood as *directed* by active persons (doctors) *toward* and *upon* passive ("patient") persons. Even some physicians have come to regard that model as deficient, but its implications continue to obscure an understanding of what is entailed in psychotherapy. Use of evocative but undefined medical metaphors of health, emotional or mental, also cloud a practical guiding image of the desired outcome of the process.

It therefore seems to us legitimate to reach for a new term to refer to the quality and form of a new relationship between client and clinician in psychological counseling, a new definition of the goals to guide that process, and a new expectation for its outcome.

The new relationship is characterized by *collaboration*. When we put the term psycho-clarity forward (Powers and Griffith, 1982), we wrote:

> The client is invited to help the therapist to see more clearly what is in the client's thought, feeling, and action, and what its effects are upon the social field.... Client and

> therapist are united in the effort to understand what is going on, what it goes on *for*, and what it costs to keep it going.... As the therapist comes to see more clearly, the client does as well.

We cautioned against the transaction typical of the more traditional approaches in therapy:

> Many therapists are trained as if their task were to pursue the goal of changing the client.... The therapist who wants the client to change is setting up for a fall. Only the client can decide when to change and what and how to change.

The new goal is one of *self-understanding*, without which a consideration of whatever might be changed is impossible. Therefore we went on to say:

> The psycho-clarity formula is: You cannot change your mind until you know your mind. You cannot know your mind until you can speak your mind, and your speech brings the private [sense] into the commonsense world. [When that occurs, your private sense of things] is no longer *unspeakable* [and, therefore, no longer *unthinkable*.]
>
> Therapy gives the client an opportunity to break the spell of the unspeakable by clarifying for the therapist [his or her private sense of what it is to be in the world]. When I know my mind I can see that while the past behavior [is now] *understandable*, it is no longer *necessary*.

The new outcome of the process is *freedom*. We concluded our 1982 article by saying:

> Only at this point is the client free to reconsider, and in that liberation may decide to do so.

Our word, psycho-clarity, is new; our emphasis on collaboration, self-understanding, and psychic liberation must be attributed to Adler who saw it first. In 1931 he stated it this way:

> Treatment itself is an exercise in cooperation and a test of cooperation.... The client must contribute his part to our common understanding. We must work out his attitutdes and difficulties together.... We must cooperate with him in finding his mistakes, both for his own benefit and the welfare of others.
>
> The usual treatment has been to attack the symptom. To this attitude Individual Psychology is entirely opposed.... What we must always look for is the purpose for which the symptom is adopted and the coherence of this purpose with

> the general goal of superiority.... With the change of the goal, the mental habits and attitudes will also change. The client will no longer need the old habits and attitudes, and new ones, fitted to his goal, will take their place (1980, pp. 72, 62-64).

"The Arrangement" in the case report that follows illustrates these concepts. At the conclusion of of our presentation of this case we will return to a discussion of the psycho-clarity process.

The Arrangement

A psychologist asked a fearful and hesitant, but intellectually vain, client, "Do you know the proverb, 'Nothing ventured, nothing gained'?" "Of course," the client replied. "Can you tell me what it means?" the therapist went on. "It's simple," the client explained patiently. "It means that if you don't try anything you won't fail." There was not a hint of guile or irony in his tone or his expression. He was innocent of how he had turned things around.

It was not a matter of organic damage, or a failure to understand the words. It was certainly not an intellectual inability to grasp the idea expressed by the proverb. It was, rather, a *use* of brain, understanding, and ability in the service of a basic and faulty attitude. What the client (whom we shall call Edward) said was true in a sense; the proverb allows for the negative implication he derived from it. *In a sense.* That is the key phrase. The sense he made of it is not the sense we commonly take from it.

Common sense is a sense we share with others, a feeling for the way life is shaped, for what it requires of us, and for what we have to offer in meeting the requirements. Edward's private sense led him into a private way of thinking that could not be shared. It was the basis for a private logic that could not be followed. In fact his private sense was opposed to the sense commonly expressed by use of the proverb, arguing against the courage required by life, and withholding assent from the willingness to take the risks and accept the setbacks entailed in any pursuit of success. The safeguards his private sense raised against his exaggerated opinion of the danger of defeat had become barriers against the demand to take part. His private argument concluded that the struggle to solve problems and overcome difficulty must be left to others. Finally (and for him, the worst of it), his sense of life did not work, and he was suffering.

Edward's safeguard against failure had failed. It could not protect him from being passed over for a desired promotion, it did not allow him to enjoy the company of friends, and it left him sexually impotent.

His wife was an affectionate, capable woman, who was advancing in her career. When he pointed to the jealousies of others and their failures to appreciate his brilliance as the reason for his difficulties, she was sympathetic. That didn't help. He only suspected that she must, secretly, be looking down on him. His safeguards did not protect him from this suspicion, or from the distance he began to feel between himself and his loving ally.

He did not know what was wrong. He could not, because he could not think clearly about it. He could not think clearly about it, because he could not put it clearly into words. To the extent that he could talk or think about it at all, he missed the point, complaining about the spite, insensitivity, or jealousy of others. He could talk about these things, at least to his wife, and so he could think about them.

He could not talk about his basic convictions and attitudes, least of all with his wife, whose successes reminded him of his failure. To put such things into words would have revealed the extent to which they were antagonistic against everyone, even against her. Had he stated his convictions, their defiance of common sense would have been revealed and his solitary rebellion against social living would have been exposed, even to him.

He could not say that he must dominate others to feel safe, that he must look down on others (including her) to feel worthwhile, or that he must impress her with his masculinity before he could respond sexually.

Language is a vehicle for meaning. Meaning is social. The meaning of meaning is that it can be shared. Edward could express his attitudes only indirectly therefore, and in disguise. He cloaked his posture of domination by unarguable statements about not letting others "push me around" or "force me to compromise my ideals." In the same way, he disguised his posture of looking down on others by focusing on shortcomings which anyone might agree were real. For example, he kept his wife off balance by reminding her of inconsequential faults about which she was embarrassed, always with the "good intention" of helping her to correct them. To account for the withdrawal of his sexual feeling, he criticized her for her "aggressiveness" in approaching him sexually, and told her that she was losing her femininity.

In a sense (private sense) he believed these things, even if uneasily. There was nothing else he could do, because there was nothing else he could say.

Thought is framed in language, which is a social possession; one thinks in a language which is not one's own. Here, as with the meaning of language, rational thought is thought that can be shared. It need not be, of course. We can keep thoughts to ourselves, as every discreet person knows. We can also state them, if we choose to speak our mind. Only the unspeakable remains unthinkable. *We can think clearly only in thoughts that can be stated plausibly to others.*

Edward was unable to state his basic convictions and attitudes because they did not make sense (common sense). As a result, they could not take form even in his own mind as rational. He had to make do with his private sense, muddled in the painful awareness that something was wrong.

Instead of a clear awareness of himself as a participant in the common life, he had constructed an "arrangement" (Adler) by which to picture his painful situation to himself (p. 263). He had to do this in a way that did not add to his feeling of falling short and of having a status of diminished worth in comparison to others. His *attitude* was that of a man who would be above others; his *conviction* was that otherwise he would be nothing at all.

His strategy, which he was unable to see, was to deflect his feelings of diminished value off onto others; first, onto his wife, the person most disposed to be his ally. He also drew on her willingness to do her part and to make allowances for his insulting behavior, as if he were entitled to draw upon this resource to shore up his faltering self-esteem. This was a dangerous game, comparable, as Adler put it, to drawing checks on the accounts of others. It was also self-defeating, because the more she struggled to understand and help, the more she appeared to him as the "better" person, adding further to his humiliation and leaving him with no way to deal with it other than by his strategy of counter-humiliation, which he intensified. Finally, she threatened to leave him. Edward's arrangement had begun to fall apart, and the remnants of his common sense brought him to consult a psychologist. He was thirty-one years old.

Edward was a first-born son. At the time of our first meeting his father was sixty-four years old, still an active research physician. His mother was sixty, an excellent cook and hostess, more modestly educated than his father, but polished in her speech and manners. She adored her husband, looked up to him as if he were a god, and did all she could to make life comfortable for him. Father had been kindly, not punitive, but his busy professional life left little time for the boy. He did note Edward's accomplishments, and was especially pleased by signs of intellectual ability. Father did not enter into conflicts with his colleagues, among whom his position was one of unquestioned respect. He was, however, disdainful of mediocrity (as he often referred to it) in his peers or among his students. This disdain was never openly directed toward his son; rather, it was expressed, as the boy saw it, by a lack of interest in anything unrelated to academic excellence. His younger sister seemed to have an easier time with father. Father was playful with her, and lavished approval on her appearance, the way she decorated her room, and the help she gave Mother. She did not do as well in school as Edward did, but Father never seemed to be bothered by that.

It was not hard to see, at least in rough outline, how Edward had formed his convictions, or how he had practiced his attitude. He was trained and had trained himself for a position above others. Superior achievements were expected of a man; anything less would be mediocre, and to be mediocre would be the same as to be nothing at all.

It was hard for Edward to see it. It sounded simplistic and stupid (as he put it), and he was brilliant. It was harder for him to see his ambition to be worth more than others, or how this ambition required others to be worth less than he, and to admire his superiority. It was hardest for him to see that his attitude and convictions forbade him any experience of fellow feeling or ease in friendship; that they spoiled any satisfaction in doing a job unless he was outdoing others; or that they robbed him of the refreshment of closeness and comfort in love, since they required that his partner remain at a subordinate distance.

He began to recognize what he had been trying to construct in his arrangement when the psychologist noted that he was then, at the age of thirty-one, approaching the same age his father was when he, Edward, was born. He was startled by this observation. He said that he had been puzzled by an uneasiness at the idea of his next birthday, a feeling he had never had before. His startled reaction and his awareness of uneasiness were intellectually intriguing to him, suggesting that some unconscious process might be at the root of his difficulties. We had found a point at which to begin the work of psychotherapy; he had entered upon the process of psycho-clarity. His meanings, for his age, his masculine guiding line, his expectations for himself and for life, all came clear in the subsequent assessment of his life-style. He was able to understand and to reconsider all his convictions and attitudes.

Precursors

Structure reduces uncertainty; it strengthens the possibility of a useful process and beneficial results. Beginning with Adler, and continuing to the present text, Adlerians have developed a variety of ways to organize the elements involved in assessing an individual's unique style of living.

An "Individual Psychology questionnaire, for the understanding and treatment of problem children, formulated with explanatory comments by the International Society for Individual Psychology" was noted by the Ansbachers (pp. 404-408) as being contained in several of Adler's publications, beginning in 1929. The Ansbachers report that Adler recommended this device as "an informal aid, not to be adhered to rigidly, in assessing a child's style of life, in learning what 'influences were at work when the child was forming it,' and in seeing how this style of life manifests itself in coping with the demands of life."

Following this questionnaire is another headed, "For Use With Adults" (pp. 408-409). In an introductory note Adler is quoted as saying:

> In case of adult failures I have found the following interview schedule to be valuable. By adhering to it the experienced therapist will gain an extensive insight into the style of life of the individual already within about *half an hour*. [Italics ours.]

A list of only eighteen questions is then offered. They follow the form of the usual medical history, beginning with, "What are your complaints?" and going on to the situation in which symptoms were first noticed, the current situation, and the person's occupation. The next question concerns the "character, and...health," of the parents and, if they are no longer living, the causes of their deaths. Then comes a question regarding the relationship of the parents to the patient. Only then is there an inquiry into the siblings, the person's place among them, and other particularities of the person's childhood situation.

Dreikurs (1967, pp. 88-90) created a longer questionnaire to be used after acquiring information concerning what he called "the subjective condition" of the presenting complaint, its onset and history, and the current social or "objective life situation" of the person. He then directed the inquiry to the person's place in childhood among the siblings, giving much more attention than Adler did to the relationships between them. A series of ratings elicited a lengthy self-assessment of the patient's childhood standing relative to the other children in the family in terms of behavior, character, appearance, and other traits. Only then did Dreikurs turn his attention to the parents, their ages and characters, and the relationship between them.

Dreikurs's students adapted and amended his work. A "Family Constellation Interview Guide" was published by Bernard H. Shulman (1973, p. 57). Shulman and Harold H. Mosak (1971) produced "The Life Style Inventory," a printed outline on which to record data. Daniel Eckstein, *et al.* (1982) expanded this in a form of their own as a "Life Style Interview Guide." Raymond N. Lowe and Betty Lowe (Appendices H and I, Leroy Baruth and Eckstein, 1981) followed the same outline with further modifications in two separate forms, an "Interview Guide for Establishing the Life Style," and "Life Style Interpretation." Don Dinkmeyer, Sr. *et al.* reported on Roy Kern's "The Lifestyle Scale" and "The Lifestyle Questionnaire Inventory" (1987, pp. 264-268). All of these follow Dreikurs in his departure from Adler's sequence, keeping the inquiry about siblings prior to that about parents and other adults.

Dreikurs stressed the importance of this priority. To him, sibling relationships were of greater consequence to the individual's creation and rehearsal of a unique style than was the example of the parents or their efforts to mold or influence the child's development. Dreikurs emphasized the other pole of parent-child transactions, possibly because it was so often overlooked or disregarded in quests for the causes of personality formation. He opposed speculations about causes, leading (as he saw) toward pessimism, fatalism, and disrespect for individuals. In one of his most widely read books he put it unequivocally: "Earlier than we realize, children shape and mold themselves, their parents, and their environment" (1964, p. 32). We agree.

In the *IPCW* we have returned to Adler's priority. Our purpose is to restore Adler's emphasis on *context*, to draw attention to the usefulness of contextual thinking, and to demonstrate its importance to students and practitioners of Individual Psychology. (Dreikurs was of course also aware of the importance of context. His term, "family atmosphere," was clearly designed to evoke it, as was his use of Adler's early image of "guiding lines" to refer to unconscious rehearsals for gender roles.)

The Psycho-Clarity Process

The psycho-clarity process rests upon a thorough appreciation of the context in which the inevitable errors made by a child can be understood as having made a certain kind of sense. If, as Adler put it, "every neurotic is partly right" (p. 334), a humane effort at identification may let us see how, as such a child in such a situation, we could have been creative enough to come up with the same mistakes.

Once this clarity is achieved, the client who was that child is able to consider those errors with a sympathetic understanding and, perhaps for the first time, may experience a sense of optimism about what life now holds open.

Until this clarity is achieved, the error cannot be seen at all; it can only be experienced in a kind of psycho-muddle, accompanied by a feeling of inevitability. Since the error lies in an evaluation of life's requirements, and in a corresponding attitude toward them, the error inheres in the person's way of apprehending everything. A way of seeing does not see itself. Just as those whose vision deviates from the norm cannot account for the discrepancy between what they see and what others report seeing, a person whose style deviates in erroneous convictions and attitudes may be aware of missing something and yet be unable to account for it. A faulty visual apparatus is one of the genetic possibilities of the organism; a faulty attitude is one of the developmental possibilities of the person.

The Life-Style Assessment procedure envisioned here follows the method provided in the *IPCW*; it calls for a thorough inquiry into the particularities of the situation in which this one person learned to rehearse and to make do with a particular pattern of errors. This procedure reflects the structure of our practice, in which two people work with the client, one responsible for gathering the material, both participating in a review and interpretation of the information with the assistance of the client, and one responsible for summarizing its implications. It allows for about ten hours to complete the work (following an Initial Interview of two to three hours). Sometimes the assessment takes as long as fifteen hours depending on the complexity of the client's personal history, on how quickly the therapists are able to make sense of the data, and on whether the client is verbose or laconic. We do not expect anyone to imitate the procedures set forth in this text in all their particulars. Clinicians who have studied with us in the AIAS Program for Professionals report that they adapt our structure readily to the requirements of a variety of circumstances.

In any case, our procedure takes much longer than either Adler or Dreikurs demonstrated were necessary for "the experienced therapist." It is true that an extensive understanding of a life-style can be gained in an hour or even in half an hour when the basic principles of assessment have been mastered and practiced; in Individual Psychology, and in the psycho-clarity process, it is also true that no fixed boundary is drawn between assessment (diagnosis) and psychotherapy (treatment). The client is engaged in psychotherapy at each step in the assessment. We therefore feel free to take all the time necessary for a systematic exploration of the story of this person's life and an attentive reflection upon the meaning of its difficulties.

The *IPCW* presents a format; this text provides a method for using it. Neither of these can be more effective than its users, a large part of whose effectiveness resides in the discretion with which they employ our material. In considering a client's history, the clinician must bear in mind that a numerical or even logical order does not dictate a fixed sequence for gathering data. We are not in search of a body of fact; our goal is to discern the pattern of an embodied life expressed in movement, the key to which lies in convictions and attitudes. Dreikurs made use of Henry Winthrop's (1959) term, factophilia, to warn against the activity of collecting more and more data without a sense of the context in which it could be intelligible. He appealed to the image of a mosaic, which may reveal its pattern even when only some of the tiles are in place. A Life-Style Assessment is not a systematic collection of a heap of tiles; it is the imaginative reconstruction of a pattern which allows each tile of information to be fitted into the context of the whole. This context, furthermore, is a pattern of movement in line with what Adler recognized as the "great line of action" of the "whole of human life...from below to above, from minus to plus, from defeat to victory" (p. 255).

Elements of the Procedure

The Initial Interview. We first meet our client for an Initial Interview of two to three hours. In this book, the Initial Interview process is set forth in three chapters: "The Initial Interview Inquiry" (Chapter 3); "Life Situation, Presenting Problem, and Life Tasks" (Chapter 5); and "Impressions Derived from the Initial Interview" (Chapter 12).

The Life-Style Assessment. The Life-Style Assessment follows and builds on the Initial Interview. Chapter 4 describes the life-style inquiry; Chapters 6 through 11 illustrate the process of reviewing and interpreting the material gathered in the inquiry; Chapters 13 and 14 offer instruction on the development of the final summaries.

The Early Recollections. Both the gathering and the interpretation of early recollections have their own techniques that are integral to the Life-Style Assessment. The process of gathering Early Recollections is explored in Chapter 4, which includes a section on special problems. Chapter 11 provides a method for interpreting early recollections, and Chapter 14 outlines a format for constructing the two early recollections summaries.

Key Features of the Child's Experience

There are features common to the landscape of childhood to which every child attends with a unique evaluation. We isolate seven such features, the evaluations of which are expressed in a characteristic pattern of movement, revealing the basic convictions of the life-style, and forming the foundations of a lifelong orientation. They are:

1. Masculine and Feminine Guiding Lines and Role Models

2. Family Atmosphere

3. Family Values

4. Other Particularities (including the ethnic, religious, social, and economic situation)

5. Birth-Order Position

6. Genetic Possibility

7. Environmental Opportunity

The outline below relates each of these features to its evaluation, indicated by a phrase following the slash (/). The first statement, for example, represents the child's identifying the "Masculine and Feminine Guiding Lines and Role Models" in parents and other men and women in its sphere, and then constructing a pattern of responses, designated here under the heading of "Gender Role Preparation."

Our effort to illustrate these ideas in a diagram (Figure 1, p. 24), risks misrepresenting the person's lively creating of a unique pattern of movement as static or determined. We rely on your imagination to see through to the creativity and subjectivity involved on both sides of the dynamic reality as you study the suggested *givens* in a child's situation (represented by the shaded, curved arrows) and the meaning and value the child *gives* to them in response (represented by shorter, unshaded arrows).

1. *Masculine and Feminine Guiding Lines and Role Models / Gender Role Preparation*

   The child evaluates the meaning of gender in preparation for taking part as a man or as a woman, concluding, "This is the way men are and the way women are. This is what I can expect of members of my gender and the other gender. Therefore this is what is going to unfold for me (as a man or as a woman)."

2. *Family Atmosphere / Interpersonal Style*

   The child evaluates the family atmosphere, set by the attitudinal and operational relationship between the parents, and between the parents and the world (including the children), and concludes, "This is what I have to expect and prepare for in my dealings with others."

3. *Family Values / Personal Code*

   The child considers the values that are shared by the parents, and concludes, "These are the issues of central importance, on which I must be prepared to take a stand."

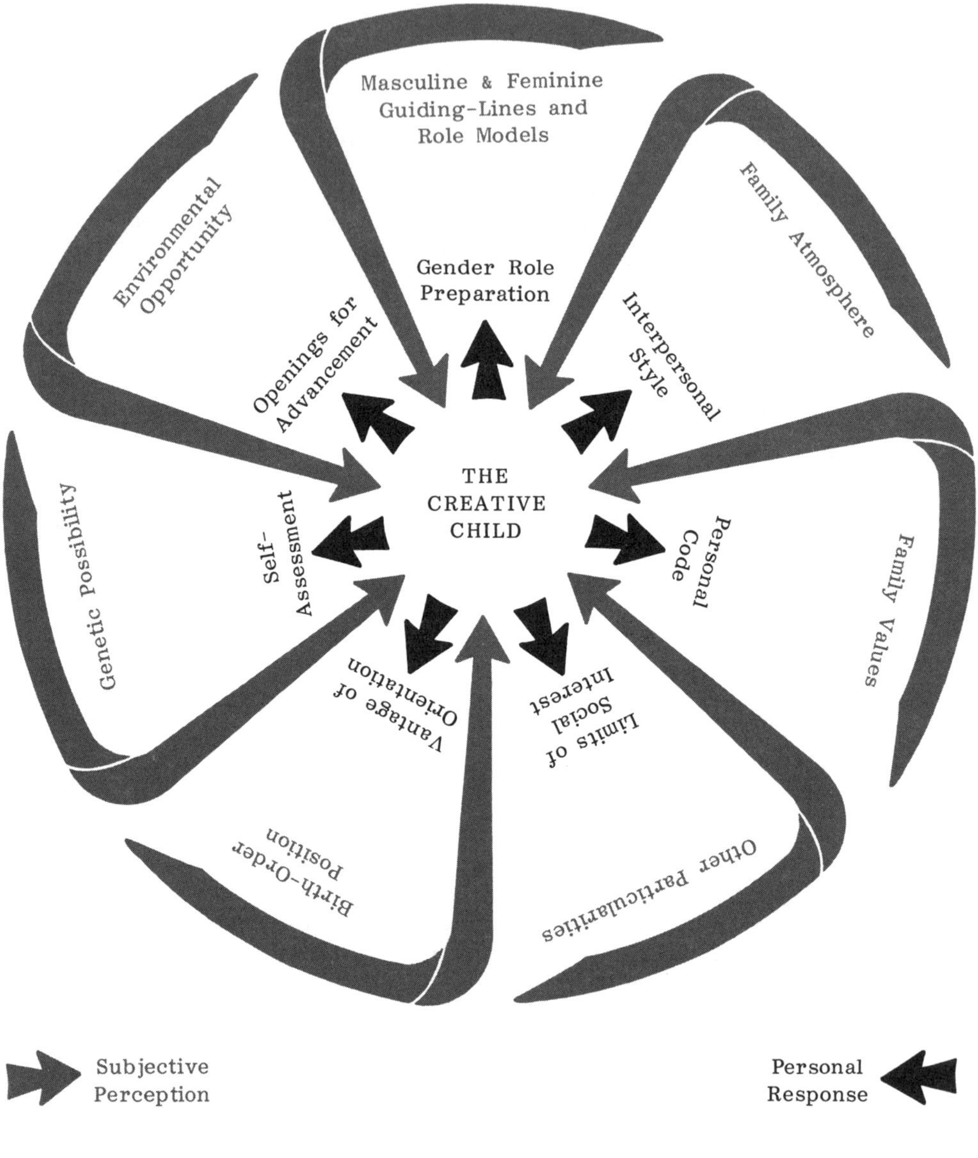
Masculine & Feminine Guiding-Lines and Role Models
Family Atmosphere
Family Values
Other Particularities
Birth-Order Position
Genetic Possibility
Environmental Opportunity
Gender Role Preparation
Interpersonal Style
Personal Code
Limits of Social Interest
Vantage of Orientation
Self-Assessment
Openings for Advancement
THE CREATIVE CHILD
Subjective Perception
Personal Response

Figure 1.

4. *Other Particularities (Ethnic, Religious, Social, Economic) / Limits of Social Interest*

   The child evaluates the ethnic, religious, social, economic, and other particularities of the situation, and concludes, "It is possible for me to make a place in the broader community on these terms, and to this extent."

5. *Birth-Order Position / Vantage of Orientation*

   The child finds a vantage of orientation among (or in the absence of) siblings from which to consider the situation of self, others, and the world, and concludes, "This is where I stand and must stand amongst others in order to maintain my bearings."

6. *Genetic Possibility / Self-Assessment*

   The child's evaluations consider the physical and mental constituents of the self as among the features of the world. These may include organ inferiorities, particular strengths, degree of activity, mental acuity, and any other perceived constitutional capacities for life in the social world, drawing the conclusion that, "These are my personal limits and possibilities for making a place amongst the others."

7. *Environmental Opportunity / Openings For Advancement*

   The child evaluates the situation as including both openings for and limitations to advancement, concluding, "This is what is open to me in life, and this is what stands in my way."

Conclusion

In Chapter 1 we set out to orient the reader to the distinctiveness of Individual Psychology's understanding of personality development and dynamics, its field of inquiry, and its method of correction. In Chapter 2 we presented an overview of the psycho-clarity process in Life-Style Assessment.

The coming parts of the book address three aspects of procedure: gathering information (Part II: "Inquiry"); going over the gathered material with the client to gain as complete an understanding as possible (Part III: "Review and Interpretations"); and finally, summarizing the conclusions the therapists and client have reached together (Part IV: "Summations of Understanding").

PART II: INQUIRY

In a considerable portion of neurotics, the turning to a physician, sometimes even to another person, is of itself enough to drive the patient on further. In approximately half of the neurotics, the call on the physician signifies their decision to get better, that is, to give up a symptom which has become superfluous or disturbing. It is this 50 per cent of "cures" that enables all schools of psychiatry to continue to live.

Alfred Adler (p. 336)

INTRODUCTION TO PART II

Part II is a discussion of items covered in the Initial Interview and Life-Style Assessment inquiries, clarifying the intent of each item and providing examples of the kinds of information they elicit in a variety of client responses. The complete outline of the items discussed in this section appears in the *IPCW*, included here as the Appendix.

The inquiry is conducted by the first therapist. After the inquiry is completed the client, first therapist, and second therapist convene for the review and interpretations and the summations of understanding. The first therapist is responsible for the inquiry, both therapists participate in the review and interpretations, and the second therapist is responsible for the summaries. (In the *IPCW*, the first therapist is designated FT, the second therapist ST, and the client CL.)

This procedure follows an innovation by Dreikurs, who used the term "multiple therapy" to designate his model for more than one therapist working with the same client (1952).

Multiple therapy enhances the opportunity for awakening the client's sense of engagement in shaping outcomes. Adler called this sense "social interest," a term he borrowed from William James as nearest to the meaning of the German, *Gemeinschaftsgefühl*. Individual Psychology's criterion for measuring the value of any therapy is the extent of the increase in the client's social interest. Here, in the very structure of the therapeutic encounter, the client is invited to experience social interest from the start by engaging with two actively interested professionals, and by working with them in a joint effort to understand the private logic of his or her own personal style. In this, the process itself offers a foretaste of the desired outcome.

The client's sense of equal engagement is further enhanced by seeing that each therapist makes individual and distinctive contributions to the work, each from a unique vantage, each in the exercise of a particular set of responsibilities.

In the inquiries, the task of the first therapist is to enter into a conversation with the client. This conversation is unlike others in that it has a therapeutic goal, and to achieve that goal it must be ordered.

The framework provided by the *IPCW* is therefore intended to guide the discussion, allowing it to unfold in a coherent manner without interfering with its conversational character.

Therapists will use the outlines and items detailed here in line with their own styles and the styles of their clients. For example, if clients move from talking about their children to talking about their siblings, there is no need to interrupt; turn the page and write the sibling information in the appropriate section of the outlines. Or, if the therapist has a sense that it is important to address the question of a client's health before asking for information about the client's parents, this is the sequence to follow. The format we present here, in other words, is to be the servant of the conversation, not the master.

The Initial Interview is organized so that the recording of apparently external facts (date of birth, place of employment, etc.) begins a process leading to a consideration of the client's current life situation, presenting problem, and self-assessment in the areas of the three universal challenges of affiliation, work, and love. The client thus moves step by step toward addressing issues of personal difficulty in the course of discussing matters of consequence to all human beings.

The first therapist is responsible for noting signs of exaggerated nervousness, hesitation, lability, jocularity, and so on. Silences or other retreats from engagement in response to particular subjects must be noted as well. These are important indicators of sensitivity, and they may show themselves at any point during the interview. The first therapist must also be prepared to offer encouragement; to keep the atmosphere light without making light of the issues; to allow time for the silences; to offer comfort and sympathy as appropriate ("I can see that this is hard for you"); to make self-disclosures when they are called for; and to maintain an interested attitude in the face of anger or tears by saying (to anger, for example), "I can see how you could feel that way," or (to tears), "Let the tears come.... What comes with the tears?"

Chapter 3 covers the inquiry in the Initial Interview, Chapter 4 the inquiry for the Life-Style Assessment itself. You will note the heading "General Diagnosis" for the first and "Special Diagnosis" for the second. These are Adler's terms. Our use of them here is intended to draw attention to our following Adler's lead in this area, as described by the Ansbachers:

> Understanding the specific life-style of the patient, his specific problem situation, and the specific significance of his symptoms...is accomplished by an initial, tentative understanding of the patient, which is gained through empathy, intuition, and guessing. On this basis Adler formed what we

> might call a hypothesis of the patient's life-style and situation. At one time, when addressing a group of medical men, he termed this step of forming the hypothesis, the general diagnosis, and termed the verification of the hypothesis, the special diagnosis. This second step consists in a careful interpretation of all the expressions of the patient, to see what bearing these have on the hypothesis. "In the special diagnosis you must learn by testing.... At first you have to guess at the cause. But then you have to prove it by other signs. If these do not agree, you must be severe enough with yourself to reject your first hypothesis and seek another explanation" (pp. 326-327).

In our experience, these two "steps" (as Adler called them), namely an empathic, intuitive guessing and a "severe enough [willingness] to reject [our] first hypothesis," are the psychological actions essential to following the living movement of another person in Life-Style Assessment. They are also the most difficult to teach, probably because they are matters of virtue more than of technique.

The virtues referred to here are not heroic or saintly, but the more ordinary and everyday ones, made possible by our interest in each other, and our imaginative capacity for identification. They are, first, the willingness to extend oneself in empathy and intuition; and second, the courage to guess. Some will lack the former because they are more interested in knowing better; others will lack the latter because they are more interested in being right (and will want more and more data to ensure that they have not overlooked anything before risking a hypothesis). As practitioners gain greater confidence in what they have to offer, they become more capable of empathy and develop more courage to make guesses. Then a further virtue is called for: the humility to acknowledge wrong or useless guesses when they are corrected or rejected by the client.

General Diagnosis

INITIAL INTERVIEW

The Life Situation (Items 1 - 20)

1. Date______________________

The date of the Initial Interview may relate to a particular recent or upcoming event of importance in the client's life, or to an anniversary of a past occurrence of importance. Bear this in mind as you inquire about date of birth, date of marriage, ages of the client's children and parents, and the dates of significant events in the lives of the parents.

2. Present Age__________

3. Date of Birth_________

The human experience of the present includes an expectation of the future and a remembrance of the past. Life-style convictions include the former and rest upon the latter. In any present moment we operate on the basis of our expectations, guided by the wisdom we believe to reside in our memories. The client's present age has an importance relative to these private and (most often) un-understood life-style expectations.

- A single, twenty-nine-year-old man said, "Six months from now I'll be thirty. I always thought I'd have everything sorted out by now, and I don't even know what I want." He had set age thirty as a big number (Powers and Griffith, 1986) by which to measure his accomplishments, and felt profoundly uneasy and anxious as his birthday approached.

- A divorced woman said, "I just turned thirty-five. Not only don't I have any children yet, but I don't even have anybody to have children with! By now I thought I'd have kids in school. I can't figure out what went wrong."

- A man, forty, and unhappily married, exclaimed, "I just hope to God the next forty years aren't going to be like the last forty. I've got to make some changes, but I'm afraid it's already too late."

Knowing the period in which the client was born also helps to establish the context in which that person developed a unique style. A sense of what life was like, economically, politically, and socially during the time of a person's childhood can be of fundamental importance to understanding his or her childhood evaluation of the world, and how, and to what extent, the current situation may challenge that evaluation.

- Harold was born in 1946. His boyhood began in the years of recovery after the world struggle against fascism and militarism. He entered his adolescence as the postwar period of readjustment, the beginnings of the Cold War, and the ambiguities of the Korean War were yielding to the prophecies of the Beat generation.

As we move forward with Harold in conversation, we consider what his experience could have been as a child, and what he might have made of the years of dislocation after World War II. We try to think of how, in his adolescence, he experienced the years when togetherness, propriety, and optimism gave way to the Cold War and the space race. Harold's interpretations of the events of his time, and his way of experiencing the world situation and mood, all have a bearing on his present movement. None of this can be clear to us unless we are thinking contextually.

4. Name, address, home phone; maiden name; full name of spouse:

Record the client's full name (including maiden name if she took a married name) and the spouse's full name. If the names are not familiar to you, inquire about their ethnic origin. Ethnicity can add to your sense of context. It may provide a framework for thinking about the client's family of origin, values, and religious attitudes. If the client is married, the names may reveal that this person married "out" of one ethnic group and "into" another, possibly perceiving the marriage as "up" or "down."

- A thirty-seven-year-old man from a Polish Catholic family had married a Protestant woman of English extraction. He had left his family religion and working class neighborhood and established a social life among the corporate managers with whom he now worked. His family refused to accept his wife. He was troubled by this, but even more troubled by his sense of disadvantage in moving among his wife's wealthy, Protestant friends in a new suburban milieu. He had wanted to enter this world, and was proud of his wife, but he had misgivings, and often felt, as he put it, "over my head."

Home address may tell something further about a client's sense of social status, sometimes even of social values.

- A woman of thirty-five gave her address as being in a predominantly Jewish community, adding that she planned to move soon, that the neighbors were "not my kind of people," and that she didn't want her children to attend school there.

5. Occupation, position, address, work phone; occupation of spouse:

This information further defines the context of the client's objective situation.

- A man of thirty-four was employed as a nuclear engineer. (Begin to consider probabilities: Such a person may place a high value on the understanding and control of details. He may be more cautious and constricted compared to people drawn to other occupations. He may enjoy tasks that involve immediate measures for determining whether solutions are right or wrong. He may appreciate being part of an orderly, predictable environment in which he knows exactly where he stands, and in which there is no doubt about who is responsible for what.) He complained, "I don't have any fun."

- A woman of twenty-nine was an accountant studying for the C.P.A examinations. She is punctual, and carefully groomed. (She may want everything to "add up," and for life to be coherent and predictable. She may have carefully chosen friends in a narrow social circle.) Here is the way she described her problem: "I'm lonely. I never seem to go anywhere or do anything."

- A man of thirty-one was a sales representative. (He may value being his own boss, may be impatient with details, and may enjoy a more free-spending, gregarious way of life than those in other occupations. He may have an appetite for spontaneous camaraderie in an ever-new group of acquaintances.) His statement of the problem was: "I can't hang on to an intimate relationship."

- A man of sixty-two was a restaurateur. (He may be a workaholic whose business is his life. He may find his identity in the spotlight with many patrons who feel special when he gives them personal attention and who flatter him in turn.) He complained: "My wife has gotten interested in a lot of other things, and wants a divorce."

- A woman of thirty-six was a furniture importer. (She may enjoy travel and excitement. She may be artistic, concerned with appearances and glamour. She may value independence, and avoid close ties. She may be self-absorbed both in work and play, and may expect to be the center of things.) Her complaint was: "My boyfriend doesn't treat me right."

Occupations attract people whose life-styles are congenial to the requirements of those occupations. Choices of occupation can help us to understand the various patterns of style, in terms of their effectiveness and their limitations, the kinds of success they enable, and the kinds of difficulty they entail.

Work address may also yield information concerning style.

- A woman of forty-two worked out of her home as a commercial artist. She valued privacy and self-reliance. She had been unable to form an alliance with a man because she feared she would have to "compromise" her freedom.

- A man of forty-eight was an insurance executive with a fashionable downtown office. He enjoyed the fast life of the city, had flirtations and affairs, went drinking with his men friends after work, and complained: "My life is empty."

Noting the spouse's occupation may also provide clues relating to the current difficulty.

- A man of fifty-three stated that his wife was a buyer in a department store. He complained, "Ever since she went back to work six months ago our marriage has fallen apart. She's never home, and nothing gets done. She has a new circle of friends, and I'm not included. I don't know what to do."

- A woman of thirty-two was married to an attorney, but said that that wasn't enough for him. He wanted to go into politics, a life she hated: "If they aren't already corrupt, they get corrupted. Ever since he got bitten by the bug, he's been a different person."

If a client moves immediately to discuss the details of the presenting problem before you have had an opportunity to gather the basic material in The Life Situation section, you can say, "It appears that this part of your life is the most troublesome. We're going to explore it together in detail, and I think we'll be able to make more sense of it if we first examine the context in which it's happening. Let's take a few moments more for the basics so that I can get to know you better; then we'll move to that subject. Is that all right with you?" We have never had anyone say no; people appreciate having the opportunity to proceed in a systematic way. The structure may even come as a relief to a client's chaotic way of thinking and talking about troublesome issues.

When there are other digressions from the topic at hand, one must use tact and a friendly confidence to guide the conversation back to the subject. "I can see that this is important to you. I'd like to come back to it when we have more time to explore it." Such an approach usually enables the client to return to the subject.

6. Preferred phone and mailing address (home or work):

A client may say, "Don't call me at the office." This person may see the office as gossipy or political, an environment in which people must be cautious not to disclose their personal lives. (This is often the issue when people whose visits could be covered by group insurance do not want to file a claim for psychological services.)

Someone may say, "Don't call me at home." It may be that this client's spouse is unaware of your being consulted; the statement may imply that a degree of trust is lacking in the marriage. It is advisable to inquire about this, to know why the spouse does not know about this appointment, and to learn the reason for the secrecy.

If a client is still living at home with parents (or a parent), this may be relevant to the presenting difficulty. It may indicate a hesitation of the client's with respect to being "on my own," completing school, or identifying and pursuing an occupation.

7. Marital status (age of spouse, how long married, anniversary, previous marriages of both spouses; or, current love relationship, how long, level of relationship):

In the review of the life tasks the issues of love and intimacy will be addressed in some detail. Here we are concerned with the objective situation. If there was also a previous marriage (or marriages), say, "Tell me in a few words what you think went wrong with your previous marriage(s)."

> - A man of twenty-seven responded, "I know my former wife would tell you something different, but I don't think she ever grew up. Whenever anything went wrong she got her mother tied up in it, and I'd always come out the bad guy. She never tried to solve anything with me. She'd just withdraw or call 'Mommie.'" I finally called it quits."

In this connection it is important to ask who initiated the divorce or separation, and what prompted him or her to act.

Ethnic background, religion, social class, etc., may be at issue between spouses. If there is a marked disparity in the ages of the partners, that may be another matter to consider. Of course, any disparity can be a source of enrichment for a marriage; it may also become a source of trouble, however, depending on the meanings the partners assign to it.

> - A man of fifty-one was in his second marriage. His wife was twenty-nine. He had adult children from his first marriage. Now his new wife wanted a baby. During their courtship he had said that he would want a child with her, but secretly hoped that she would give up the idea after they were married and caught up in their new life. Contrary to this hope, she was pressing him and threatening to leave. He wondered, "What's wrong with me? I like children, and I love her. Why am I unwilling to go through with this?"

8. Children (names, ages, sex; deceased children and other pregnancies; adoptions, difficulties of conception; from other marriages):

The importance of this information may not show itself immediately, but the data fills out a picture of the client's life experience. Later you may find a significance in the dates of the children's births, or the timing of the pregnancies, or the dates of other events connected with the children. (A correlation may show itself at Item 22: "When did it start? What else was going on in your life at that time?")

> - A man, forty-nine, was having marital difficulties, and was considering divorce. The trouble had begun fifteen years before. We asked, "Wasn't that about the time Jennie was born?" It turned out that he had felt overburdened by the birth of this child, their fifth, born five years after the next oldest. He was then having financial problems, hadn't wanted more children, and felt that his wife had "tricked" him into the pregnancy. From that time on he had felt resentful and betrayed, and as if he were all alone in the task of making a living and providing a life for everyone: "Now I'm almost fifty-five, and it's time for me to have my own life, before it's too late."
>
> - A woman of thirty-eight was the mother of three children. Six years before, while she was away from the house, her husband, a physician, was looking after the children. He had stepped into the house to get a drink when the middle child, then four, ran into the street and was hit by a car.

> Even though the father then rushed to the scene of the accident and saved the child's life by dint of his medical training and competence, the client felt unable to trust him ever again, and had come to see him as vain and uncaring.

You may learn that the client married after the beginning of a pregnancy. Many first-born children "arranged" the marriages of their parents unawares. Sometimes the result is a good marriage, sometimes not.

> - A man of forty-two had "had" to marry his wife. He had also had to drop out of school and give up his ambition to become a lawyer. He was angry and resentful: "I did that for her, not for me. She's never appreciated it. The least she could have done for the past twenty-two years is show a little gratitude. I saved her reputation, and it cost me my life. I never would have married her if it hadn't been for the pregnancy."

The birth of a child may have other consequences.

> - A stockbroker, thirty-six, had been the baby of his family and his mother's favorite. He married a much younger woman who had been doted on by a grandfather, and who expected her spouse to pamper her. The relationship was stormy, with neither of them feeling adequately served by the other, but there was a lot of money for each of them to spend, and they managed to stay together for ten years. Then she decided that she didn't want "to miss out" on the experience of having a baby; when the baby arrived, she was absorbed in catering to the infant. The client felt abandoned and ignored, and said he "couldn't handle it."

Adoptions, miscarriages, stillbirths, abortions, and children who are handicapped or placed in institutions should be noted. So also should artificial insemination or any sexual difficulty, which may be an indication of diminished compatibility, trust, and confidence in the marriage.

> - A couple unable to have children after several years of trying to conceive adopted two children in rapid succession. Within five years they were considering divorce because, as the woman put it, "We argue all the time, we don't enjoy each other's company, and we don't have anything in common."

An exaggerated idea of the responsibilities of parenthood can also be at the root of a difficulty in conception.

> - A thirty-year-old man was in despair over a marriage in which, "everything is good, except the main thing. We can't have children."

He and his wife had consulted fertility experts, and she had been told that she had an "infantile uterus." They had agreed to adopt, but when the time came for a decision she had faltered and offered a host of reasons for delay. He felt betrayed, and was considering divorce. The whole line of his ambition as a man was in the direction of being a successful father, a task at which (to his mind) his own father had been defeated by his mother's depressive personality.

At our urging, he brought his wife with him for a meeting. She was reluctant, because as she put it, a consultation with a psychologist was a sign of "weakness," and she hoped her mother would not learn of her having resorted to it. We saw an opportunity, and asked them not to discuss children in any connection for six months while we worked with them to find out how two people, so clearly fond of each other, were experiencing so much difficulty. They agreed.

Within six months she was pregnant. She had come to see that the feminine guiding line set by her mother had left her with the conviction that motherhood was a heroic task, and that only when she was equal to taking care of anything and everything on her own, without anyone's help, would she be equal to it. When she was liberated from this constricting idea, she was able to conceive. They are now the happy parents of three healthy children (and he has greater respect for his father).

Also, in the inquiry about children it is important to note any special alliances between either of the parents with a particular child.

- A woman of forty-eight complained that her husband was so involved in the life of one of their grown daughters that she felt overlooked and disregarded. He in turn accused her of "selfishness and callousness" regarding the daughter's continuing difficulty, and husband and wife were estranged.

9. Level of education; military experience; religion:

This item elicits further information regarding a person's history and range of experience. A client may offer important evaluations as well as provide unexpected information while reporting the facts.

- A man of thirty-three reported that he had an M.B.A., and that he was the first person of his family to complete any degree, saying, "I've felt a little uneasy around my father ever since I finished college, and now that I have a master's degree it's even harder." When we asked what had happened between them, he told us that he felt as if he had "surpassed" his father and his family's working class position: "I feel like a misfit in my own family."

- A woman of thirty-eight had an M.S.W., and said, "Of course, I only got that degree after I left the convent."

- A woman of forty-one had dropped out of school and made a career in advertising. She had been promoted to the senior management group in her company and felt unequal to the position: "I'm not only a woman; I'm an uneducated woman."

Military service (or the lack of it) may be reported matter-of-factly, or your asking about it may stimulate further revelations.

- A thirty-six-year-old man said that he enlisted to get away from an intolerable family situation: Father was a drunk who brutalized Mother, and she wouldn't do anything about it.

- A thirty-seven-year-old client had another reason: The primary family value and training was a fundamentalist pacifism against which he volunteered in an act of defiance.

- A man of thirty-four said he was a "conscientious conceptor," explaining that he had married and had a child immediately to avoid the Viet Nam draft. He felt he had "gotten away with" something, and suffered with an uneasiness that he had not gone with his friends, some of whom had been wounded or killed. "What kind of man am I?" he wondered.

In addressing religious affiliation we pose the matter this way: "Tell me about your religious orientation and practice, if you have one."

- A woman of twenty-seven said, "My family is Jewish. It was a social thing for them, and I hated their attitude. I decided to do it right if I was going to do it at all, and I keep a kosher house now. In fact I chose my husband, in part, because he was so strict about it."

- A man of forty-one said, "I was brought up Catholic, went to Catholic school, the whole bag. I got out as fast as I could. I leave it alone, and it leaves me alone. I'd like to be a Presbyterian, but I haven't done anything about it."

We asked what made Presbyterianism attractive to him, and he said, "It isn't emotional. They're not all hung up on guilt."

- A woman of twenty-nine said, "I'm Catholic. Church, and everything related to it, was important to all of us when we were growing up. Going to church was special. We were together, we all looked our best, and there was the music, and the flowers. It was the only beautiful thing in my life."

- A woman of twenty-eight reported, "My father was a fundamentalist minister. We couldn't go to movies, watch TV, play cards, or smoke. It's really funny in some ways. The

> teenagers figured out that the only thing we could do was have sex: They never even talked about that, so we must have decided that it wasn't forbidden! We were not part of the town. They looked down on us; we looked down on them. I got out of there as fast as I could. But, even though I don't belong to a church, whenever I feel down I go to the nearest church to pray. I don't know why I do that."

10. Parents (intact marriage, divorced, or separated; remarriages of parents; if parent deceased, date and cause; CL's age at time of any family disruption; parents' current life situation and state of health; other adults present in preadolescent household):

With this subject we begin to form an impression of the masculine and feminine guiding lines. We start with, "Was your family intact in your growing-up years?" Then, "Were there any other adults living in the household?" And, "Are your parents living?" We want to know the year and cause of death (if one or both has died); these things may impinge upon the client's private expectations of sickness, health, and longevity. We also want to know about the parents' marriage, whether it was intact or whether they divorced or separated; whether either one remarried. Sometimes the record is uncomplicated and straightforward (though it will always yield some information worth exploring during the review and interpretations); sometimes the record is more complicated because of disruptions and changes in the family relationships; at other times the client will respond to the question in greater than expected detail, as if to draw your attention to an issue related to the presenting complaint.

> - A woman of forty-three was executive secretary and office manager for the owner of a new company. She had gone to work for him five years before, on a temporary basis. This was when her husband, then forty, was recovering from the first of a number of stays in hospital for a degenerative disease that limited his ability to work. Since then the company had grown; she was regarded as "indispensable" by her boss, who paid her well, relied upon her, and took a personal interest in her life and her problems.
>
> She reported that her father died when he was sixty-five, eight years before. "He was healthy all his life, and went to work no matter what. I doubt if he missed a day. He had a stroke just one month after he retired. My mother's still alive at sixty-eight. She developed a severe digestive problem after Dad died -- no diagnosis. It worries me. She came to live with me about six months after Dad's death; I didn't want her living by herself. You know, she was one of those women who never worked. My father wouldn't hear of it.

> Only once, when he was on strike, he let her work nights in a restaurant, but he hated it, and so did I."

This woman came to us complaining of intermittent depression, agitation, and sleeplessness. It was not hard to see that her expectations for a woman's place in the world were not being met: A man was supposed to support and care for a woman; a woman was not supposed to work at all (much less be "indispensible"). She laughed when we pointed out that anyone growing up as she did would be likely to feel disoriented, perhaps misled, and probably resentful. From that moment on she began to feel better about herself, more accepting of her unforeseen responsibilities, and more free to enjoy the self-esteem that she had gained with her employer's encouragement.

> - A man of twenty-nine reported, "My parents divorced when I was eleven. I never saw it coming. My stepmother, Joyce, married my Dad when I was twelve. My stepfather, Harry, married my mother when I was sixteen. I think Mom waited to see what Dad was going to do, and whether it was going to work out with him and Joyce. She really wanted him back. I think he already had something going with Joyce while he and Mom were married. I always thought so, and I always resented Dad and Joyce. They really wrecked my life. I still have a hard time being civil to my Dad."

This man had come to us because he had broken his engagement three times from the same woman, who remained devoted to him. He said that she was "perfect" for him, but that "I lose my nerve at the thought of the responsibility of marriage."

11. Siblings (list by first names from oldest to youngest, placing CL, deceased siblings, and Mother's other known pregnancies in their ordinal positions; using CL's age as a baseline, note the difference in years between CL and siblings; in parallel columns note step-siblings and CL's age when they entered the family; note present whereabouts and occupations of all siblings):

Here we establish the client's position in the birth order of the children. It is important to know not only about surviving siblings, but also about any miscarriages, deaths, stillbirths, or siblings placed in institutions. Following Adler, we often discover that a healthy child born after such events and difficulties involving earlier-born siblings has come into the world as a "revelation" (p. 377) and may have grown up with an aura of invincibility.

Birth order is not to be mistaken for a determinant of the individual's style of living (see Chapter 8); birth-order information is important in that it gives us an idea of the particular vantage from which the child viewed and assessed self, others, and the world. As Adler put it:

> There has been some misunderstanding of my custom of classification according to position in the family. It is not, of course, the child's number in the order of successive births which influences his character, but the *situation* into which he is born and the way in which he interprets it (p. 377).

For this reason empirical studies, inspired by Adler's emphasis upon the significance of birth order, have often been inconclusive and unsatisfactory. In no other area of this inquiry is Adler's general maxim more to be taken as an imperative: *"Alles kann auch anders sein"* (Everything can also be otherwise) (p. 194).

- A woman of twenty-three came to see us because she didn't "know what to do" with her life. She was one of two children, with an older brother. As she reported it, "I was the baby. My brother Jim is three years older; he's a lawyer."

- A woman of thirty-six complained that she couldn't get along with men. She had been the only child of her parents until her two brothers were born, one when she was fifteen, and the other when she was seventeen. She reported that she was embarrassed when she was in high school and her mother became pregnant. "How could she have done that to me?" She also reported that her mother had always had "female trouble," and that it was after an operation to rectify this that Mother had been able to conceive again. This woman did not enjoy sex and had the idea that it was "the only thing men are interested in."

- A man of forty-two was in torment over his marriage to a woman seven years younger, who had told him she didn't love him, and who was having an affair. "She's so naive. I'm afraid to think of what would become of her if I left." He was the first born of three, with a brother three years younger and a sister six years younger. He was his mother's favorite. "Dad worked hard and wasn't around much, so it was Mom and I, and the little kids, and I helped her out. I went to work when I was twelve. My hypertension was diagnosed when I was thirteen years old."

- A woman of thirty-one was the first of four. "The only one who bothered me was my brother Tim; he was eleven months younger than I. He was always getting into trouble, and fighting, especially with me. If he hadn't been so bad we would have had a nice family." This client consulted us because she was having problems with her son.

12. When you were a child, if anything could have been different, what would you have wanted it to be?

This question may uncover something of the direction of a person's hopes, striving, and ambitions. It may also elicit information about disappointments in life, and, perhaps, the client's claim to being a victim of circumstances, with a right to bear a grudge against others and the world. Adler noted that goal directed movement can only be understood "as the individual's efforts to secure for himself what he interprets, or misinterprets, as success, or as his way of overcoming a minus situation in order to attain a plus situation" (p. 181).

- A woman of fifty-five was an only child. "I would have liked to have an older brother. It was so hard to always have to be the ideal daughter, to have to be perfect. My parents doted on me, and I never had a moment's peace. With an older brother, I would have had someone to share all that pressure. Maybe I could have done something on my own. Maybe I could have had some fun."

- A man of forty-one was the first-born and only son, with six younger sisters: "I would have wanted more privacy and more space. I never had a room of my own; there was always a baby in it. My parents went on having children even when they couldn't take care of the ones they already had." He felt deprived then and continues to feel deprived. He has struggled all his life to create his own world. He owns his own business, and has a large, comfortable house, which he maintains as a bachelor. He came to us because he found it "impossible to keep employees. I can't work with anyone."

- A man of thirty-eight reported, "I would have wanted my father to be able to hold a good job. He was always out of work, and there was never enough money. The fights Mother and Dad had over money never ended. They had it tough, and they made it tough on each other. I swore that would never happen to me." He was a successful politician. He always knew someone with whom he could make a deal, get a job, get ahead. He was rarely home, and his wife wanted a divorce. He was amazed: "Why would she want a divorce? She's got everything she could possibly want! What more does she want? I'll give it to her!"

13. Are you currently under a physician's care? What for? (Note type of problem; if the "presenting problem" which brought CL in to see you is a physical symptom, see Item 21; note signs):

A psychological investigation is not complete without a thorough inquiry into any physical problem. Whether or not it relates to the presenting complaint, it has a meaning to the client. You should also be prepared to inquire about any signs of a possible physical disorder, whether or not the client refers to them. A client's failure to refer to an obvious disorder is significant in itself, and should be understood.

> - A man of thirty-seven reported that he was a compulsive overeater. This was connected to his presenting complaint (to which we turned at this point in the inquiry). His physician had sent him to Overeaters Anonymous. He said, "When I work the program, I can lose weight. A month ago I dropped out of the program, and I'm gaining again. It goes in cycles, and seems to depend on two things: How busy I am at work, and whether or not my wife shows any interest in me." He appeared to be moderately overweight, looked tired, and showed little energy.

If a client reports a physical symptom and has not consulted a physician, we insist upon a medical examination. Any symptom, indeed any illness, may serve the purpose of psychological expression, which we will want to help this person to understand; however, an illness also has physical effects that must be interrupted before they crystallize into permanent damage.

14. Are you currently taking any medicines?

Note the purpose for which any medicine has been prescribed, the name of the drug, the dosage, how long the client has been taking it, and its effects and side effects. Sometimes side effects first come to the attention of the psychotherapist. Further, it is not safe to assume that the prescribing physician will always be alert to their occurrence, or even aware of the frequency with which they may be associated with the drug. A consultation with the physician may be called for, and you will have to obtain the client's written permission for this purpose before you proceed.

> - A woman of twenty-four, barely more than five feet tall, had consulted a physician six months before our meeting in an agitated and depressed state over the deterioration of her marriage. The physician prescribed an antidepressant drug with a tranquilizer. Since then she had gained over twenty-five pounds, and was unhappier than ever. We turned to the *Physicians' Desk Reference* and found that weight gain is a frequent side effect of the drug she was taking. Just knowing this was an immediate source of encouragement to her. Psychological counseling restored her self-confidence, and her weight gradually returned to normal when she stopped taking the medicine.

15. Date of last physical examination:

We routinely recommend a physical examination if the client has not had one within the past year. Even when there was an examination during the past year, we may recommend another if the person has since experienced catastrophic stresses. If the client does not have a personal physician we refer to a local clinic which does a thorough exam on a sliding fee scale. The clinic sends a complete report directly to the client, who may then review the results with our assistance.

- A woman of forty-six said, "I don't want to go. If I do, I just know they'll find something wrong with me." Her mother and sister had died of cancer, and she suffered with the expectation that she would also have the disease. We were able to persuade her to consider the possible damage her pessimism and fatalism could do to her general health. A physical examination revealed a mild nutritional anemia which was treated with iron and vitamin supplements. She began to see how her discouragement had kept her from maintaining a proper diet, leaving her more vulnerable to any illness, including the illness she dreaded.

16. Name, address, and specialty of physician(s) being consulted, if any:

Be prepared to give a referral to an appropriate specialist, if this appears to be necessary.

- A woman of thirty-eight was fearful of many things, including dentistry. "My teeth and gums are rotting, and I'm terrified of going to a dentist." We referred her to a dentist who is psychologically sophisticated, and who was able to establish a relationship with her one step at a time, beginning with simple instructions on dry brushing and the gentle use of unwaxed dental floss, and going on to the painless process of correcting her bite by equilibration. He went with her to the offices of another dentist, who was an expert in root canal surgery, and stayed with her through the procedure. She became fearless, and enthusiastic about the restoration of her mouth, even to the point of wearing braces!

17. General health (energy level; appetite; sleep; exercise; level of sexual activity; use of alcohol and drugs, including "recreational drugs"; tobacco; caffeine. Note physical signs):

We ask, "How would you describe your general state of health at this time in your life?" This gives us the opportunity to go on to inquire about specific health issues, if the client has not already addressed them in responses to the four preceding items.

> - A man of forty-two made an appointment to discuss his career plans. He was a corporate manager, considering an entrepreneurial venture in partnership with a friend. He made no reference to marital difficulties until we asked about his level of sexual activity and degree of satisfaction in that part of his life. He responded, "My wife and I haven't had sex in six years, at least!" It later unfolded that his idea about occupational change was connected to his hope of being able to earn enough money to satisfy his free-spending, pampered wife, in the hope against hope that, if he provided better, he might regain her respect, and with it her love.

Sometimes a client's worries about his or her own patterns of drug or alcohol use will come forward here. We will be alert to inquire whether any of the others involved in the client's life worry about it as well. Active substance abuse of any kind interferes with the possibility of psychological investigation. You must be alert to every subtle hint and to any small cues in this area, since the phenomenon of denial is inherent in a pattern of abuse. Often you will be unaware of any trouble until it is blatant.

> - A man of twenty-seven, whom we had counseled several years earlier, and whom we had seen intermittently since then in connection with his career difficulties, called the office on a Friday evening to describe himself as suffering with a severe panic attack. We engaged him in conversation, and detected a very slight slurring of his speech. We asked how much he had had to drink in his efforts to calm himself down, and he admitted to having consumed a six-pack of beer. We pointed out that alcohol was likely to increase rather than diminish extreme anxiety feelings, and asked whether he would be willing to stop drinking alcohol for the remainder of the weekend, to use warm milk to induce drowsiness, and to call us on Monday to report on how he was doing.
>
> On Monday he called to say that he felt much better, that he had talked with various members of his family during the weekend, and that he had decided to enter a hospital with an inpatient alcoholism treatment program. He did this, and subsequently has made good use of the Alcoholics Anonymous program, and better use of further psychotherapy.

In the discussion of general health, as in other matters covered in the inquiry, it is important to note if the client is aware of any marked change in condition, either positive or negative. If so, we pinpoint the period when it became apparent as closely as possible, then ask, "What else was going on in your life at that time?" By asking this question we may identify what Adler called the "exogenous factor" (p. 296); that is, an event in the client's life which facilitated, provoked, or invited the change. The significance of the exogenous factor in understanding the client's difficulties, including health problems, cannot be overestimated. It may lie in an event that, to all outward appearances, would seem relatively unimportant, such as a birthday, a promotion, or a move. The meaning of the exogenous factor will only be understood from within the context of the client's private convictions, expectations, and values. It can tell us a great deal about the limitations of the life-style, for it typically relates to a challenge for which the person felt and feels somehow unprepared.

> - A man of thirty-four had muscle spasms and aches in his right arm. They began about four months before he came to see us, at the time of his marriage. He felt burdened by the responsibility of having a wife, who (in his picture of what was required of him as a man) would expect him to be her "strong right arm."

18. Previous counseling or therapy (when, reason, type, with whom, how long, outcome):

The purpose of this item is to identify previous times of crisis in the person's life, to discern whether there is a pattern to these crises, to assess "therapy readiness" in the present encounter (the person's expectations of success), and to learn what this client has found to be either encouraging or discouraging in a therapeutic relationship.

Here note also whether or not the client has come to see you while still in a therapeutic relationship with someone else. In such a situation there are several possibilities, and they must be addressed. The person may have come at the recommendation of the other therapist, or may have suspended work with the other therapist for the duration of the work with you. This would, of course, be acceptable. If the client proposes to continue working with another therapist while consulting you at the same time, however, it is not acceptable, and you must make it clear that a decision is required before you can proceed. It is not to a client's advantage to work with two therapists who are not consulting together in multiple therapy. Differences in approach and emphasis become sources of confusion at best, and at worst defeat the collaborative nature of therapeutic work, with the observations of one therapist used to negate the observations of the other.

> - A man of forty-four had been in therapy off and on for nine years before he came to see us. He had worked with a Jungian therapist, and a Gestalt therapist; had studied Neurolinguistics extensively; had gone to a Freudian analyst for several years; and was currently working with an eclectic therapist. He felt he was not getting anywhere, and told his

therapist that he had decided to consult us in an Initial Interview, and that if he got something out of it he planned to terminate his work with the other therapist, who agreed to this plan. About the outcome of all his previous therapy he said, "I've learned a lot, and gained a great deal of insight, but I still feel that there's something fundamentally wrong with me that's never been resolved." We said, "Maybe that's what's wrong." He was startled, and asked what we meant. "Maybe your idea that something is fundamentally wrong with you is a mistake, even a form of vanity, a special idea of yourself as handicapped, having to struggle more than others to achieve as much as you do." He agreed to a Life-Style Assessment, which revealed the foundation for his idea: the hostility of his mother and his maternal grandmother (with whom the family lived) to his father, who came from an ethnic group which the two women regarded as inferior.

19. Referral source:

If we do not already know, we ask, "Who referred you to us?" (We typically learn this during our first telephone contact.) Knowing the referral source provides information about the person's network. If clients are unwilling to confide this information to us we do not make an issue of it. We find that as trust develops they will come back to the subject at a later time, sometimes later in the Initial Interview.

- A woman of twenty-four did not tell us how she came into contact with our practice until we had seen her several times. Then she said, "I didn't tell you who referred me because I didn't want you to know I was dating Jim (one of our former clients). I thought you would disapprove." Jim was twelve years older than she and divorced.

20. Emergency contact (name, address, phone, relationship):

At the beginning of our work together we ask the client to give us the name of someone with whom we have permission to make contact in case of an emergency. This can be important in the event of a suicide threat, or a need to arrange a stay in hospital.

- A woman of twenty-seven called us in the midst of a paranoid terror. We agreed with her that she should be admitted to a hospital, and called our psychiatric consultant to make the arrangements. We then told her that we would ask her contact to be with her until the admission could be scheduled. The contact was able to spend the afternoon with her and take her to the hospital.

The Presenting Problem (Items 21 - 28)

21. What brought you in to see us? If a physical symptom, describe location, sensations, intensity, frequency.

This question may appear superfluous, coming as it does so far into the interview. But it is often a relief to a person to have an opportunity to answer other questions first, and the relationship established in covering them makes this question all the easier to address.

> - A man of thirty-seven, within two weeks of his thirty-eighth birthday, said, "Few things in my life are constant. I am one of the most talented people I know, but my talents are stretched in so many directions that I feel I am spread thin. I seem to spend my whole life maintaining all my talents instead of focusing on one and moving it forward. I also do this with women.
>
> "The second thing is that I am afraid to express myself. Can you imagine a professor who is afraid to express himself? Isn't that nuts? What I mean is that I'm afraid to take a stand on anything. I hear myself saying, 'Now let's take a look at the other point of view here,' when I know damned well that the other point of view is horse-shit that can't be defended intellectually.
>
> "The last thing is that once I've accomplished something in an area, I think to myself, 'O.K., now I've done that. Why should I do more of it?' And I find myself moving on."

It turned out that our client was fighting against a rigid, limited, and inflexible masculine guiding line (see Chapter 6), which threatened him with the idea of sterility. When this man was born his father was thirty, an autocrat and a self-made businessman full of braggadocio who ruled his household by browbeating his wife and children, and by insisting upon having things the way he wanted them. He claimed this by right, as the provider, and Mother went along, as if in awe of him. Then, when the client was eight years old, Father's business failed as the apparent result of his refusal to accept advice about a shift in the economic climate. Father was never the same; Mother never understood or accepted the change in the family's financial circumstances, and complained about it constantly. The client saw the tables turned between his parents, and ascribed it all to Father's obstinate determination to stick to things and prove himself right.

Some people are focused and articulate in response to this question, and spell out their difficulties in an orderly way. Others present a torrent of undigested ideas, complaints, and experiences. In a case of the second kind, it is up to us to guide the client toward the setting of priorities, and toward an organization of the issues.

Occasionally people do not know how to answer, but even these tell us something in response to this query, from reports of a general uneasiness and anxiety about life to accounts of things that are "no big deal," but somehow remain troublesome.

Others tell us that they came in under duress from a spouse, a boss, or a parent. We want to know what provoked these concerned persons to apply this pressure.

The presenting problem may refer to the chronic and troublesome behavior pattern of a person who has long been aware of it, and is at last prepared to sort it out. On the other hand, it may be a situational crisis for a person who is asking for short-term help to manage it.

Many of our clients get what they want from the Initial Interview, and that is the end of their therapy. Others choose to conclude their work with us after completing a Life-Style Assessment. Still others continue their work with us in order to reconsider all the implications of the interfering ideas isolated in the Life-Style Assessment.

22. When did it start? What else was going on in your life at that time?

Here we have another opportunity to isolate the exogenous factor and, perhaps, to employ Adler's "organ dialect" (p.310), or organ jargon, theory (Griffith, 1984), as we were able to do in the following case.

- A woman of thirty-eight suffered with chronic back pain. She reported that the trouble began when she was a senior in college. She had wanted to head for New York and become an actress, but her parents insisted that she go on to nursing school, arguing, "You'll have something to fall back on. You can always get a nursing job."

- A man of forty-eight had lost his job in a corporate takeover two weeks before he came in. "Until now, I've felt that this is a big world, and there will always be a place for me. Now here I am on the street with no place to go, and no fall-back position."

23. Have you noticed a pattern?

Sometimes this has been established already, and the inquiry at this point is unnecessary. If not, the question may represent a new idea to the client.

- A woman of twenty-nine said, "It's the story of my life. No matter what I do, my father objects, criticizes, and puts me down, over and over again. I have an idea it's to get at my mother and doesn't have much to do with me, but that doesn't help. It also doesn't help to have Mother support me, because she won't do it in front of my father. She just pretends to go along, and lets him do this to me."

24. What happens as a consequence of having this problem? Who is most affected by it?

Take these questions one at a time. It is always best to maintain the conversation without allowing it to become an interrogation. You may get the answer to the second question in this item from the client's response to the first one, and not have to go further. What we are after here is the function of the symptom, and its possible "target."

- A man of thirty-four said, "When I have headaches my wife is very solicitous. She has taken this very well. I usually have them when I get home from work, and she makes me lie down and take it easy."

- A man of forty-seven responded, "When I blow up at work, it's very effective. I have a reputation for being tough, and I get a lot of cooperation when I begin to get impatient with my people. But I know that it's no good; I also get a lot of complaints about it."

25. What have you done about it until now?

Here again, we may already have an answer to this question. If not, we want to learn what the client has done, or tried to do, about the symptom, complaint, or presenting problem. This may help us to find the private value of the difficulty, and the hidden reason the person has for maintaining it.

- A woman of twenty-seven, still in competition with her sister, said, "I've tried to point out to her how wrong she is, but she won't change. She seems determined to cause trouble for me with Mom and Dad."

26. How do you explain this situation to yourself?

The person's own assessment of the difficulty may reveal the question of self-esteem that is involved.

> - A man of fifty-three presented the problem of not getting his work done on time. He said, "I have too many people to manage. I get there early every day and stay late. When I get home in the evenings, I work. And I'm not only doing my own job. I pick up the pieces for everyone in my department. No one does the work as well as I do -- they all say that. But then there's not enough time to do what I have to do."
>
> - A woman of thirty-four presented the problem of procrastination. "I can't decide what to do first, or how to do it, so I put things off...and off...and off. Then I have to scramble to get the job done before the deadline. It feels absolutely great to go in with my work on time! But I'm in agony thinking about it for days, weeks, sometimes months before I do it."

27. How would your life be different if you did not have this problem?

Dreikurs referred to this question of Adler's (p. 332) as "The Question." It is an integral part of any Initial Interview:

> The examination begins with an inventory of the subjective symptoms and complaints of the patient. They represent his *subjective condition*. The next step is an investigation of the *objective life situation*. This consists of a careful examination of his participation at work, in social contacts, and in his relationship to the [other] sex, uncovering existing conflicts and dissatisfactions. The connections between the subjective condition and the objective situation is established by the question, "What would you do if you were well?" The answer will reveal the dynamics of the existing psychopathology (1967, pp. 105-106).

The Question is also of great importance in differential diagnosis of physical symptoms. Dreikurs specifically pointed to this in a discussion of the psychological purpose of physical symptoms:

> (The technique) consists of the "question." The patient is asked what would be different in his life if he were well. The answer indicates against whom or against what condition or situation the symptom is directed.... (The answers) indicate why the patient is sick, if the illness is entirely neurotic, or that he uses a physical ailment for such purpose. Such neurotic superstructure may be revealed in the case of an actual organic pathology (1967, pp. 114-115).

The following three examples will help to illustrate the usefulness of this technique. The first represents neurotic use of an organ weakness in the circulatory system, without any diagnosis of organic disease or damage. This is a single man of thirty-one, who has been medically treated for migraine:

> If I didn't have these headaches I'd go out more socially. I would have more time for myself, and I'd do things I enjoy. Now I use my spare time to recover. For some reason week-ends are the worst. Some Saturdays I just lie in bed. If I were able to go out more socially I'd be able to find a woman.

The second example is of a neurotic superstructure over a diagnosed organic disease process. This is a young married woman with recurrent episodes of ulcerative colitis:

> My house would be organized and decorated. We could entertain. My husband says that he's embarrassed to bring people home as things are now. It's funny. My bedroom is finished, but after five years in the house, the living room and the den aren't. I used to cook and throw parties, but not any more. Now I just "stew." Oh, I get things done, but only by the skin of my teeth, and never under pressure. That just puts me to bed!

Finally, an example of suspected neurotic behavior ruled out by the diagnosis of a physical ailment. This is a young couple presenting a marital disturbance brought on by the husband's suspicion that his wife has lost interest in him. When he sits with her after dinner in the early evening, and tries to have a conversation about events of the day, she falls asleep. Aside from this, they both describe the marriage in positive and affectionate terms. Here is part of what she said:

> I don't understand it, and I'm embarrassed to talk about it, because I can see how he must feel. I'd feel the same way, if the shoe were on the other foot! I fight to stay awake, and I want to talk with him, but as soon as things get quiet and relaxed I'm gone. It's not only with him. I fell asleep on the basement stairs once, and woke up on the floor at the bottom. It's a wonder I didn't break something. And it's misery for me to ride the bus! As hard as I try not to, I'll just go straight to sleep as soon as I'm comfortable, and as often as not I miss my stop.

Her reply to The Question was that nothing would be different in her life, except that she wouldn't suffer the embarrassment of falling asleep so frequently and so abruptly. The disorder did not interfere with her functioning in any debilitating way, since, when she was active and engaged in taking care of the children, cleaning house, or doing any other physical work, she was almost always free of the symptom, and fully alert. Nor did the "misery" of her embarrassment restrict her from continuing to ride the bus whenever it was necessary.

Our clinical impression was that she suffered with narcolepsy, an hypothesis strengthened by the fact of the couple's being black, and therefore from a group at greater risk for this disorder. We referred to a neurologist, who confirmed the diagnosis, prescribed the appropriate medication, and put an end to the couple's need for further psychological consultation.

28. What do you expect will come out of our work together?

The discussion will tell us something about the person's relative optimism or pessimism, which is a key index to therapy readiness. Some clients have been to many therapists before coming to see us. In some cases it may even be surmised that they have moved from one to another in order to maintain the symptom with a clean conscience. Therapy can be a sideshow in itself, one of many excuses or rationales for not getting on with the real business of life, and even a way of certifying a person's being inadequate or unprepared for those tasks. When being in therapy is part of a neurotic arrangement we can expect to be told something like, "When my therapy is over I'll be able to address the problem of ____________" (fill in the blank with love/work/friendship).

- A woman of thirty-five said, "I have a good marriage, but my husband wants a baby and I don't. I told him that I can't deal with that until I get my head straight. I hope you can help me."

- A parishioner went to see the curate of an urban parish with a host of problems. His wife had left him, and he had the sole responsibility for the care of two young children. He was about to be evicted from his apartment, and he was in danger of losing his job. He attributed all his difficulties to a conspiracy being directed against him by the Elks Club, the Presbyterian Church, and the Democratic Party. The priest recognized a paranoid arrangement, but felt incompetent to be of help to the man. Gently, he recommended that psychiatric help was needed. "You're absolutely right, Father," replied the distraught parishioner, adding: "As soon as I can get these Elks, Presbyterians, and Democrats off my back, the first thing I'm going to do is go to a psychiatrist. This whole thing has shot my nerves."

In this case, pastoral counseling was his side show; by means of it he was evading a realistic reappraisal of his failed marriage, hoping to gain some measure of sympathy, and (by concocting such a dramatic explanation to account for his troubles) to salvage some scraps of self-esteem.

The Life Tasks (Items 29-34)

LOVE

29. Situation. Tell me about your love relationships. (If CL lacks relationships of emotional or sexual closeness, ask: How do you account for this?)

Key prompting questions: What makes a man a "masculine" man to you? What makes a woman a "feminine" woman? How do you compare yourself to your list of associations for your own sex? Do you experience difficulty in expressing love and affection for others? Difficulty in receiving such expressions from others? What does your partner complain about in you? What do you complain about in your partner? Describe your first encounter with your partner. What was there about him or her that impressed you at that time?

Note that the *IPCW* uses the term "prompting questions" here. We prefer a free flow of conversation to follow out of the instruction ("Tell me...etc."), but sometimes the client does not know where to begin, or may overlook key issues. In such a case one or more of these questions may serve as a guide.

The questions about masculine men and feminine women are designed to reveal the client's gender guiding lines in a brief sketch. Requiring little reflection, the replies express biases regarding the two sexes, naming qualities, competencies, and attitudes that are likely to be related (either directly or antithetically) to the person's basic perceptions of mother and father. Here are a few examples, male and female, with ages noted in parentheses:

Male (30)

Masculine	*Feminine*
The way you walk; tone of voice; way you handle yourself; a strong person, able to handle your own problems.	Not loud; not aggressive; visual (how she's built); soft; warm; someone who can comfort you.

Male (53)

Masculine	*Feminine*
Strength and endurance, both emotional and physical.	Warm; empathic; a kind of teacher (for example, my daughter taught me how to play handball. I never would have tried it if she hadn't conned me into it!).

Female (37)

Masculine	*Feminine*
Gentleness; intelligence; humor; nurturing.	I think of negatives: not girlish; no ruffles; not a tomboy either; not dumb; not up tight, more laid back. (This is harder for me. I'm pretty clear about that "masculine" man!)

Male (36)

Masculine	*Feminine*
Provides whatever is needed, no matter what it takes you to do it; you can right any wrong, and whatever befalls, you can correct it.	Looks.

The question, "How do you compare yourself to your list of associations for your sex?" prompts a self-assessment:

- A man of fifty-six: "I stack up pretty well. I don't think my wife would agree with me, but I'm pretty comfortable with it."

- A woman of forty-two: "I am loving and giving. But I'm afraid to be flirtatious. I envy women who aren't afraid!"

- A woman of twenty-three: "I'm not like this at all. I'm not feminine in any traditional sense. Isn't it odd that I'd have a list like that? Actually, I'm uncomfortable about this whole issue."

- A man of forty: "I don't do very well with the 'toughness' and being able to handle situations. I'm O.K. on the 'caring' and 'sensitivity.'"

Here are some examples of responses to the questions, "Do you experience difficulty in expressing love and affection for others? Difficulty in receiving such expressions from others?"

- A man of forty-eight: "I can really dish it out. I treat my girlfriend like a princess. I hug her a lot. But I don't want her to move in on me. Actually, she's sort of unhappy about this. I don't even like her to give me presents."

- A woman of thirty-two: "My mother says I'm thoughtless, that I don't show her enough attention. She's not a warm person. She's so defensive. With other people it's easier for me, but still a problem. I like it when they're warm with me, but I'm still a little awkward in the way I respond."

The next two questions ("What does your partner complain about in you? What do you complain about in your partner?") can elicit further information about the masculine and feminine guiding lines, and the client's training for cooperation with the other sex.

- A man of forty-four: "She says I don't communicate with her. As she puts it, 'Once I cross that line with you, it's as if I don't exist.' She says I'm not affectionate enough. I tell her she talks too much. Also, she's quick to anger. She flares up. But once the anger is out, it's forgotten. I can stonewall, and I bear grudges. I wish I were more like her."

- A woman of thirty-seven: "My boyfriend doesn't like it that I'm a Democrat, and that I hate to cook. He complains about my temper too. I blow my fuses, especially when he interrupts me, which he does a lot. Then he complains that I don't speak up calmly and directly. So, I don't like the interrupting, and I don't like that he smokes and that he's married. I complain about that a lot."

- A woman of twenty-eight: "His mess drives me crazy. He's a pack rat. Also, he's overcommitted, tries to do too much, and is never home. He doesn't like the way I try to organize his life. He says, 'Leave me alone.' But I can't. Organization is important to me. He also doesn't like the way I worry about him. But he's out on the road, in all kinds of weather! How can I not worry about him?"

The last two of these questions ("Describe your first encounter with your partner. What was there about him or her that impressed you at that time?") are directed by the FECK ("First Encounter of the Close Kind") concept (Belove, 1980). The character of the relationship can be discerned in the story of the first encounter, which reveals the qualities that attracted the two to each other. Their movement in the story is a paradigm of the ensuing transaction between them. They may continue to rehearse this transaction successfully, or it may have failed them in meeting the challenges of the current situation, leaving one or both of them discouraged.

> - A man of thirty-six: "I met my wife at the laundromat. We only spoke casually. She had beautiful eyes, and was attractive. She seemed to be a professional, or at least someone who used the language correctly! Also, I liked the fact that she was cautious. She didn't want to carry on an extended conversation with a stranger, and wouldn't tell me where she lived. That was feminine. I asked around, and tracked her down. Finally we went out, and it turned out that we liked a lot of the same things. She has always controlled the relationship, though; her cautiousness again, I guess. It keeps me in line."
>
> - A woman of forty-one: "I didn't like him when I first met him. But he was very persistent, kept calling me up and asking me out. I resisted until I saw him again at a party. There he was, surrounded by a lot of friends. I saw that he had a strong personality, and was the leader of the group. He was attractive and outgoing. Before, I had thought that he was too aggressive. He paid a lot of attention to me that night, which I liked. He's too busy now."

30. Goals. What do you want to improve or change in this area of your life?

In eliciting an ambition to improve or change the present situation, we learn about purpose and get hints of privately perceived stumbling blocks to moving forward. On the other hand, the reply may indicate that this is an area in which the person is experiencing success; therefore talking about it can be a source of encouragement.

> - A woman of fifty: "I don't know if I want my husband to come back or not. I have so much resentment. He's hurt me so much. If he could be like he used to be, then I'd want him."
>
> - A woman of twenty-four: "I want to get married, but my boyfriend doesn't. He says he thinks things are just fine the way they are with our living together. But to me it's just

like playing house. I want a real house, and children. How can I get him to change?"

- A man of thirty-four: "I'm happy with this part of my life. I feel happily married. My wife and I have a lot of fun. What worries me is the job situation."

WORK

31. Situation. Tell me about your work. (If CL has no occupation or is currently unemployed, ask: How do you account for this? Explore interests and ambitions in this area.)

Key prompting questions: What has been most satisfying to you in the jobs you have held? Least satisfying? What other work have you done? Why have you left those jobs? Are you aware of anything about the way you work that causes trouble for you (e.g., procrastination)? Do you feel appreciated at work? How do you evaluate your relationships with others at these levels: superiors, peers, subordinates? Members of the other sex?

The client's perception of areas of personal effectiveness and ineffectiveness, and an evaluation of these, are invited by the first of the prompting questions, "What has been most satisfying to you in the jobs you have held? Least satisfying?"

- A woman of forty-four: "I like the technical part of being a nurse. I didn't like being a floor nurse who took care of people. I liked working with the doctors in intensive care where I had a lot of medical responsibilities. I was very competent in those areas. On the floor they complained that I didn't work fast enough. They were pushing patients through there like cattle, and we were really overworked. I never felt like I did a good job. I liked the feeling of being a member of the team in intensive care, and the doctors liked my work."

- A man of thirty-six: "My present job is blah. There isn't anything new for me to learn. The challenge is gone, and I'm getting stale. I'm not afraid of responsibility, and I make good decisions. They respect me. But if it isn't exciting, it just doesn't interest me. I don't know how much longer I can keep it up."

In the prompting questions, "What other work have you done? Why have you left those jobs?" we are looking for a pattern of experience and attitude.

- A man of sixty-three: "I've done a lot of different things. I've worked since I was fourteen. Summer jobs in a grocery, in a factory, you name it. When I've left, it's been to move on and move up. In college I got into business administration courses, and realized that was what interested me. I'm not interested in the product. I can work in any industry as long as the pay is good and I can live the kind of life I want."

Self-evaluation is invited by the question, "Are you aware of anything about the way you work that causes trouble for you?"

- A woman of fifty: "I don't delegate. We're under a lot of pressure. It's a lean, mean company. This has become more and more of a problem for me."

- A man of forty-seven: "I'm disorganized. I don't stick with a job until it's done. I get distracted by my thoughts about other things. I leave the paper work, and make phone calls; or I stop making phone calls, and go to the paperwork. I'm my own best interrupter."

- A man of twenty-nine: "I don't do the follow-up work. I love new projects. Once they're in place I lose interest in them, and depend on others to do the detail work -- which they don't like. I get complaints about this."

- A man of fifty-six: "I procrastinate. The Bar Association has brought two complaints against me, based on my client's reports to them. I do good work, but I can't seem to bring it to completion in an appropriate length of time."

"Do you feel appreciated at work?"

- A man of fifty-three: "No. I move too fast for them. If they could fire me, I believe they would. Luckily for me, my immediate boss has a lot of clout. As long as he's there I'm untouchable. I like making decisions and acting. I don't like waiting for authorizations from upstairs. When I can't get decisions pronto, I just go ahead. So, even though I'm generally unappreciated, the person who counts appreciates me."

- A woman of thirty-two: "My peers are jealous because of my success, and they aren't very nice to me. This troubles me. I'd like to be a team member. As it is, I'm a loner. I'm a very successful salesperson, though, so I have that going for me. The others think I'm a snob. When I try to be friendly and helpful, they think I'm faking."

"How do you evaluate your relationships with others at these levels: superiors, peers, subordinates? Members of the other sex?"

- A woman of forty-two:

Superiors: "Good, cooperative, mutually satisfying. I work best when I get encouragement, good feedback, and have the freedom to set my own objectives."

Peers: "It's a team effort. I think we respect each other's areas of expertise."

Subordinates: "I expect them to do a good job. And I like to see them succeed. I think they work well with me."

Other sex: "Great. It's women I can't work with, if they're in authority. I don't know. It just doesn't sit right with me. Usually I feel that I know more than they do, and that they shouldn't be there."

- A man of thirty-seven:

Superiors: "Fine."

Peers: "Not so good. I'm quite a bit above them in educational level, so I don't enjoy them. They hang out together socially, and I don't take part. I don't think they use their brains."

Subordinates: "Good."

Other sex: "There are very few of them in the industry. I feel kind of sorry for the ones who are. They just don't fit in. I try to help them out."

32. Goals. What do you want to improve or change in this area of your life?

- A man of forty-one: "I wouldn't want to change anything. I really like my situation; I can see it growing and getting even better in the years ahead."

- A woman, thirty-five: "I want to quit my job and go back to school. I like working in the travel business, but I know that I can't move as far up as I want to unless I have more education. I thought this was one business where not going to college wouldn't matter, but I've learned that I just have to know more about everything."

- A man, thirty-three: "When I finish law school, I'd like to specialize in family law. There's a real need for sensitive men in this field."

FRIENDSHIP AND COMMUNITY

33. Situation. Tell me about your friends and your life in the community. (If CL reports few or no connections with others, ask: How do you account for this?)

Key prompting questions: From where do you draw your friends? How many close friends do you have? How often are you together? What do you do? Do you have friends of the other sex? How do your friendships end? How much do you feel you are able to confide in your friends? What sort of impression do you think you make on people the first time they meet you? Does this impression change over time? If I were to call one of your close friends and ask, "What do you value in (CL)?", what would he or she say? What kind of connections do you have in your community?

"From where do you draw your friends?"

By this question we inquire into the extent of the client's social interest. It is telling if the friends all derive from the family of origin and the extended family, or from members of the ethnic or religious group in which the client grew up. When the loyalties and affiliation of a person are not extended into the wider community, we can expect to see an increased intensity of symptoms and disturbances. The extent of the social interest and the severity of the dysfunction are in an inverse proportion to each other.

- A woman of thirty-nine reported that she had no friends. Her social life was limited to her sister, her brother-in-law, nieces and nephews, and her widowed mother. There was no man in her life, and she described her colleagues at work as "competitive and unfriendly."

- A man of twenty-seven reported that he drew all of his friends from his circle at work. "We're all techies. We go out drinking and talk computers. The group includes a couple of really bright women. We keep sex out of it."

- A man of fifty-one reported, "One of my gripes is that my wife doesn't make her own friends. She gets mad at me because I don't always want to include her in my evenings 'on the town' with my buddies. I tell her to get some friends of her own. My friends come from work, from my health club, and from my connections with United Way and other activities in the community."

"How often are you together? What do you do?"

- A woman of twenty-six: "My best friend is a sorority sister from college. We have lunch together at least once a week. I tell her my troubles, and she tells me hers. I stay in touch with a couple of girlfriends from high school. It's been hard for me to make new friends in the city. I don't like the bar scene, and I don't know what else to do to meet people. People at work aren't suitable. They don't share my interest in the arts."

- A man of thirty-one: "I don't have a big group of friends, but I'm happy with that. I was always the type who had one 'best friend.' So I prefer a small group. We do lots of things: Sailing, skiing, tennis."

"How much do you feel you are able to confide in your friends?"

- A man of thirty-eight: "I can tell Andy and Joe anything. They know all about my divorce and the troubles I'm having. They give me good advice."

- A woman of thirty-two: "I keep them at a distance. I like to keep it light. When I have trouble I talk to my father or my brother. I don't want my friends to know about it."

"What sort of impression do you think you make on people the first time they meet you? Does this impression change over time?"

Most clients have not thought about these questions before, and are intrigued to think about them. Some "have no idea," which may be an index to how little social effectiveness they experience in themselves. The degree of self-confidence and self-understanding may be revealed.

- A woman of forty-eight: "People see me as friendly. I'm a good listener, and I'm honest. I don't talk much, but when I do it's because I have something worthwhile to say. I keep my friends a long time. I give them a lot of attention, and they appreciate it. They can rely on me. They know I'm there for them when they need me."

- A woman, twenty-five: "They think I'm aloof and maybe a little too quiet. I like to feel my way into a situation, sort of size it up before I get too involved. I think they see me as attractive and intelligent. After they get to know me they see my sense of humor, my talent, my warmth and caring. I think some are threatened by me, especially men."

- A man, thirty-six: "I know what I want them to think, but I don't know what they think. I want them to think I'm intelligent, articulate, suave, and put-together. The only thing I'm sure of is that they see me as tall!"

"If I were to call one of your close friends and ask, 'What do you value in (CL)?', what would he or she say?"

- A man of twenty-two: "They'd say that I'm loyal, that I care, and that I'm supportive."

- A woman of twenty-eight: "I don't know what they'd say. Well, I give them good advice. They know I'm sincere and that they can count on me."

- A man of fifty-three: "They know they can count on my support -- if I agree with them. If I don't agree, they know I'll tell them. So I guess it would be my bluntness that they would value most."

"What kind of connections do you have in your community?"

- A woman of sixty-seven: "I've lived in this town all my life. At one time or another, I've been involved in the church, in the schools, in different charity activities, on the library board, and so forth. I've given that up now. It's my turn! Now I want to go to Florida."

- A woman of thirty-five: "I'm active in the women's work of the synagogue. I feel that I have an obligation to do that as long as my children are involved. I don't especially enjoy it, but what can I do? I feel this way about a lot of things in my life: I ought to do them, so I do."

- A man of forty-one: "I'm active in the church. I'm on the Vestry. It's important to me. I used to be a Catholic, so it's like I've found a new home, and I'm glad to feel 'at home' in it. I also do volunteer work with The Little Brothers. They take care of old people. I keep thinking about what it will be like for me when I get old, since I have no family. I hope The Little Brothers will be around then."

- A man of twenty-four: "I don't have any connections in the community. My parents know everyone and are real active. I'm just going to school. I can't see ending up like them. I want to get away and travel."

34. Goals. What do you want to improve or change in this area of your life?

- A man of twenty-nine: "I'd like to be a better friend, more consistent, less volatile. I'd like to be very consistent in my conduct, and get balance in my life -- social, marital, professional, religious."

- A man of thirty-four: "I'd like more and closer friends, and a more active social life. I'd like to feel comfortable among strangers. I used to, at home, when I was young. Then I came to the U.S. to school, and never really went back. It's never been the same for me."

- A woman, thirty-two: "I want to feel that I can say what I want. Other people seem to feel free to do that, and it always surprises me! I just kind of go along with whatever is happening. Then I get resentful."

Conclusion

In this chapter we have presented the *IPCW* format for the Initial Interview inquiry, along with samples of responses elicited by each of the numbered items it includes.

In the next chapter we move on to the inquiry process in Life-Style Assessment, with a detailed consideration of the way information about the client's position in the childhood family can be gathered, and with a guide to eliciting and recording the client's early recollections.

This sequence makes sense in terms of the organization of the book, but a reader may not want to consider more information about inquiries without seeing how we use the data gathered in those processes. Skip to Chapter 5, "Life Situation, Presenting Problem, and Life Tasks," to see how we work to make sense of the data in our review of it with the client, where we test our understanding and our interpretations. The final step in the Initial Interview is the composing of the summary of the material; the method for this procedure is covered in Chapter 12.

Chapter 4: LIFE-STYLE ASSESSMENT INQUIRY

We divide the Life-Style Assessment inquiry into two sections. First we systematically record a thorough description of the members of the person's family of origin, their relationships, and their circumstances. This gives us a sense of the social dynamics and organization (the "family constellation") in which the person encountered the tasks of life. With this as a context for understanding, we then elicit and record memories of specific incidents that occurred in the early childhood situation ("early recollections"), to gain a picture of the evaluations the person made (and makes) of life.

The form we use for the investigation into the family constellation has two parts: "Part I: Parents, Other Adults, Milieu"; and "Part II: The Situation of the Child." The form for recording early recollections provides space for eight stories of childhood experience, plus (for reasons we will explain below) a ninth recollection. (See *IPCW*, pp. 10-21, for the complete outline.)

This is, of course, a formal way of structuring the work. For the therapist it has the advantage of keeping the discussions with a client disciplined and to the point. For the client it provides a reassuring sense of direction, frequently welcomed as an antidote to the disorientation that occasioned the consultation. Even so, we remind readers that a living conversation is never so neat as to fit a formal structure for recording the data derived from it.

A client's memory is likely to be stimulated during the family constellation inquiry so that some early childhood recollections will come to mind then, prior to the place in the outline at which you intend to ask for them. Each of these recollections should be recorded at the time it is presented, on a separate sheet of paper which can be interleaved with the other data as a kind of footnote. Because these recollections are prompted by the material under discussion, they do not have the same projective quality or value as those memories that the client presents without an awareness of any context or reminders. They are important, however, and we take them into account when we compose the "Summary of the Family Constellation" (as you will note in the following case). Later, when you are making the formal record of early recollections (unprompted by anything other than questions such as,

"How far back can you remember?" and, "What is the next memory that comes to mind?"), the client may recall some of these same incidents again. Make a fresh record of these memories then, encouraging the client to tell the story once more as he or she is now remembering it.

This chapter includes a verbatim transcript of the Life-Style Assessment inquiry in "The Case of Dan." We have protected confidentiality by disguising all identifying material, as we have also in all other cases referred to in this book. To introduce The Case of Dan, the transcript is preceded by a synopsis of notes from Dan's Initial Interview, and the summary of impressions derived from it. Without discussion here of the methods used in shaping them (which are covered in Part IV) the three summaries of the life-style data conclude the chapter.

THE CASE OF DAN

Synopsis of the Initial Interview

Dan was forty-five years old. He had been separated for eight months from his wife, Eileen, their fourth separation in fourteen years of marriage. Before marrying they lived together for two years. He had a stepdaughter from Eileen's first marriage; he and Eileen had a daughter eleven years old.

The disturbance between him and Eileen was the presenting problem. He said that they loved each other, "at least we both say that we do." Their relationship was stormy, and he reported that he had acted "violently." When asked to define this, he said that he had never struck his wife, or in any other way physically abused her. He had "raged and sworn" and struck his head against the wall in "displays."

Dan had one sibling, a brother three years younger, who was married and had no children. Douglas was a violinist with a metropolitan symphony orchestra.

Dan's original family was intact. His parents (Mother, seventy-three, and Father, seventy-six) still lived in Virginia, in the original family home: "They went through some rough periods, but stayed together, and are very happy and contented now. It's funny, because when I was a boy I was always afraid she would leave him. I felt sorry for her, somehow. She was very ambitious, and Dad certainly was not, though he was terribly bright. She was always disappointed. When I look back on it now I can see that he was a hard worker, and a good provider, but it was never good enough for her. I never saw my father get angry with anyone but her. I guess her complaining got to him." Father was described as arthritic, but "in good spirits"; Mother as having been troubled for twenty years by a smoker's cough, but "she refuses to go to a doctor, and is very active physically."

He assessed his own health as "generally good, though sometimes my back goes out. I can stand the pain, but I can't stand the immobility." He does not report any trouble arising from the use of alcohol, drugs, or food, and is not under a doctor's care.

He had been in therapy with another psychologist for six months, and decided to try someone else because "I want the process accelerated." When asked about the outcome of the therapy, he said, "He helped me to define some problems." Dan said that he had described himself to the other psychologist, "with a smile," as "indecisive," and told him, "I'm a person who likes to be told what to do. Either help me to become more decisive, or tell me what to do." Asked what his present goal was in therapy, Dan replied, "I want a better feeling about myself and a better understanding of why my relationship with Eileen is so difficult. I want an answer to the question, 'Can we make a happy marriage?' I also want to be better at making decisions, being understanding, and sharing affection."

Dan said that the trouble between him and Eileen had started the second year after they met, before they began living together. "I was already aware that we were going to have some struggles. When we met she was still married to her first husband. I was doing well and was happy and carefree. She was very unhappy. Her husband was an elitist, a rather learned man, from a family that was socially 'above' hers. He was very condescending toward her, more a mentor than a husband. It hurt me to see it, because she struck me as a remarkably bright and 'gutsy' sort of person who deserved better. I was always very shy with women, and never thought of myself as attractive to them, at least not to the ones I saw as attractive. She had striking good looks, and I was impressed by how friendly she was toward me. Her husband's coldness, and before that her father's indifference to her, had left her with some pretty bad feelings about herself. She had the idea that she was unloveable. I knew better, because I had fallen in love with her."

He reported that she left her husband for him, "and then, almost immediately, she became very insecure, and accused me of infatuation, of being incapable of true love, of being immature. It was always, 'If you love me, prove it, show me that you love me.'"

He said that he had "put a lot of effort" into this task, had given up some attractive job offers, and had moved to another state, "where she had always wanted to live. But it was never enough. She says I'm selfish, that I don't recognize her emotional needs, and that I don't share my feelings. Well, I guess I am rather selfish, and I do have a hard time trying to guess what she wants from one day to the next. I don't feel able to share my feelings with her, except for my anger."

Work. Dan reported that he was a metallurgist, currently manager of a large research project. He liked working with people from a wide variety of backgrounds. "I like synthesizing something out of nothing in my work. I like organizing a team out of disparate pieces, bringing order out of chaos. Some people philosophize forever; I like to get things done." He then added, "Eileen has played a heavy hand in the course of my career. She made the decisions about where we lived and what jobs I would take."

About working with his peers, he said, "I felt competent until my present job. Most of the men are recent Ph.D.s, and have lists of publications as long as your arm. They regard themselves as an intellectual elite."

He reported that he got along well with subordinates, but added, "I'm a little afraid of supervising them. I don't find it easy to force people to do things, though I can organize teams on a project."

He said that he worked well alone, and avoided supervision. "I can never tell where my boss is at. He's hard to read. He always knows more, or at least appears to. He's intellectually intimidating to me. I think he'd say of me that I'm a 'soft' person, which isn't exactly a compliment among 'hard' scientists."

His goal in this area: "I don't know what I want to do. I love wood working and puttering around, and I love music. Maybe I should go into furniture design. It's ironic, though; I got my Ph.D. so I could be secure in a job and able to do whatever I wanted to do. Now, it's as though I'm stuck with metallurgy because of it."

Love. Dan said that he had trouble expressing affection for women, "except my daughter. I'm very affectionate with her." He reported impotence, not only with Eileen, but with other women as well. "I can't get close to people. I don't know what to talk about." His first experience of impotence "was when Eileen forced me to make love to her because she wanted to get pregnant. She said we *had* to have a child. She had had a couple of abortions before that, and I had begun to draw away from her, especially after the second abortion. But I do love Eileen, and I wish our marriage could work out."

Friendship and community connections. Dan reported that he had a few close friends, none of whom lived nearby, even though he had lived in the same neighborhood and worked at the same job for two years. "I've begun to change that in the past few months, since Eileen and I have been apart." He had good friends in other states, but saw them only occasionally. His best friend was a woman. They talked on the phone "a great deal" and have considered living together. His next best friend was also a woman with whom he had had a "periodic" love affair. "It was a 'same time, next year' type of thing. I've drawn away from her now. She's a real 'earth mother' sort of figure. My other friend is a new, modern woman -- very clear, direct, ambitious. We're both opposed to marriage, but we're considering living together, or at least in the same community. We'd like to be close."

Of his male friends, he said, "It's mostly casual. You know, a drink after work. I've always felt shy around people, especially girls and women. It's always been a problem for me. Eileen says that it's my emotional immaturity and self-centeredness. The friendships I do have don't end though; they just change. Eileen faults me for that, too. She says, 'You're forever looking someone up; you live in the past.' I suppose she's right; it may even be part of my trouble with Eileen. We've been separated four times, but we never end it."

He believed that his friends valued him for being easy to talk to, understanding, sympathetic, and sensitive. On first meeting, "they see me as open, friendly, and easygoing. It doesn't always hold up. I reach a point where I can't be supportive, where I switch off. It's because I'm afraid they're going to demand something I can't cope with. In a way, I keep people at a distance. I need to be thought well of, and if they really knew me, they'd find out that I'm not as sensitive as I'd like to appear. I can be pretty selfish, too."

His goal in this area was to have a wider circle of friends. "I've been going hammer and tongs with Eileen, and haven't had time. In the last six months or so I've realized that other people are more important to me than I used to think they were."

> [Note: Immediately after reviewing the above data with the client and the first therapist, the second therapist dictated the following summary of impressions.]

SUMMARY OF IMPRESSIONS DERIVED FROM THE INITIAL INTERVIEW

Dan is emerging from a great defeat, reluctantly separating himself from an ambition which promised everything if it could be attained, but which demanded that he give more than everything he had in exchange, and, when he had given it, still proved unattainable.

The ambition appears to be based on a misunderstanding in which Dan long ago pictured manhood as an *achievement*, and was consequently unable to enjoy it as a *given*.

In the course of his childhood training the questions of sexual identity, personal power, domination, and submission seem to have been very much in the forefront, possibly because of Mother's struggle to demonstrate her importance, and her struggle to have Father work harder in order to insure it.

It appears that there was a general atmosphere of struggle in Dan's childhood family, with Mother energetically pushing, and Father trying to resist and comply at the same time. Further investigation may uncover the lines of this struggle in detail.

Dan probably wanted to be a good and diligent man like Father, but did not want to be in the service of a demanding, managerial woman like Mother.

As the first-born son he might have disarmed Mother by working to remain her favorite and to become her protege, learning from her how to manipulate, and then manipulating her so as to gain the advantages of her protection and pampering.

With other women it was a different matter from adolescence on. What he hoped for with them was to emerge as the Real Man that Father had appeared unable to be. This would require that he combine intellect with striving for accomplishment, and do so in such a way as to demonstrate a superior "goodness" which would mark him as "sensitive" to the "needs" of the woman. Then he would be able to rule without having to fight for domination.

He would be all things to a bright, gutsy, but unappreciated and unhappy woman, making her happy, and making it unnecessary for her to complain ever again. Thereby he would demonstrate to his own satisfaction that he had solved the problem of manhood by making an alliance with a powerful (and powerfully resentful) woman who would look up to him, rely upon him, be grateful for his superiority, and give up her resentments by yielding to the argument of his "goodness."

The problem that he hadn't foreseen, however, lay in the fact that the more superior, the more admirable, and the more able he looked, the more would be demanded of him, the more he would be required to be endlessly and generously concerned to make it up to the inferior woman for her disadvantages, and (the trickiest part of all) to prove to her that he was worth looking up to by never looking down on her.

Until now, his way of dealing with the insoluble problem he had set for himself (that is, the problem of making the Unhappy Woman happy) was to work harder at finding a solution. Only now is he ready to acknowledge that all the lore of the metallurgist is still unequal to realizing the alchemist's dream of transmutation: Lead remains lead, and gold remains gold, and gold (like a woman prepared to be happy with him and with life) is where you find it.

> [Note: The following is a verbatim record of the inquiry in the Life-Style Assessment in "The Case of Dan," following the form of the *IPCW*, pp. 10-16.]

Special Diagnosis

LIFE-STYLE ASSESSMENT

CL's present age 45 Date XX

Family Constellation, Part I: Parents, Other Adults, Milieu

1. Father's name Ronald Occupation warehouseman

   Age at CL's birth 31 Age, if living 76 Or, at death ____

   Yr & cause of death ____ CL's age at death ____

2. What kind of a man was your father when you were a child, up to age 10 or 11, in the pre-school and grammar school years? Consider activities, personality, health, level of education, and values (i.e., what was important to Father):

He always wanted a daughter. My brother and I both knew it. He even had a name for her: "Evelyn." He didn't take care of himself. Mother waited on him. He was quiet. He seemed very capable in a quiet sort of way. He wasn't able to go into the army -- bad feet -- but he was in the Civil Defense or something during the war. He always seemed to be there to take care of us, my brother and me. Dad sang hymns. I remember his singing hymns with me sitting on his lap. He kept a "victory garden," and he used to take me out back to work in the garden with him.

Dad never hurried. Mother would shout at him, "Hurry up or you'll miss the bus." He'd say, "Never mind. There'll be another one." He used to take me to see his father, my grandpa, who'd always be sitting in his chair in the kitchen with a cat on his lap. My grandma and great aunt were both paralyzed -- my great aunt was born with some sort of "creeping paralysis," as they called it then. Grandpa looked after both of them.

My dad flirted with women, but there was never any indication that he was unfaithful. Dad's really a good, earthy, sensible human being. Very little ever bothered him, except my mother. Mother said that he wasn't very good with sick people, but I could never understand what that meant, since she was never sick, or at least never admitted it if she was, and he always seemed to me to be kind to his mother and my great Aunt.

Dad was self-made. I don't know if he finished eighth grade. He learned fast, and was really a genius at figures. He was always very healthy as a young man. He was a good worker.

3. How did he relate to you and the other children?

I think Douglas was his favorite. Maybe this was a reaction to Mother's favoritism toward me. I didn't really perceive this in the early years, though; I began to see it when I was a teenager. He'd discipline us with verbal threats and occasional smacks, but he was never cruel. Mostly it was just by his presence and authority. We weren't afraid of him. I don't have any idea what he wanted me to do with my life. There just was no indication. And he was fairly liberal about my behavior. Not much bothered him.

4. How do you see yourself now as like Father? Unlike Father?

I'm like him in that I don't expect too much of people. For example, I've guided my children; I've never dictated to them. Also, I like working with my hands, and I like cats. I think I'm easy to talk to -- as he is now. I'm different from him in many ways. I'm achievement-oriented. I'm much more energetic -- going places, doing things. I will hurry, and I will worry. I went on to higher education. He never regarded education as important. He said, "I left school at fourteen. That was good enough for me."

5. Tell me briefly about Father's background and family of origin.

[Inquire into CL's relationship, if any, with Father's siblings and the paternal grandparents, and CL's impressions of each of them.]

Dad's family is very diffuse. His brothers and sisters weren't close. They got into fights and arguments. When I was eight or nine Dad and two of his brothers had a scene at my grandmother's funeral, and he hasn't talked to them since. Mother said that Grandpa spoiled and idolized Dad. There were seven or eight children. I think that there were two girls and five boys, and that Dad was one of the youngest. My grandpa was a gardener. I know they were very poor, and that they all left school quite young. I told you that my grandma wasn't well. Yet she raised those kids.

My mother said that Grandpa couldn't stand to be around sick people. She said that my grandma was treated very badly by Grandpa, but I didn't see that. My mother was always saying to me, "For God's sake, don't grow up to be like an Allen!" In other words, don't grow up to be bad-tempered, inconsiderate, and someone who can't stand sick people.

6. Mother's name Edith (Edie) Occupation housewife

Age at CL's birth 29 Age, if living 73 Or, at death ________

Yr & cause of death ____________________ CL's age at death ___

7. What kind of a woman was your mother when you were a child, up to age 10 or 11, in the pre-school and grammar school years? Consider activities, personality, health, level of education, and values (i.e., what was important to Mother):

She was energetic, busy as a bee, hard-working, quick, kept a nice house, cooked good meals. She was very ambitious for me. She hung over me when I was growing up. It was "nose to the grindstone" for me. She encouraged me to work hard -- really beyond my ability. I remember that I got real low scores on the SATs. She made me take them again, and I did better. But that was later. She was determined that I wasn't going to be deprived of the opportunities that came with higher education. I also remember her getting *very* angry with Dad.

Early Recollection: I was three or four years old. I was sitting on Dad's lap. He's singing to me or telling me a story. Mother walked in holding a carving knife, and said, "I could cut your throat!" He says something and she shouts at him and leaves the room.

Most vivid moment: The look of hatred on her face when she says it.

Feeling: Frightened.

She demanded that I look spotless, well-groomed, and that I was perfectly behaved. She sewed and ironed. I wasn't supposed to get dirty. I had to be careful. At age six or seven, I had a couple of baby teeth knocked out. Later, I broke the bottoms off two permanent teeth and she screamed at me, "You'll be disfigured for life!" She was horribly upset. It was a mortal blow! She wasn't concerned about the pain I was in!

Early Recollection: I was eight. I woke up with a crick in my neck. Mother took me shopping. She kept telling me to straighten my neck. She got very angry. She said, "I'm ashamed of you. You're stupid, dumb, an idiot," or words to that effect.

Most vivid moment: Her trying to force me to straighten my neck up, and I really couldn't.

Feeling: This is unfair! I felt very self-conscious and ashamed. I also felt inadequate: I felt I *should* be able to do it.

She treated me like a showpiece and protected me against my will. She'd intervene with my teachers, for instance. I felt pressure all the time, especially from the time I entered school.

She got colds very easily, but she'd "carry on." She was a martyr. She stayed up and suffered. She had three or four miscarriages when I was young. Even at these times she'd be on her feet. She'd say, "I've got to feed your father and you. Your father's useless, and you're a bungler."

My mother hadn't been able to finish high school, much less go to college, and she always resented it. There wasn't enough money in her family for that, not in those days. She was very musical, played the piano, and sang. But she never could afford a piano. She felt she'd married beneath her when she married Dad. They were both of English ancestry; she always said her people were of "better stock" than the Allens because they'd been here since colonial times, and the Allens hadn't come over until 1885. I don't know if there's any truth to any of that.

8. How did she relate to you and the other children?

She was really focused on me. Douglas had an easier time of it. She always claimed that Douglas and I had equal attention, but we knew it wasn't true. She had a lot of expectations: Be well-educated, look good, dress well, be well thought of by *everybody*, be in the top ten of your class. I stayed in the middle -- I was too talkative in school. She always said I could do better. She'd go through periods after my report cards when she wouldn't talk to me for a few days. I felt cast out and uncomfortable, and it really worried me. Oh! -- *and* I had to have good manners. I was in the spotlight -- I mean *her* spotlight -- always.

> *Early Recollection*: I was nine or ten. I'd been trying to make a little wooden house for my cat. Mother said, "You're a bungler -- a jack of all trades and the master of none." I remember walking into the kitchen and telling her that I was having trouble making the house. That's when she said that. Dad had only chuckled at all the nails I'd used.
>
> Most vivid moment: When she said it to me.
>
> Feeling: Inadequate. "I can't do anything right." That was the thought I had about myself. Awful.

As I said, if I did anything she didn't like, she'd withdraw her love and affection. She was always drumming into me, "Don't grow up to be an Allen." She'd say, "You're acting like an Allen." And, "I never did want to marry your father. He made me. He kept pestering me. When you kids grow up I'm going to leave your father." Whenever she said that I'd be scared for her. She'd be alone and friendless in the world.

9. How do you see yourself now as like Mother? Unlike Mother?

I'm like her in that I'm energetic. And for long periods I can be patient and uncomplaining. And I'm ambitious -- not so much in terms of career and making a lot of money, but in terms of being thought to be proper, intelligent, informed, well-read. I'm not like her in terms of endurance. I can't endure what she endures. In the end I'll kick back. She always implied that she stayed in it "for the children." I couldn't do that. I am more tolerant than she is, but not as giving. I always heard, "Your mother does anything for anybody."

10. Tell me briefly about Mother's background and family of origin.

[Inquire into CL's relationship, if any, with Mother's siblings and the maternal grandparents, and CL's impressions of each of them.]

There were more than ten children in her family. She was near the bottom, the second or third youngest. The one next younger to her died when she was in her twenties. He died of TB, and she stayed with him and took care of him during the illness. She said, "He was everything a man should be: Sensitive, loving, and kind." She came from a very close family. They all looked out for each other. I knew her mother better than any of my other grandparents, perhaps because she was the only one who came over to our house. She died when I was nine or ten years old. I remember her as kind, gentle, and soft-spoken, and in the background, barely a real presence of any kind.

I didn't know my grandfather. I guess I saw him a few times, but I don't remember him. My mother *never* talked about her father. He was a carpenter who was in and out of work, and drunk as often as he was sober. He ruled with an iron hand. Three of Mother's brothers and sisters still live together. They never married. I can't really be sure about Dad's family; he *says* they're English, but Mother's *is* English, through and through.

11. Parents' relationship. Tell me about how your parents got along with each other when you were a child. (Were they affectionate? Was one of them "the boss"? If they argued, what about? Who seemed to initiate the trouble, and what was the outcome? Did you take sides, openly or covertly? How did you feel about the trouble? Did you feel sorry for one of them?)

They had a very stormy relationship. I always felt insecure. I was scared of the fights and of my mother's temper. Dad would shout back at her. There was an awful lot of shouting and insults and swearing. They *never* touched that I ever saw. They were *never* affectionate in any way. In fact, Mother wasn't affectionate with anyone. She hardly ever touched me. She would give me a little peck every now and then. That's *all*. I tend to think I sided with my father, but mostly I was just frightened. Mother was the boss -- *always*.

12. Other significant adults. Tell me about any other adults who were important to you when you were a child. (If not already clear: Describe the character and role of any other adults living in the pre-adolescent household. Describe other adults who impressed you as a child, either positively or negatively.)

My father's brother, Uncle John, was a very funny man. I enjoyed him. He always had something good to say about me, and treated me as if I had important ideas and interests. He had a big house and a big garden. He was a plumber, and made a good living. Also, I'd go with Dad to see my great aunt when she was in the hospital. She was a very sharp, touchy woman, and difficult to talk to. She'd given me a violin, and when we went to see her she'd always ask me about it. We kept up the lie that I was doing fine with it, though in fact I didn't play. It was Douglas who played, and I had given him the violin.

Then there was Aunt Jill. She was a big, no-nonsense woman, not affectionate, but not unkind. She just wouldn't hesitate to tell you what to do.

On my mother's side there was Aunt Carla. She's the second oldest of my mother's brothers and sisters. She was a large, mother earth type. She ran a small business, a newspaper and magazine stand. She always sent presents -- magazines and books. That was kind of nice. She never married. And my mother's brother, Ned. He was called the "black sheep," but I never knew why -- still don't. I thought he was very nice and generous. He never married either.

13. Family milieu. If not already clear, inquire into: Socio-economic, ethnic, religious, and cultural characteristics of the family, and into the family's standards and values.

We felt we were better off than the others in the neighborhood. Our house and yard looked nicer, we ate better, and I was better dressed. Of course, nobody had a car or TV -- it was during the war, and it was a poor neighborhood. Even in our situation some of the rooms in the house were shut off sometimes. It was a fairly rough area, and Mother didn't want me to play with the other kids. She couldn't keep me from it, but she didn't like it and she'd lecture me about it.

Ethnically, I suppose it was about as mixed as it gets in a working class neighborhood in a city in Virginia. Of course, there weren't any Black people. Not in those days! Dad was a kind of "Archie Bunker" type in his thinking. You know, "Jews are all moneymakers, out for themselves." All the standard prejudices. The funny thing about it was that, of course, he didn't really *know* any Jews, except for the people who ran the dry cleaner's, and with them he was always the soul of polite good manners. So I grew up with all that, and I've had a lot to learn.

I was steeped in the Episcopal Church. Sang in the choir and so forth, although it dawned on me as I got older that we were a little out of our league there, in terms of class. But it was part of Mother's thing. She always referred to us as "Anglicans"! My father didn't go, by the way -- another bone of contention between them, and another opportunity for her to lord it over him. But my father was a religious man, in his own way.

He was into simple pleasures. He read all the racing sheets, and put a few bucks on the horses now and then. Mother hated that. She'd always say, "If he weren't a gambler we'd have more money." Being honest was *very* important to my mother, and gambling didn't fit with that. You should be hard-working. Don't look for charity, and don't look for luck. Take care of yourself, keep your problems to yourself, be suspicious of your neighbors, and believe in Heaven.

Family Constellation, Part II: The Situation of the Child

Sibling Array

Using the following page, array the names of the siblings from oldest to youngest, across the page from left to right. Include CL, and any siblings deceased, or separated from the family and living in institutions or elsewhere. Also note Mother's other known pregnancies terminated by abortion, miscarriage, or still-birth, entering them in the appropriate ordinal positions. Using CL's age as baseline, note the difference in years, plus or minus, between each of them and CL. Include step-siblings, and note CL's age at the time they entered the family. Use the following items to guide the discussion with CL, placing appropriate information in the boxes on the following page.

14. What kind of children were you? Describe each of the children, beginning with yourself, with respect to personality, health, and activities.

[See page 80 for an illustration of how the data for Dan and his brother was entered on the "Sibling Array."]

15. Note any subgroupings among the children: Who played with whom; who fought and argued with whom; who looked after and took care of whom; who taught and guided whom.

We played together a lot. We scrapped (I'd win). The issue was who'd be boss. He did what I said.

16. Note how each of the children distinguished himself or herself from the others; for example, by taking the place of the one who was:

academic/Dan	the problem child/neither
athletic/Douglas	religious/Dan
artistic/Douglas-violin; (Dan-painting: I'd paint with Mother.)	socially successful/Dan
	handicapped/neither
	the good child/both
entrepreneurial/neither	sickly/Dan

17. If any of the children was handicapped or sickly, note the child's and family's attitudes toward the difficulty.

I had asthma and allergies. I was hospitalized once when I was four. We coped. I wouldn't get more than a few days off from school. It was "tough it out." It was a "carry on" attitude. About my teeth, Mother's solution was, "Don't smile!"

SIBLING ARRAY

DAN (45)		DOUGLAS (-3)	
I don't know what kind of a kid I was. It's very difficult to answer. Very conscientious. Very intent on being seen the "right" way: - good behavior - polite - not rough - a gentleman I was very talkative. I tried hard at school. I was bullied a lot by neighborhood kids beginning about 8 or 9. They were rough. I'd get my head kicked. My mother would always run to the neighbors: "Look what your Johnnie did to my Dan!" I was sick with asthma from age 2 until I was 16 or 17. I usually couldn't take part in gym. And I was allergic to chlorine, so I couldn't swim in the summers.	(Note: Mother had "some" miscarriages between the births of the two boys, and possibly before Dan and after Douglas: "I'm not too clear on this.")	Much more popular than I was. He was easygoing ... just took things as they came. He was well liked. Easy to play with. He did what I wanted him to do. He never made any trouble. He was in excellent health.	

18. Which sibling were you most like? Least like? In what ways?

Like Douglas: We were both musical, though he really got into it, and worked to learn the violin. We both had tempers, and still do. It was the only way to get any relief from Mother's nagging. She'd back off, but for me the price was high. I hated her cold silences. We also both took schooling seriously enough to go on through college.

Unlike Douglas: He was more laid back than I was, more easy-going. He gave Mother the impression that he was going along with what she wanted, even when he wasn't. He'd just say, "Yes, Ma'am," and then do as he pleased. It amazed me. He'd fidget when he was nervous. I'd blabber. I'm a workaholic, and I think he's got his life more in balance.

19. To what extent did each of the children accept, reject, or modify the family's standards and values?

We both went along, for the most part. Douglas was a little less controllable, especially when he got older, but generally we both went along. We always put up a front of being good.

20. Childhood chronology. If not already clear, note any changes in the course of childhood and adolescent development experienced by CL as major events or turning points (e.g., a divorce, a move to another community), and CL's age at those times.

The main thing was that we were both different from the other kids. We wanted to go to college, to get out. That made us different.

21. What were your favorite stories, TV shows, fictitious or historical characters? What was there about them that you liked?

I was a reader. I liked adventure stories. I read all the Hardy Boy books. I remember the kids. I read the Nancy Drew books, too. My aunt who had the newspaper and magazine stand got them for me. I liked Nancy Drew. She was different. She was spunky, ready for anything, daring. She'd get into scrapes. She was gutsy! She went where the boys went.

22. Did you daydream? What about?

I didn't daydream, but I had terrible nightmares.

23. Do you remember any night dreams? Describe. How did you feel when you woke up?

I don't remember what they were about, but I had them, and I'd be terrified. I remember Mother's telling me about a nightmare she had when she was pregnant. I don't know if it was when she was pregnant with me or when. There was this huge spider coming up over the end of her bed. It would keep coming, and she'd wake up in a sweat.

24. Did you have any particular fears as a child? How did others respond?

I was very afraid of spiders. I wonder if it had anything to do with that nightmare? I was afraid they'd get on me and devour me. Mother and Dad were nice about it, sympathetic.

25. Was food and eating an issue in the household? In what way?

You had to eat everything on your plate. And you had to stay at the table until you finished it. We just did it, that's all. That's the way it was.

26. What were you good at? What did you most enjoy?

I liked acting and drama, painting, drawing, and singing. Later I played softball. When I was a kid I roller skated. But I was asthmatic then, and couldn't do a lot.

27. Was there anything you did not enjoy? Anything that was particularly hard for you?

Lots of things. School. Arithmetic. Writing. It was never quite good enough. I talked too much, and I had some trouble with being accepted and making friends.

28. Did you experience difficulty in your mental or emotional development? How was this addressed in the family? In school? How did you feel about it?

Well, that's a pretty broad question. I suppose if I did have some difficulty, I wouldn't have known it then. We wouldn't have noticed! It was "tough it out," all the way.

29. Think back to your early years, up to age six or seven. What did you want to be when you grew up? What was there about that that appealed to you? How and when did this change?

I didn't have a clue. Once we had to write a paper called, "A Day at Work." I was about eight or nine, I guess. I wrote about being a shoe salesman! My attitude was, "just do the job." Oh, another thing: I loved trains. There were lots of trains when I was little. I loved the engines. Big, huge, steam engines. You'd feel the earth shake when they went by. I used to write down all the numbers of all the engines. I considered being an engineer, but it wouldn't have been considered the right job by my mother -- or anyone. It was manual labor, and I saw myself in an office. Not that I knew what people did in offices!

30. Describe how you got along in the world of the neighborhood. How would you characterize your role among the children (e.g., leader, follower, jester, outsider, etc.)? Did you have friends of the other sex?

I was O.K. in the neighborhood when I was little, just one of the kids. When I got to be eight or nine I started getting bullied. I was identified as a "sissy" then, and never shook the label. I was always shy and ill at ease around the others, especially the girls. We didn't play with girls on our street.

31. Describe how you got along in the world of the school. Was your role in this setting different from your role in the neighborhood? If so, in what ways, and how do you account for it? Did you have friends of the other sex? How did you get along with teachers? What were your favorite and least favorite subjects, and what was there about them that you liked or disliked?

Well, in school we were separated when we got to junior high. They called it "tracked," and it was supposed to be very progressive. I was in the top group -- in the middle of the top group. The kids from my neighborhood weren't in it, so it threw me in with another type of kid. Actually, they were the rich kids from other parts of town. So my group from then on was very different. It was hard, and it made my life in the neighborhood harder than it had been. After my teeth got broken they started calling me "toothless Danny." That hurt.

One thing that affected me all the way through school, especially in high school, was my accent. Real southern, or, "southren" I should say, with an emphasis on "backwoods southren." When I was thirteen I tried out for a part in a play. They said, "Your acting is great, but your accent is terrible." I sounded "common," so I didn't get the part. I was stunned.

About teachers: I got along with them all right, except that I was too talkative. I jabbered. It was nervousness. My favorite subject was science. It was so orderly. And, I could memorize everything and learn it easily and get good grades. And I liked the projects. I didn't do too well in arithmetic; later, though, I liked algebra and higher mathematics. I liked sorting out the word problems.

32. Describe your bodily development in childhood, and how you felt about it. How did it compare with that of your peers? Consider height, weight, strength, speed, coordination, vision, hearing, anomalies. Did you have any special difficulties (e.g., bed wetting)?

I bit my nails all of my childhood, right to the quick. I was average, neither too short nor too tall, fast enough. Worst for me were my teeth and my curly hair. I got teased about that. I wanted straight hair. I had a tendency to be skinny, but that was O.K.

33. Describe your sexual development, and your sexual experience and initiation. How did you learn about sex? How did you feel about the bodily changes that took place at puberty? (Females: How old were you at the menarche? Describe what happened. Did you understand what was happening? How did you feel about it?) Describe your experience as a sexual person during adolescence and young adulthood, and your evaluation of yourself at that time.

I didn't have any sex education. It was unheard of then. All us kids in the neighborhood talked to each other. If we asked our parents, they'd ignore us or tell us the dumbest things. My mother actually said that I came out of the doctor's "little black bag." I didn't learn about intercourse until I was thirteen. It's hard to believe we were so ignorant! But when I did learn about it, it seemed reasonable to me. We had cats. It made sense.

What didn't make sense was to think about my parents: "They've seen each other without any clothes on! They've touched each other!" I was intrigued. I thought, "Gee, my parents have actually had physical contact."

When I hit puberty I ran into trouble with girls. There had been a couple of girls in grammar school I'd liked. When I was about fourteen, I began some sexual exploration. We'd feel each other under the desks -- put our hands under each other's clothes. That was as far as it went for me.

I didn't actually start dating until I was about eighteen, and I didn't sleep with anyone until I was twenty-five, when I was engaged -- later it fell through. Anyway, we had intercourse. It was probably awful for her. I was so reticent. It was so mechanical. I just kept thinking, "Quick! Something's going to go wrong!" I just rushed through it. I was terrified that I'd get her pregnant. That fear was part of what always kept me away from women.

> [Note: After reviewing the above data point by point to clarify an understanding of Dan's training and self-training for an approach to current difficulties, the second therapist dictated the following summary. This procedure is further described in the Introduction to Part IV.]

SUMMARY OF THE FAMILY CONSTELLATION

ST dictates the Summary of the Family Constellation to FT in the presence of CL at the conclusion of the review and interpretations of the family material (*IPCW*, p. 17).

Dan grew up as the older of two boys, psychologically the first-born son.

The family atmosphere was one of disturbed security. The security lay in knowing that Father would provide for and protect the family; the disturbance lay in knowing that Mother would, nevertheless, be anxious, unhappy, and dissatisfied.

The family values emphasized by Mother and Father included hard work in caretaking of what one has (house, garden), and religious feeling.

The masculine guiding line set by Father stressed a kind of relaxed cheerfulness and steadiness, together with a balanced temper and a practical intelligence capable of flashes of brilliance. Father was also capable of putting up a show of fighting back, and knew how to pursue his own interests quietly even when opposed (playing the horses). Grandfather confirmed the masculine guiding line in his loyalty to the women in his life. Uncle John enhanced the masculine guiding line through his sense of humor and relative material success.

The feminine guiding line set by Mother stressed a fretful, ambitious, pessimistic, and temperamentally unpredictable busyness. Mother was better than others, and yearned to be among her betters. Mother's failure to express warmth was confirmed as characteristic of femininity by the attitudes of Dan's Great Aunt and his Aunt Jill, both of whom were cold. Even Aunt Carla, a generous, comfortable woman, kept her distance by "sending" presents, and by not making an alliance with a man.

Dan stayed ahead of Douglas by sharing Father's interests, and by being Mother's chief object of interest. Mother, who saw her life in tragic and heroic terms, was determined to see to it that her sons would succeed in ways that had been foreclosed to her by what she regarded as unfair circumstances.

It was difficult for Dan to understand Mother's fretfulness about appearances, about striving, about education and moving up and out in the world, and about Father and his alleged inferiorities.

In the world of the home Dan apparently imitated Father's way of quietly enduring Mother's agitation, which led to his enduring her fussing over him as well. He also imitated Father's temper outbursts, by means of which he (and Father) were able to gain occasional relief from Mother's pressure. In Father he found a source of acceptance, but no standards by which to measure progress. Mother, who praised him when he met her standards and chastised and withdrew from him when he did not, provided the source of judgment.

Douglas, three years younger, made a place for himself by leaving the first-place position to Dan, uncontested; by staying out of trouble; and by developing an easygoing, friendly attitude toward life. Seeing that Mother's focus on Dan was the source of Dan's troubles, Douglas contrived to stay out of Mother's way, and out of her "spotlight."

Dan found another source of acceptance in his Uncle John, whom he often saw in Father's company. John encouraged Dan, took pleasure in the boy's efforts, recognized his intelligence, and, like Father, did so without judgment.

In the world of the neighborhood he was able to do well enough without striving, buttressed by a sense of being "a cut above" the others that carried him through his difficulties with them. His good appearances, maintained by Mother, and the good appearance and steadiness of the household, probably sustained him in this idea.

He managed well enough in the world of the school until adolescence, when everything changed: He now found himself propelled into a new group of peers, and compelled to assess his personal situation against the background of a much wider social world.

Dan suddenly saw himself as a very small duck in a very large pond. His uncertainty about his place in the larger world, beginning at this time, continued to express itself in his hesitation to engage with the other sex in caring intimacy until in his mid-twenties he could make his first effort to do so under the protection of a formal engagement.

In adolescence, all of Mother's complaints against Father's lack of ambition, and all of Mother's warnings against Dan's being "like the Allens," previously hard for him to understand, came to make a certain kind of sense to him: Appearances in his new world were much more important than he had thought. It was not enough to look good; he would have to sound good as well, with the proper accent. He came to see that Mother's brand of ambition and striving were essential if he wanted to better himself. (Unlike Father, he could not afford to miss any buses; for him, another might not come along.)

The question that confronted Dan at the threshold of adult manhood remained: How could he prove himself to be a man unlike the Allen men? To do this, he might suppose, would require that he set out in quest of an unhappy woman, and then demonstrate that he could make her happy by becoming whatever she wanted.

Record of the Early Recollections

Before we return to the inquiry in "The Case of Dan," it will be useful to offer some observations on the process of eliciting and recording early recollections.

An early recollection may be a complete story with beginning, middle, and end, or it may be an account of a single moment; it may describe activity, or it may be limited to the memory of a sensory perception.

For the purpose of a Life-Style Assessment, an early recollection is defined here as a memory of a single incident of early childhood experience, preferably referring to occurrences in the first eight or nine years of a person's life, prior to the onset of puberty.

Note that this definition distinguishes an early recollection from any report of an experience that does not focus on a single occurrence.

Phrases such as "I remember one time..." or, "Once when I was..." indicate the introductions to early recollections.

Reports, by contrast, characteristically begin with "We used to..." or "We always..." or "Lots of times I...", phrases that do not refer to a focus on a particular incident.

Reports often contain early recollections which, with a little prompting, come into view. If you ask for an early recollection and the client proffers a report, simply inquire, "Are you remembering something that happened one of those times?" or, "Do you remember one time when that happened?" If the answer is no, proceed to an early recollection by asking, "What is the next thing you remember from your childhood?"

Make a marginal note of any reports which you receive in the course of recording early recollections. They may stimulate further recollections during the review and interpretations, and they can help to clarify a context for the interpretation of the early recollections themselves. (See Chapter 11 for a fuller discussion of early recollections.)

Gathering the Record

Begin the process of gathering the record of early recollections by telling the client: "The next thing we have to do together is collect a few stories from your childhood, from before the time you reached puberty, up to, say, age nine or ten. I'd like you to tell me some incidents you remember from that period, beginning with the very first thing you can remember."

The Life-Style Assessment inquiry anticipates that a record of eight recollections will provide an optimal amount of material for interpretation. It is of course possible, and sometimes necessary, to work with fewer early recollections.

It is most important to strive, as far as possible, for a *verbatim* record of the early recollections. If a client likes to give long, discursive accounts, this may prove to be difficult; with a little practice you will learn to distinguish the recollection itself from irrelevant introductions and stage-settings. The goal is to obtain first-person narratives using the client's exact language. Example:

> I was about three, playing in the front yard. As far as I can remember, I was alone. There was a fence around the yard, a picket fence. I was making mud-pies.
>
> Most vivid moment: My hands full of mud, sort of squeezing it between my fingers.
>
> Feeling: Just great! Fabulous!

After the first recollection is recorded ask, "What's the next incident that comes to mind?" Make it clear to the client that the memories need not be recalled in chronological order. Accept whatever arises after the recollection just presented. There is an internally coherent, artistic arrangement in the sequence of the early recollections which is, in itself, of psychological importance, and therefore of value to a psychological investigation. This sequence should not be disturbed by the imposition of a temporal ordering. (See Chapter 14 for an analysis of this artistic arrangement.)

When the client has presented eight recollections say, "We have all we need for this record. Is there any other memory that is important to you, and that you haven't had a chance to tell so far in our work together?" Often a client will say something like, "Well, there is just one more," and go on with, "I thought of this a little while ago, but it didn't seem important enough to mention"; or, "Yeah. I didn't want to tell you this one, because it's sort of unpleasant [weird, embarrassing, scary, etc.], but I think about it a lot. Now that you ask, I guess I may as well tell you about it."

There is a tension involved in holding a memory back and wondering whether to report it. When you say that you have enough memories in the record, the tension is relieved, but the client remains uncertain whether it makes sense to withhold information that might better be explored. Then, when you present this further opportunity to get it into the record, the tension will often break, and the client will confide material that enables you to get a fuller understanding.

Special Problems in Gathering Early Recollections

1. *Not remembering*

Sometimes, even before we begin the inquiries in a Life-Style Assessment, the client will report being unable to remember anything from childhood. The review of family material usually stirs reminiscence; by the time we arrive at the recording of the early recollections a complete store of incidents is almost always available to the client's memory.

Sometimes, however, a client will not remember specific incidents from before the age of eight or nine, or even later. Do not make an issue of it. Stay with the format of asking for the earliest memory, and then recording the others as they are presented. Bear in mind that memory serves to maintain the individual's orientation. In most cases the basis of this orientation was established by four or five years of age, and the first memory dates from this period. Failure to remember back before a much later age can be taken as the sign of a disorientation that occurred, and of a reorientation that began at that time.

> A client could not remember an incident from before he was twelve years old. He knew about his life before that age, and could report that he had grown up on an isolated farm. As the much youngest of three boys he was his mother's companion and helper in the house, while his brothers worked the farm with his father. He attended a one-room school where he was one of fourteen children of various ages. When he was twelve he began to go by bus to a consolidated junior high school, where hundreds of young people were enrolled. For the first time in his life he found himself in a group of boys who were age mates, among whom he was able to take his place in team sports and other activities.

This man's failure to recall specific incidents from before the age of twelve reveals the disorientation and reorientation that he experienced then. The impressions he had of self, others, and the world before he was twelve were no longer useful. It was necessary to evaluate everything afresh in the new situation, which he had done successfully. He provided a rich set of early recollections from the period between ages twelve and sixteen. (Later, as his work in therapy progressed, he did recall incidents from his earlier years, and was able to integrate their meaning into his new awareness of himself.)

2. *Absence of affect*

When asked, "How did you feel at that moment?" (the "most vivid moment" in the story), a client will sometimes say, "I don't know." A feeling expresses an evaluation. If I tell you how I feel about something, I tell you where I stand relative to that issue. Those who have rehearsed the posture of not letting others know where they stand are often unable to recall feelings in their early recollections. Do not press for a feeling when none is reported, and, above all, do not suggest to the client what he or she "must" have (or even "probably") felt in the situation. Empathy is required of you, as is the courage to guess; the aggrandizement of another person's subjectivity is forbidden.

There are other motives for being unable to recall feelings:

> A man of forty-two recounted eight early recollections with no hesitation. He was, however, unable to recall a single feeling in connection with any of these incidents, even though the first therapist had patiently encouraged him to take his time to focus on each memory. During the review of the material with the second therapist, he readily identified feelings for each of them. The first therapist was a woman, the second therapist a man. According to this client's masculine and feminine guiding lines, the judgment of a woman was not to be trusted under any circumstances, and he would not entrust his judgments to a female therapist.

3. *Inclusion of family constellation early recollections in the formal record of early recollections*

During the task of recording early recollections, clients will refer to incidents that were recorded during earlier inquiries, or that came up and were discussed during sessions of review and interpretations. A client may say, "I'm thinking about the time my grandfather and I were picking apples. I already told you about that. Do you want me to go on to another story?"

We say, "No. Let's include that here." Then we ask the client to tell the story again while we enter it into the record at that point.

4. *Historical accuracy*

Sometimes people say, "It probably couldn't have happened this way, but this is the way I remember it." Assure the client that you are interested in the way he or she remembers experiencing the incident, and that historical accuracy is not important for this purpose.

The client may say, "I'll have to talk to my sister about this. I'm not sure about it." You can respond that this would be interesting, but that for the purposes of the assessment, it isn't important to know how anyone other than the client remembers the incident. (It will be useful for such a client to discover that others remember incidents differently, since they had a different significance for them.)

5. *Dreams as early recollections*

The client says, "I remember this dream I had when I was a kid. Should I tell it to you?" The answer is yes. Dreams are experiences. Any dream qualifies as an early recollection if it is remembered as taking place during the childhood years, and can be recalled as a single incident. This is true also of recurring dreams which the client had over extended periods of time, even many years, provided that a single occurrence can be recalled.

6. *Photographs as early recollections*

The client may wonder, "I don't know if I remember this, or whether I only know it from a photograph." Here, there are two possibilities: the client has reconstructed a memory of the incident during which the picture was taken, or the client is recalling an incident of seeing the photograph. Ask, "Can you picture yourself in that situation in your mind's eye? What's happening?" The client may respond,

> "Yeah. I'm standing in front of the swing -- like in the photo. I'd just gotten off, and my sister's been pushing me. She's not in the picture. She's standing by the tree. She's angry because I won't push her, and I'm kind of pleased with myself for having gotten away with it."

Other times the response is,

"I can't get it. All I see is the photo." If the client recalls the incident of seeing the photograph (of looking at it, of discovering it, or of being shown it by someone), and if this took place in childhood, the early recollection will be something like this: "I remember the first time I saw that picture. I was sitting on the sofa with Mother, going through an album. She pointed it out to me. I was pretty excited."

7. *More than one "most vivid moment"*

When asked, after recounting an early recollection, "In all of this, what is the most vivid moment?", the client replies, "I remember two things vividly. The first is riding the bike by myself -- the moment when I was aware that Uncle Bill had let go of the seat, and I was on my own. The second really vivid thing is when I lost my balance and fell over, and the bike fell on me." Ask how the client felt at each of the two moments, making a record of both responses in the numbered space for the early recollection.

8. *"Bum rap" and "good rep" stories*

One may recall being told a story about oneself in the course of one's childhood and be unable to recall the incident which the story claims to portray. Such a story may burden the client with a "bum rap" (that is, a charge of faultiness based on allegations of which the client feels innocent, or at least unaware). Another such story confers a "good rep(utation)" on the client (which can also be experienced as a burden, something which the client feels obliged to live up to).

- A woman recounted a family story that is told about the time she dumped her baby sister out of her carriage, causing the baby to cut her head, and requiring that she be taken to the hospital for stitches. Although the client could not recall this incident, she had felt badly about it all her life. Whenever the sister failed to perform well at anything, some family member could be counted on to refer to the accident: "It's your fault. If she hadn't hurt her head this wouldn't have happened." Even though there was usually a joking, lighthearted quality to these statements, the client felt anxious and uncomfortable in the face of them. It was as if she were being reminded that she was, inescapably, a person expected to cause harm, an idea she tried to compensate against by being overly solicitous and cautious.

- A man reported that, although he cannot remember the incident, it appears that he saved his brother from certain severe injury and possible death by grabbing the child as he was about to fall through an open upper-story window in the family's apartment. "I dislike hearing that story. I'm no hero, and I'm not a guy who thinks and acts quickly. Every time I hear that story I feel like they're talking about someone else. I guess it happened, since they all say so, and my father was there at the time and saw it, but I always feel inadequate when I hear it. I'm an ordinary guy, and they expect too much from me."

These "stories about me," which are not subjectively remembered as part of one's own experience, but which can be imaginatively pictured, may be thought of as "imposed early recollections" or "imposed personal myths." The effect they have on a person's self-image and sense of what is required in life may invite strategies of safeguarding, or other special struggles to meet the expectations of others. While they are not authentic early recollections, we must take them into account when we are framing "The Pattern of Basic Convictions."

THE CASE OF DAN
(continued)

[Note: The material below follows the form of the *IPCW*, pp. 19-23.]

Record of the Early Recollections

Ask for CL's Early Childhood Recollections (ERs). After recording the account of the recollection, narrow its range to the moment most vividly recalled, as if in a snapshot capturing a moment in the action, and ask how CL felt at that moment.

Prompting questions: How far back can you remember? What is the first incident or moment you remember in your life? Tell me about it. How old were you at the time? What is the most vivid moment in the action of the story? How did you feel in that moment?

Note that the first ER to be recorded is to be the first incident of memory. ERs recorded after the first need not be in chronological order. After recording the first ER, ask, "What is the next thing you are able to recall from before age 9 or 10?" Or, "What comes up next from your childhood before age 9 or 10?"

---

1. Age $3\frac{1}{2}$

I remember when my brother was born. It was cold and dark, January. The weather was bad. I remember the doctor coming in -- it was common for babies to be born at home in those days. He had a big black bag. I remember being alone outside the bedroom door and not being allowed in.

Most vivid moment: Standing outside the door; the door was ajar.

Feeling: Frustration. I thought, "There's something going on in there that I'm not allowed to share in or see. Why aren't I?"

---

2. Age 3

It was during the war. I was playing in a sandbox in the yard. There was an air-raid drill. Do you remember those? It was afternoon, the sky was blue. Mother came out and rushed me into the house. I didn't want to go in.

Most vivid moment: Mother coming out looking very worried, picking me up and taking me in.

Feeling: Frustration. I thought, "Why don't you let me do what I want to do, which is to stay here?"

Record of the Early Recollections (continued)

3\. Age 4

Sleeping over at a friend's house in a basement. Sort of a recreation room, but it hadn't been finished. It was cold and damp down there.

Most vivid moment: Going down into something dark, damp, unpleasant.

Feeling: Reluctance. I didn't want to go.

4\. Age 5

I'm in the kitchen with my mother. There's a spider on the ceiling. My mother sees it and she freezes.

Most vivid moment: Mother being immobilized.

Feeling: Real insecure. I was aware that my mother was scared, and that made me feel insecure.

5\. Age 5 or 6

We were all out together, Mother, Dad, me, and Douglas. We came to a busy intersection. Dad got Mother to hold my hand and Douglas's hand. We stepped out to cross the street. All of a sudden a car swerved toward us. Dad sort of tackled us all and pushed us out of the way, shouting, "Look out!" He almost got hit himself.

Most vivid moment: Dad being capable. He was calm in a way: He just did what he had to do. He just acted. Threw himself at us to make sure we'd be O.K.

Feeling: Safe. I thought, "My Dad's strong and protective and capable."

6\. Age 6 or 7

I was walking to school. I noticed that a building that had been across the street from my school wasn't there any more. There were bulldozers there in this hole pushing dirt around, and the building was gone. It had just vanished!

Most vivid moment: Seeing that enormous hole and realizing that the building was gone.

Feeling: Wow! I felt a sense of wonder at it. A tinge of excitement. Sort of, "Look what people can do! Look what *Man* can do!"

Record of the Early Recollections (conclusion)

---

7. Age 8

At school we had a fire drill. Our teacher, Miss Johnson, led us down a long corridor and the line slowed down. I was standing in the hall, waiting to go on. I saw an empty socket, and I stuck my finger in it and got a shock.

Most vivid moment: Getting shocked.

Feeling: Embarrassed. I pretended that nothing had happened and didn't tell anyone. I thought, "They'll think I'm stupid." My arm tingled and hurt all day.

---

8. Age 5

My brother fell into the lake at the park. He was a toddler, two years old. We were playing by the lake together, sort of squatting down and playing on the concrete edge by the side of the lake. I looked up and saw this coat floating on the water. I just stood there and looked at it. I was aware that Douglas wasn't there, and that his coat was in the water, and I remember thinking, "But where is he?" Then someone grabbed the coat, and there was Douglas.

Most vivid moment: Seeing the coat floating, with Douglas nowhere in sight.

Feeling: Astonishment! All I saw was the coat -- it didn't register with me that Douglas might be under it, so I was astonished. He was gone, and there was his coat.

After recording eight early recollections, ask CL if there is any other recollection that is important to him or her that has not been recorded in the Life-Style Inquiry to this point. If another early recollection is forthcoming, record it here:

Age________

N/A

Most vivid moment:

Feeling:

[Note: See Part IV for a thorough discussion of the way early recollection summaries are developed.]

ER SUMMARY: THE PATTERN OF BASIC CONVICTIONS

ST dictates the summary of The Pattern of Basic Convictions to FT in the presence of CL at the conclusion of the review and interpretations of the ERs.

Life is centered around the mystery and wonder of Woman.

I don't know how I fit into it. Somehow I feel kept from entering into acquaintance with the feminine heart of things, as if I were not allowed to share in and to know the mysteries of intimacy even when the door is partly opened to me.

At the same time, I feel unable to move freely on my own in the world, under the open sky, because of the power a woman is able to exert over me.

I don't want my life to molder in some narrow place for the sake of my friendly feelings toward someone.

A woman is able to throw fright into me by her being frightened. There is no need for it. Being afraid is no help against danger anyway.

A man knows enough to take sensible precautions, and to do what he can and must do in the face of difficulty.

I am impatient with being shepherded by a woman. I want to find out for myself what life is all about. If I have to take my lumps I am prepared to suffer in silence, especially when I am embarrassed by my difficulties. I'm afraid that anyone to whom I might confide my pain would fail to sympathize and may only think that I'm stupid.

Even so, I am in awe of what I am discovering about the wonders of human power and human possibility.

There is more to life than meets the eye, at least my eye. I am astonished at how much I have failed to see, when life itself is at stake, and it is imperative that I learn to see clearly. I am aware that I have needed the assistance of others to save me from disaster, and I can take some comfort from the thought that nothing goes so far wrong (as long as we're still alive) that it can't be set right again.

[Note: After allowing time for the client's reaction to "The Pattern of Basic Convictions," the second therapist presents an enumerated statement of "The Interfering Ideas."]

ER SUMMARY: THE INTERFERING IDEAS

This summary is also dictated in the presence of CL, immediately after the presentation of The Pattern of Basic Convictions.

1. He has some idea that the door to intimacy and belonging is closed to him when, in fact, he knows it's open.

2. The meaning of closeness with a woman is mixed up in his mind with the idea of his freedom being restricted and his courage being undermined by her fears.

3. He has some notion that his sense of wonder and curiosity is an idiosyncrasy, and that he cannot expect to find sympathy or understanding for the difficulties he experiences because of it.

4. He has an exaggerated idea about masculine competence, as if he believed that a Real Man can do everything, and is left feeling like a wide-eyed boy in a world of wonderful men.

Conclusion

In this chapter we have set forth the process of gathering family data and early recollections according to the format of the *IPCW*, illustrated by "The Case of Dan." (Note that we return to Dan's case in Chapter 13. There, Dan's family constellation summary serves as the model on which we base our discussion of how this section of the life-style summaries is developed and presented.)

This brings us to the end of Part II, "Inquiry." The next step in the psycho-clarity process is the review and interpretations of the material with the client. Part III, Chapters 5 through 11, is devoted to explicating the various aspects of this task.

PART III: REVIEW AND INTERPRETATIONS

Anyone who wants to understand Individual Psychology correctly must orient himself by its clarification of the unitary purposefulness of [the] thinking, feeling, willing, and acting of the unique individual. He then will recognize how the stand an individual takes and the life-style, which is like an artistic creation, are the same in all situations of life, unalterable until the end -- unless the individual recognizes what is erroneous, incorrect, or abnormal with regard to co-operation, and attempts to correct it. This becomes possible only when he has comprehended his errors conceptually and subjected them to the critique of practical reason, the common sense -- in other words, through convincing discussion.

Alfred Adler (1979, p. 52)

INTRODUCTION TO PART III

Individual Psychology and the psycho-clarity process based on its findings do not allow for the traditional medical distinction between diagnosis and treatment. These terms fit a model of interaction in which one person seeks a thorough knowledge (diagnosis) of another's state of being, and then applies an appropriate corrective (treatment) to the other person's disorders.

The "convincing discussion" Adler refers to is, by contrast, an inherently collaborative effort. The corrective to one's own psychic suffering and sense of social maladjustment is gained by a "thorough knowledge" which recognizes and understands the errors in one's own private logic. Paradoxically, however, this most personal of responsibilities cannot be exercised on one's own. A collaborator is needed, skilled in the task of subjecting hidden errors "to the critique of practical reason, the common sense." The errors in the client's private sense of the world are fatefully and hopelessly pitted against the community; the therapist serves, therefore, not only as a faithful worker with the client in the struggle for clarity, but also as a representative of the community, negotiating an end to hostilities.

The meaning of this encounter can be misunderstood. It is not between a therapist who is all common sense, and a client whose sense is all private. No discussion of any kind could occur if the client did not share in any way in the sense we have of our common life, and of what it requires of us. No convincing discussion will occur if the therapist does not know, through firsthand experience, what it is like to be guided by biases, and blind to one's own errors. The psycho-clarity process does not take place between a therapist, above, and a client, below. A little quatrain warns us against the uselessness of such a posture:

> The toad beneath the harrow knows
> Exactly where each tooth point goes;
> The butterfly upon the road
> Preaches contentment to that toad.
>
> Rudyard Kipling (Bartlett, 1968, p. 871)

In simplest terms, the collaboration of client and therapist is in itself the fundamental and primary corrective to errors in the client's private logic, which are "erroneous...with regard to cooperation." The effort to understand the life-style is already contrary to the maintenance of a private sense, since understanding is by definition something that can be shared. Here, diagnosis is treatment.

This is why everyone who writes on psychotherapy and counseling of any kind emphasizes the importance of rapport. To us that word means the alignment of goals, or working together in quest of the same objective. This is not always easy to maintain. The anti-cooperative errors in the private sense of a discouraged person distort the meaning of any movement toward collaboration. You can expect to be set up as an expert and put down as a failure, all in one deft move.

An advantage, therefore, of the psycho-clarity process for assessing the life-style is that you and the client are engaged, right from the start, in the pursuit of something the client wants. In the review and interpretations you are drawn together into the work. Wanting to be understood, and having to help you to understand, the client, almost inadvertently, begins to share an understanding with you.

A caution is in order here. Remember that people seeking any kind of psychological counseling are likely to be confused and disoriented. Disorientation is hard to endure. It leads to disorganization and a frantic, wasteful dissipation of energies. This is why survival trainers warn us that if we are lost in a wilderness, the first thing we must do is sit down, focus attention, and take our bearings. Panic is a threat to life. In the pain of it, people are suggestible. When we lack clarity, we crave certainty. Fanaticism (both political and religious), esoteric cults, and arcane pseudoscience of all kinds appeal to this craving. Charlatans feed on it. Psychotherapists can exploit it.

For example: A client was told by a clinician that he was "a depressive." He took this in as information about himself, but not without a response. He evaluated the "data" and gave it a meaning. To him, this was not an academic matter. Even a depressive has to live and make his way, and he had to figure out how. He formed an expectation ("I will be sad"), and an ambition ("I will bear up under it nobly to demonstrate my goodness, apologizing for its inescapableness as an excuse for the trouble it causes others"). To those who sought to cheer him up, he offered a game try at a cheerful face; if his inconsolability was felt by them as a reproach, he pleaded the excuse of his "disorder." It was the best he could do. As his therapist had said, he was, after all, "a depressive."

It is better to avoid labeling. Stick to the task of understanding the person's training, self-training, and rehearsal for life as it has taken place until now. When an understanding is gained, and the social meaning and consequences of the movement are clear, the symptom can make sense to the client; it is only by means of such understanding that anyone is able to consider changes.

The client comes to the therapist with "problems." As Powers has put it, the therapist's task is to reveal these problems to be solutions, faulty solutions to the problems that confront us all in making friends, making a living, and making love (Griffith, 1984, p. 439). Each of these problems requires of us that we cooperate with others for their solution. The client's "erroneous, incorrect, or abnormal" convictions, upon which the faulty solutions rest, have left cooperation out of account. The substitutes for cooperation all involve some form of coercion. With respect to each of the three problems of life set for everyone, it is as if the client were privately thinking something like the following:

> *Making friends*: In order to make people like me, I have to be (beautiful, good, intelligent, impressive, rich, strong, etc.) enough to be irresistible to them.
>
> My problem is that I am too (plain, bad, dumb, ordinary, poor, weak, etc.) to be sure this will happen.
>
> *Making a living*: In order to get as much money as I want I have to have (a boss who appreciates me, a helping hand, the right connections, a better education, the ability to do everything right, the proper knack or talent, etc.).
>
> My problem is that (my boss is a jerk, nobody gives me a break, I don't know the right people, my parents wouldn't pay my tuition, I get nervous and make mistakes, my brother inherited my father's abilities, etc.).
>
> *Making love*: To warm up to someone I have to know that [he or she] is (considerate of me, kind, sensitive to my needs, undemanding, reliable, respectful of my freedom, etc.).
>
> My problem is that I keep running into people who (are out for themselves, selfish, want things their way, are unwilling to meet reasonable expectations, are not there when I need them, refuse to bend, etc.).

Lacking here is friendliness, eagerness to make contributions, and an interest in enhancing the lives of others and sharing affection with them as they are. What is left is a pattern of manipulative strategies, claims to positions (or conditions) deserving of special treatment, self-elevation, excuses, suspicions, and reproaches against others for their imperfections.

Until now, the client worked things out tolerably, and the faulty ideas of a hidden private logic were never challenged effectively. The ideas did not invite clear challenges, because they never expressed themselves in open statements, only in a general movement. Whenever the effects of that movement were opposed by others as onerous, they could be defended by the declaration of good intentions, by rationalizations, and by appeals for greater sympathy, as in Edward's case, discussed in Chapter 2.

Now the individual confronts or anticipates a situation that will not yield to the usual strategy of movement; the style brings this person to the narrow end of the wedge. Clients know something is wrong; they do not know what it is, or what to do about it. They are addressing a current difficulty in the same way in which they have dealt with all their previous difficulties in life. This time there is no resolution. In this situation they are lost. Consider the man whose only tool is a hammer; he tends to perceive everything as if it were a nail. If the situation fails to respond to his hammering, his only idea is to hammer all the harder.

Life-style operates something like that. We have trained ourselves to respond to life's problems in a particular way. If a problem will not respond, and we do not know another way to solve it, we hammer all the harder in our practiced way. We can only do what we know how to do.

During the review of material gathered in the inquiry, therapist and client work together to learn how the client came to this overreliance on hammering, and to consider how other skills, undervalued until now, are available to the client to be studied and practiced. The chapter that follows gives an example.

Chapter 5: THE LIFE SITUATION, PRESENTING PROBLEM, AND LIFE TASKS

This chapter consists of a transcript of a review of initial interview data, together with the text of the "Summary of Impressions" derived from that interview. Except for minor changes made to protect confidentiality, it is a verbatim transcript.

As the conversation proceeds, you will be able to see the development of the ideas proposed, tested, and modified as we go along. This follows Adler's description of his own work (1963, p. 1):

> I may very well, at first, make an error in interpretation which will come to light later on as the case unfolds. If so, it will not discourage me. I am aware that I am in the same position as a painter or sculptor, who at the outset does whatever is suggested to him by his experiences and skill. Only later on does he check his work, strengthening, softening, and changing features to bring out the correct image.

[Note: After the first therapist gathered the client's data, using the initial interview format of the *IPCW*, and after a brief break, the client ("Harry") and both therapists convened to discuss and clarify the information.]

THE CASE OF HARRY

JG: Now, Harry, what I'm going to do is tell Bob what I've learned about you. If you want to say something more, or if I didn't get it right, please interrupt me at any point.

Harry: O.K.

JG: And you and Bob will go off into your own conversations as we go along.

RLP: For example, if I don't understand something, I'll ask you to clarify it for me. And, it'll be interesting to you as we go along to hear whether Jane did "get it right."

Harry: (Laughter.) O.K.

JG: Harry is thirty years old. He was born July 20, 1956.

RLP: So you had your thirtieth birthday two months ago. How do you feel about being thirty?

Harry: It's O.K., but sort of unsettling.

RLP: In what way?

Harry: I don't know. Well, probably because everything is unsettled right now.

RLP: Maybe we'll want to come back to this topic of your birthday. For now, let's go ahead.

Harry: O.K.

JG: Harry's been in Chicago for four months. He moved here from Davenport.

RLP: That's just across the Mississippi from Moline, isn't it?

Harry: Yeah. That's my hometown.

JG: He's currently in partnership in a printing business.

RLP: That's a business that's foreign to me -- except as a consumer.

Harry: It's foreign to me, too. I've had a lot of professional dealings with printers before, but I've never been on the inside before. I'm learning the business strictly from scratch. I came here without a mentor, though there are people who are helping me.

JG: You'll learn more about this bold act as the story unfolds. (JG and Harry laugh.) He's not married, and has never been married. He's having an on-again, off-again, in, out, hot, cold love affair with a woman named Debbie who is getting her M.B.A. degree at the Wharton School. They met in college at Ohio University. He's known Debbie for a long time. However, it's only been a little over a year since they actually began their love relationship. Before that, she was dating someone else who was in the group Harry was in.

RLP: So you were social acquaintances for some time, and became lovers about a year ago.

Harry: Right. It started when we saw each other at a party. She was looking for somebody to take a trip to Florida with. I said, "Fine, I'll go," knowing full well that maybe this would be a chance to start a relationship with her.

RLP: Oh.

JG: Harry completed his degree at Ohio in economics, then returned to Davenport to join the family business. He's not been in the military. When I asked about his religious affiliation or interests, he said, "I'm Jewish. I'm not very religious, but I am very Jewish. I have strong ties with the religion." He says that he's not a practicing Jew right now.

RLP: But you clearly identify yourself as a Jew.

Harry: Well, I'm very involved with Jewish affairs. I guess I'm a practicing Jew. I'm just a practicing Reformed Jew...

RLP: Oh, I see.

Harry: ...as compared with most of my relatives, who are very Orthodox.

JG: You don't practice to that extent.

Harry: Yeah. Not to that extent. I guess I am pretty religious.

RLP: So you're observant -- as much as you can be in the culture.

Harry: Right. Right.

JG: He says, "I'm very intense over the fate of the Jewish people and Israel, though I'm slacking off on that." He then told me about the family business in Davenport: "I was in a good family business, making a lot of money, and I was getting involved in Jewish community affairs. However, I didn't get along with my father on the job, so now I'm trying to do something else that appealed to me." He was in the family business for eight years. "I was miserable, and felt I should get out. Debbie was the catalyst. She gave me the push, because she said that she would never want to live in Davenport." Since his move, she says to him, "Don't try to put it off on me that you left." He says that he doesn't do that, but she sometimes feels like she is responsible, because of the ultimatum she gave him.

RLP: Uh-huh.

Harry: All along she said, "Don't make your decision based on me. I don't want you to do that."

RLP: Because it wasn't contractual. She wasn't saying, "If you leave, then I'll marry you."

Harry: Right. On the other hand, she was saying, "If we do stay together, it can't be in Davenport." I mean it's a "Catch-22."

RLP: It's possible that we'll stay together, but not in Davenport.

Harry: Right.

RLP: But, if you leave Davenport, it doesn't add to the possibility of our staying together. That's not, by itself, sufficient cause.

Harry: Right.

JG: This is the main issue about which Harry is here today: What's going on between him and Debbie. He says, "I want to marry her, but she seems to be throwing up roadblocks. But then, the funny thing is that when I back off, she's all over me." For example, if he doesn't call her for a couple of days, she calls him and "has eight or nine things she wants to tell me."

RLP: Where did you say she is?

JG: In Philadelphia. At the Wharton School.

RLP: Is she the same age as you?

Harry: Yeah. She's a few months younger.

JG: His problem is that he can't concentrate on his work, make his reputation, make his new career work out for him, because he is too distracted by the situation with Debbie.

Harry: Did I say that? Did I say reputation? I don't care about that. (Laughter, all join in.)

JG: No, that's my word. I meant, to establish yourself as a success in the new business.

RLP: Making connections, and so forth.

Harry: Right. Right.

JG: Debbie keeps saying, "I can't tell you what I am, or am not going to do." She blew up at him just the other day because over the weekend Harry got together with some of their group of mutual friends, and he was surrounded by happily married people. It made him feel like he wanted to move on the whole thing. He kind of challenged her on the phone by telling her, "I've given more than you have, and whenever I do something that you want me to do, then you throw a roadblock in my way." And she blew up.

Harry: We've been having a problem where she felt like she's fallen out of love and isn't attracted to me the way she was, but now I'm her "best friend" type of thing. I wanted to confront her, and I said, "Well, why have you fallen out of love?" And she says, "I can't tell you. I really don't know why. I don't know what's happened. Maybe it'll get better." She'd be very happy to talk about other things, but not that. And I finally kept pressing and said, "I'm having a lot of trouble up here, and when you've had trouble I've helped you through (and this, that, and the other), and you haven't been a big help to me right now. And besides that, every step of the way you've thrown up another roadblock. First it's, 'Well, I can't see you this weekend'; that's a roadblock. Or, now you're telling me you're not in love with me, but you don't know why." And I finally got her to say something, and she said, "You always expected more out of this relationship, more than I have," and she left it at that. She really didn't talk about it any more. But that pretty much is the situation I'm in. I have pushed from the start. Like I said, I saw that trip as a chance to start a relationship, and...

RLP: So you had high hopes and ambitions of its developing...

Harry: Yeah. I still do, and I still push. And, she likes me to push, but then the pressure gets too much. She likes certain aspects about it. So that's what happened: I pushed too much.

RLP: She likes being courted, but doesn't want to be wedded.

Harry: She doesn't like being tied down. Really, at this point she doesn't have any desire to go out with anybody else -- or it doesn't seem that way. But she doesn't like the idea of her freedom being squashed. I don't know.

RLP: We mustn't spend too much time figuring Debbie out. You're the one who comes to talk with us; she doesn't.

Harry: (Laughter.) Yeah. That's what I said to her. I'm spending all my time trying to figure out what she's thinking, and what I need to be spending my time on is coming up with something productive for myself to deal with, especially at work.

RLP: Yes, sure, because your life is at stake.

Harry: Yeah.

JG: Mother and Father are both living. Mother's now fifty-five, and Father is sixty. It's the original marriage for both of them. They've been married thirty-two years, and live in Davenport. Both are in good health. Mother has a job working in a lawyer's office. Father is in a grocery business that Harry's great-grandfather founded. There are some other relatives who also partly own the business.

Harry: Yeah. His brother owns some of it.

RLP: The grocery business?

Harry: Right. Wholesaling.

JG: Harry is the first of four children. He is followed by Sidney, his brother, two years younger. Sidney is in the family business now and is having some of the same experiences with Father, but is responding to them differently -- as we could expect. Gail, a sister, is about three years younger than Harry, and Burton is seven years younger. I asked him about the groupings of the children. He said, "We were one group. We were all treated pretty well." Gail wasn't special, even though she was the only girl. Harry and Sidney "got along pretty well," though they fought a lot. But that's "just growing up." When I asked how much younger Gail was, he wasn't really clear about it. "Well, I guess about three or so years younger. Something like that."

RLP: The first three of you were born pretty close together, weren't you?

Harry: Yeah.

JG: Burt was a lot younger, but Harry still thinks of this as one group of kids. He doesn't think of Burt as a tag-along, younger child. About his own position as the first born, he said, "I paved the way."

RLP: That was your job!

Harry: (Laughter.)

RLP: No wonder you have the daring to go off on new ventures, to launch out into a new world. You're used to it. You were raised to pave the way.

Harry: Well, we've all pretty well done that. My brother Sidney, for instance.... I've more stayed at home in some ways. I feel like I ran back home! When I finished school they said, "You've got to go to work." So I said, "I'll go to work here." I stayed there. My brother, he left school a number of times, and he went and traveled. Sold whatever he had and took the money and traveled. And he finally started in the business when he was in his late twenties, and he's able to cope with it better.

RLP: You paved the way.

Harry: Yeah. Yeah. I guess.... Yeah. For somebody to go and do that stuff.

JG: I asked Harry what he would have wanted different, if he could have had something different when he was a child, and he said that it was a pretty good life for him as a little boy growing up, that things got more difficult later.

We then talked about his health. He said, "I'm not as energetic as I'd like to be. I'm too heavy." I asked when he perceived himself to be overweight, and he said, "I lost a lot of weight two years ago. About a year ago, I went to Florida with Debbie. Then, some months later, I started putting it back on. I was bummed out with my situation and I started to binge." He sees himself still doing that. "I still don't exercise. I was agonizing over leaving my job and making the move." Generally, he sleeps well. Recently, in the past two months, if he doesn't sleep well, it's because he's thinking about his job.

RLP: Two months ago you turned thirty. Things should be settled by now, shouldn't they? By the time your father reached thirty he was married and had a child.

Harry: Right. Yeah.... That's true.

JG: We talked about alcohol, drugs, and so forth, and he doesn't perceive himself as having any difficulty with these, though he said that, among things of this kind, cocaine could be the biggest problem. "I never did it a lot, and since I've been in Chicago, it hasn't been a problem. But, you know, if I'm with people who are doing it, I'll probably do it." He doesn't, though, see himself as someone who would go off into a cocaine oblivion.

RLP: A lot of people do.

Harry: Yeah. I know. But I think it's changed. I don't see the guys around...

RLP: They're not around. They're gone!

Harry: (Laughter.) It does bother me, because I think I could become an addictive-type personality. If somebody threw it in my face, or gave me the money for it, maybe I'd do it. But at this point it's certainly not a problem for me. I guess I could blow my life savings on it, and in six months I'd be over and done with.

RLP: It's a very seductive drug, because it presents an enlargement of possibilities. It brings about a drug-induced mania that's very attractive to people.

Harry: My bingeing on eating has kept me away from it.

RLP: Bingeing on eating is a little different. It's more an effort to console yourself for a feeling of emptiness. You recognize it?

Harry: Yeah. It makes sense.

RLP: Because you do feel empty. You have an empty heart. You want someone to embrace. You can't fill your life, so you fill your stomach.

Harry: And what's the difference with a cocaine binge?

RLP: That's to satisfy the ambition to be elevated...to be great and to be grand.

Harry: I could satisfy that by doing my job right.

RLP: Sure you could, but that takes work! Cocaine is a shortcut to those feelings. People with high ambitions are vulnerable to the cocaine habit. It gives them a feeling of power, grandeur, majesty.

Harry: Yeah. That's the feeling. But I've never had the desire to do it at work, or take massive quantities of it like I've read about.

RLP: It's dangerous. A dangerous drug.

Harry: That really is interesting...the difference between cocaine and food binges.

JG: Not only is there the Debbie-related emptiness, but here's a person who's uprooted from his whole world he's known all of his life.

RLP: Family, community.

JG: Yes.

Harry: I was wanting to get away. I was even bingeing there. I felt empty there, too.

RLP: It wasn't satisfying to you.

Harry: Especially near the end, when I was going to the psychiatrist.

JG: I'll be telling you about that. First, I'd like to finish this about his current health. You should know he's not under a doctor's care. About a year and a half ago his blood pressure was a little elevated, and required some medication. Then it got O.K. He's not taking medication now. He feels that he should have this checked out. He has a physical every year, and will be having one soon. About the psychiatrist, I asked him what he had found out. He said, "I found out I was stubborn -- which I already knew -- and that I don't take criticism very well -- which I also already knew. It was a disaster."

RLP: How much did you pay to find these things out?

Harry: (Laughter.)

RLP: I always wonder when they say things like that, who does take criticism well?

Harry: (Laughter.) Well, I did find out some things about myself. The reason it was a disaster was more from the fact that it didn't help the situation. My father always harped on that business about my not taking criticism very well.

RLP: Right! That means without having you complain!

Harry: That's what it's always been.

RLP: Yes. He wants to feel free to criticize you without your complaining about it.

Harry: Yeah. Those were the things my dad was saying... that I wouldn't take criticism. The psychiatrist was trying to go back and get to the deeper roots of the relationship, what's really happening. He finally said that I was reaching out for my father's love, and I wasn't getting it from him. But that was totally over my father's head.

RLP: Over your father's head...

Harry: Yes.

RLP: He couldn't understand why you would want it.

Harry: (Laughter.)

RLP: Well, he was innocent. He didn't know what was going on either. What you want is for him to respect you. You want him to treat you as an equal. You don't want always to be in the position of the one who is being criticized by somebody who knows better. You also want to have something to offer.

Harry: Yes. And we had a business relationship and he couldn't draw the line between business and personal. And he made no attempt to. The main thing I was supposed to remember was that I was the employee, and that he was having to run the business. He'd always say, "Well, this can't be run this way or that way." But you (JG) probably have this down.

JG: As a result of the counseling -- which lasted about three months -- Harry said, "The doctor and I understood what the problems were, whereas my father wouldn't see the problem. He would just dismiss it. It aggravated me and made me mad. The outcome was, the doctor said, 'Well, you can't get along with your father, and you ought to leave. You are making the effort, and your father is not responding.'"

Harry: Not that I was making the effort, but that I understood the problem better. But even if both of us had understood it, it may not have become any better. But, with him not understanding it, it really wasn't getting any better, because I was still just going back and, even understanding it, I was still doing the same things. It made me even more upset that he didn't understand it, that he just dismissed the advice.

JG: Harry's response to this idea that he ought to leave was, "I never wanted to leave the money. I still don't feel I've been dealt with in an equitable manner." In terms of the money situation and this feeling, Harry said, "In the company I was pretty much doing everything he was doing. He'd be out of town a lot, and I'd be running the company. My brother came to work then, and gave me an out. When I was there, whatever went wrong was my fault. Everything's got to be perfect. Father would rail on my 'mistakes,' but his mistakes were 'judgment calls.'"

Harry: Now that I hear that, I can probably make a more accurate statement. His feeling was always that the bottom line was that no matter who made the mistake, it comes back to you how the business operates. If somebody makes a mistake, or something goes wrong, it's your fault eventually, because you're going to have to deal with it. In that respect he was right. He always felt there was a right way and a wrong way to handle a thing, and the right way was always his way.

RLP: Sure.

Harry: It was, "It's not your way or my way; it's the right way to do it." But the right way was never my way; it was always his way. He wanted that. And, my mistakes were always very objective mistakes. They were very clear-cut as to how I'd made a mistake. But when he made the same mistake, it was a "judgment call," and maybe it wouldn't even be a mistake. And a lot of my mistakes weren't mistakes in the end, either. There's no doubt that I can't run the business the way he does after thirty years. I suppose there was an intense rivalry between the two of us.

RLP: Well, some of it's on his part. He had some fear, if he felt it was so important that he keep such a close eye on everything.

Harry: It's everything I read about small business. They can't let go.

RLP: It's hard. He has some sense that it's up to him to maintain control of it. There's some pessimism in it, some fear that, "unless I hang on and watch everything, it'll all go to pieces."

Harry: That's exactly what he said: "Two years from now there wouldn't be anything here." And he feels that way. When he gets really angry and says what he feels, he says, "This place won't be here in two years. I'll go to Arizona."

JG: Father also said that Harry was lazy, and Harry said, "I was." He lays it to resistance to Father's constant criticism and nagging. He says, "From high school on they saw me as a problem child," although this is something Harry really doesn't understand. An example he gave me was, "I went with a girl older than I was, who'd been divorced. That drove them crazy. They wouldn't say anything; they'd just stand around being nervous."

RLP: How old were you?

Harry: Eighteen. She was twenty-two. It was a work situation. I can understand why they thought I was a "problem child," although I never thought that I was.

RLP: Not at eighteen. You're not a child any more.

Harry: (Laughter.)

JG: Then at college. They told him, "We were worried about you at college," when he wouldn't go to classes or something, and they'd find out about it.

Harry: In my third year, I stopped going to classes for a while, and they got a card from the college listing all my incompletes. They said, "It must be drugs."

JG: They told him, by way of explanation, "You're a member of that generation."

RLP and Harry: (Laughter.)

Harry: And then they said...my mother still believes this to this day!

When I left town, she had a good cry. Her boy was leaving town. And I told her I was just so angry with my dad and all, and she said, "We've always known you were a member of that generation." This is after I'd been working in the business for eight years! Well, "that" generation is at least five years older than me, if she's talking about the sixties, and that's what she was talking about. She just...she's out of touch.

RLP: She's frightened.

Harry: O.K. If it's that simple.

RLP: Sure. Sometimes there's a kind of pessimism that anything that can go wrong will go wrong. You don't have to be Irish to believe in "Murphy's Law." Even a Jew can defer to it. Your parents have the time-honored idea that they can make life better by warning you against making it worse.

Harry: (Laughter.)

JG: Harry says about all this "old business" between himself and his parents, "I file all this stuff away, and never forget it." He's got a great litany of difficulties he's had with his mother and father.

RLP: Yes, because it feels like a "vote of no confidence" to him.

Harry: Right. Being away from them makes it a whole lot easier.

JG: He went on to say, "Now my only problem -- since that's not so pressing -- is the anxiety of a new job and the situation with Debbie. I'm not sure if I'm in control or not."

RLP: I don't understand what that means.

Harry: Well, I'm not sure either. (Laughter.) The problem is, I'm not dealing with it. It would be real easy to say, "Well, I've got to stop thinking about what Debbie is thinking about, and just go on and do my job better." But I stand around speculating about what Debbie's thinking all the time, and how am I going to make the situation right. And I go into my job and I don't do what I should be doing there because of that, and I'll turn around and go home and eat a lot, and I won't feel like going to work the next morning. Then I'll go out of town and be with my friends over the weekend and have a good time, and come back thinking about that. You know...it's just...that's my problem: I can't do what I should be doing.

RLP: No, you can't because you're wrapped up in the idea of control. It's reflected in your endless thinking about what Debbie is thinking, and your question, "Why have you fallen out of love with me?" This is, by definition, an impossible question to answer. Why anybody falls *in* love with anybody can't be very closely answered. It's about as clear a choice as there is, to fall in love with somebody, but it's hard for us to account for it. "Why?" is always a hard question to answer in any case, because it leads to speculation. It is especially to be avoided in intimate relationships, where "Why?" feels like an adversarial question. "What?" and "How?" make for an easier set of questions. They refer to facts, to things that are givens, things that invite a further decision. You and your father, though, aren't content with those two questions.

Harry: (Laughter.)

RLP: You and your father are both interested in trying to control events, and to manage the thoughts and feelings of those around you. In your case, if Debbie doesn't think what you want her to think, you're left to wonder, "How can I get her to think that way?"

Harry: That's right. That's exactly right!

RLP: And your father operates the same way. You're a slice off the old salami.

Harry: I hate to be told that. I was told that once before. We were told that we're so much alike that we just react like each other.

RLP: Well, sure. If you're looking for apples, you look under apple trees.

Harry: (Laughter.)

RLP: You grew up under his tutelage. The two of you want to be in charge, and that's part of the conflict between you.

JG: So the control -- or the lack of it -- in the situation with Debbie is similar? That's the situation that precipitated Harry's calling us.

Harry: Yes, that and the fact that I'm not performing. I'm not giving my job a chance.

RLP: True, but Debbie is the distraction from it.

JG: Yes.

Harry: I think so. You know, I want to make sure that I don't find something else to distract me. I want to discipline myself more. I'm just thinking about it, instead.

JG: Thinking instead of acting.

Harry: Yes. That's what I'm doing. I'm not taking action.

RLP: No, you're thinking *instead* of acting. If you knew what to do, you'd act; since you don't know what to do, you think about it endlessly. That's what obsessive thinking is.

Harry: That's right. That's right.

JG: He said about Debbie, "I need a better way to deal with it. It's fifty-fifty whether it'll work out. I need to cope with it." Then he kind of pictured a scenario: "I'll be this loving boy who'll get used up and thrown out on the street. I'll let her take advantage of the situation. I have a fear that it won't work out. And what I should be doing is having a good time right now, and not be thinking about long-range commitments, marriage, and all that stuff. I was really hurt this weekend, being with my close friends who are happily married. Debbie rarely feels the way I feel, and she rarely wants the same things I want." Then he itemized a few things: "First, it was leave Davenport. She would get nervous living there all of her life. She was ecstatic about it when I left."

Harry: Yeah. She was.

JG: He went on, "Then, it's that she's not sure now. She says she doesn't love me, and she's not sure what happened to that feeling." And third, "She keeps throwing up road blocks." Then (and this is Harry, quoting himself to Debbie), "You've needed help. I've been there for you." And, she responds to him, "You've always wanted more out of this relationship than I have." He commented to me parenthetically, "Debbie is insecure. She had a hard time in school. I know she's competent, but everything always gets to her." She wanted an M.B.A. and applied to a number of places.

Harry: Yeah. And she was accepted at two places that were top-ranked. Now she's at Wharton, and she feels that she lied her way into it.

JG: She says, "I bull-shitted my way in, and now they're finding out that I'm nothing."

Harry: Here I am spending all my time worrying, getting into that whole rationalization and everything else. And I probably should just be letting it take its course.

RLP: I don't know what you should be doing, but...

Harry: I guess that's what I'm asking.

RLP: ...but I know there are some other choices.

JG: I asked Harry how his life would be different if he didn't have this problem -- this distraction with the unresolved Debbie situation -- if she were committed to him, and he said, "I'd try to make a success of what I'm trying to do, then we'd pick a place where we wanted to go, and we'd get married. I'd be happier on less money, or maybe I could make the kind of money I want doing what I'm doing. Debbie doesn't want to marry a wreck."

RLP: Who does?

Harry: (Laughter.) Yeah. I don't blame her!

JG: He said, "She doesn't want to be part of my insecurities. I asked her to stand by me now, and she said, 'Fuck off!'"

Harry: NO! Did I say that?!

JG: Yes.

Harry: No.... Yes, *I* said it. Yeah. But *she's* not saying that. She's just saying, "Don't show me your insecurities all the time," which I can understand because she has so many herself. I think that bothers her.

RLP: She feels bullied by it.

Harry: O.K. O.K. That's probably it.

RLP: She's bullied.

Harry: By the insecurities?

RLP: Yes. You're bullying her.

Harry: I understand that. I really, fully understand that.

RLP: She doesn't like it. She feels pressured. More pressure, accusation, suffering. It all winds up to be bullying. Listen: "I stood by you when you needed me, but you don't stand by me when I need you."

Harry: Yeah, but that was a very short sentence.

(Harry, after a moment, laughs. Laughter all around.)

RLP: It doesn't matter what size it was. The point is that it did harm. She was hurt by it, and offended by your bullying.

Harry: I know. I understand that.

RLP: It's like a very small bomb. Or a very small bullet...

Harry: (Laughter.) I understand...but I finally got her to say something that...that finally cleared up a little of my head...that made me realize that I was pushing her.

RLP: Yes.

Harry: She'd never say to me, "You're pushing me too hard."

RLP: You'd never say that to your father, either. But you felt it. Any pushing at all is too much. It doesn't work. In love, especially, it doesn't work.

JG: I asked Harry what he wanted to come out of today's meeting with us and he said, "I have to put Debbie in her own compartment, and sort out the work area of my life. I want to be able to not binge and not sit around obsessed with Debbie, or obsessed with anything that takes my mind off work, like bingeing."

After this we talked about love, work, and friendship from other points of view. I asked Harry about what kinds of qualities come to mind when he thinks about a "masculine" man, and the first picture in his mind was a bunch of body builders in a magazine advertisement. Then, "Well, I guess getting a lot of dates makes a man masculine."

Harry: I don't know.... Did I say that? It's hard for me to...it doesn't sound right.

RLP: O.K. What would you rather put in place of it? What does distinguish a man as masculine to you?

JG: Yes. You said, "Someone who is very sure of himself, someone who is aggressive."

Harry: Domineering...which is what Debbie called me. That's what she said.

RLP: "Aggressive" can become that.

JG: On the feminine side, "The way they dress -- like makeup. I'm trying not to think of stereotypes. I want to deal with people on a personal level. But my ideas of masculine and feminine probably are stereotyped: Probably the dominant person and the submissive person. But I don't like that picture."

RLP: Especially when it doesn't work. You've picked a woman who is not about to submit. Submission doesn't sound like Debbie's style.

Harry: No. That's true!

RLP: I don't suppose that M.B.A.'s are submissive types, generally. They're decision makers, or at least they want to be. They want to take control of a situation -- run empires. You said to me on the phone that she wanted to go into the investment banking field. We don't want our investment bankers to be submissive, do we? When we have a lot at risk, we want them to maintain tight control, and be decisive, I should think.

Harry: She's worried that she's not like that, but she is.

RLP: That she's worried that she's not, only shows her determination to be that way.

Harry: Oh?

RLP: Same for you. You're afraid you're not, which shows your ambition to be that way.

Harry: Hmmm.

RLP: Otherwise, you wouldn't think about being decisive or being in control at all. Not being decisive enough doesn't enter my thinking, unless being decisive is pretty important to me.

Harry: (Laughter.) Makes sense. I understand that.

RLP: That's the line of your ambition.

JG: I asked then about his first encounter with Debbie, and this is the story he tells: "I met her when I was in college, and she was dating a friend of mine. I felt, there's this beautiful girl, she's Jewish, I like her. We had similar backgrounds and interests. I wasn't lovestruck by any means. Then she was asking around at this party, looking for someone to drive to Florida with her, and I thought, 'Here's a chance to develop a relationship with her.'" This group of friends, he says, is quite clannish. Both of them have been in the group a long time.

He went on to say, "I was in some bad relationships prior to our getting together, and so was she. I saw something that I wanted, and I went out and got it. But now she's holding back. At this party -- and I hadn't seen her in quite a while, and she had dated a bunch of other guys in between -- we sat together and talked for a long time. We had a lot in common, and we had fun. I thought, 'I'd like to have a relationship with her -- how can I do that?' Then this opportunity came up."

I asked Harry about his ability to express affection toward her, and receive affection from her: "I have no trouble expressing affection with Debbie. Probably I'm too aggressive."

RLP: There's a hint in there that you were sensitive to the fact that she'd also been in some bad relationships -- perhaps with your friend, since it was on-again, off-again -- and you had some feeling that she shouldn't have to have that kind of trouble...such a beautiful, sensitive woman; that you appreciated her, and that she might want to have someone who appreciated her and enjoyed her. You said something that hinted at that.

Harry: Well, yeah. Why wouldn't she want that? I want that. I suppose everybody wants that.

RLP: That's probably true. But in her case you saw someone who had not been appreciated, and who might be especially grateful for your appreciation.

Harry: No, no, no. I didn't know she had had bad relationships until I knew her better.

RLP: Oh, you didn't?

Harry: I knew she was going out with some guys. I mean, I found out later, afterwards. Maybe that's tinged my thinking since.

RLP: So at the time you only knew that you liked her a lot.

Harry: Yeah.

RLP: That she's a very attractive woman.

Harry: Yeah. But it's not that she's such an attractive woman; it's that I'm attracted to her.

RLP: What is there about her that makes her attractive to you?

Harry: I really don't know what it is. Although lately, when I've been losing my grip on the whole situation, not letting it play out its course, forcing issues, I don't know what I like about any of that any more.

RLP: Well, you're sort of angry, and...

Harry: Yeah. I guess I have to let it play its course, or whatever. I don't know what you were going to say.

RLP: Well, I don't know what I was going to say, either. I only know that in matters of love a good motto is, "If at first you don't succeed, quit, quit at once."

Harry: (Laughter.) Well -- so, if she does turn around, what would happen? Would we have a miserable life?

RLP: Well, you would if this is a sample of it: On-again, off-again, back and forth.

Harry: That's what it is. That's what it boils down to.... "Quit, quit at once." (Laughter.)

JG: Harry went on to say...

Harry: "Quit, quit at once." That's great. O.K.!

(All laugh.)

JG: He goes on to say, about receiving affection from her, "I'd love affection from her, but it's not there right now. It always was more me than her." He said that there was a time when they'd "rush off into the bedroom together," but now he says, "I guess that probably was more me than her, because she's just not sexual right now. She's turned me into a 'best friend.' And she's so nebulous about it. She says, 'I don't know what's gone wrong.'"

RLP: She probably doesn't.

JG: He added, "When I approach her physically, she says she needs more space; when I'm playful she says, 'Don't be a nerd.' She wants certainty in her life, and I can't provide her with that."

Harry: That's just me, rationalizing.

JG: He says, "I expect too much out of the relationship."

RLP: You want her in your life, and she does not want to be in somebody else's life. She's having trouble enough figuring out her own life. She was happy to have *you* in *her* life -- she invited you to come on her trip! It didn't occur to her that you were going to ask her to come into your life -- to come on your trip. The moment that idea came up, she said, "I don't want to live in Davenport," which was the symbol of it.

Harry: Uh-huh.

RLP: For you to be in her life was all right. For her to be in your life wasn't very comfortable to her.

Harry: That's interesting.

RLP: That's how it sounds.

JG: She wants you on her terms.

Harry: Well, yeah. That's what I've been trying to say: She sets the terms.

RLP: Sure. She thought you agreed to the terms. She wanted a companion for her trip to Florida, and you were happy to join her. It was attractive to you to have the chance to be with her, because you were hoping it would develop into something. That would have represented a new set of "terms." But it doesn't sound as if Debbie is at a point in her life where she's able to make an alliance with anyone. She's too busy trying to figure out how to complete her studies, her education, her training, and to establish her competence in her own field.

Harry: Well, this is a better way to rationalize the whole thing to myself. It makes sense to me.

RLP: If I am correct, you don't have to rationalize anything. You just have to recognize that she doesn't want to get married. She wants to be your best friend. Best friends want their best friends to find someone else to marry.

Harry: She wants to get me out of her life.

RLP: Yes, if you don't want to be friends with her, and all you do is bring pressure into her life in an effort to change the course of her life.

Harry: And she wants to be nice about it.

RLP: Yes, and, if you want to get married, she'd like you to find someone who wants to be married to you as you are, right now.

JG: Someone who will "take the pressure off me," as Debbie put it to you.

RLP: Yes.

Harry: It's not going to be enough just to ease up on her -- and still be with her.

RLP: I don't think so. You've led her to believe that you want her to marry you, and your hope that she may come around to that is experienced by her as a pressure. You've led me to believe that she doesn't want to get married. She doesn't feel sure enough of herself, of her own competence in her chosen field. She has her own project to complete. She wants a sense of having completed something for herself.

Harry: Are you saying that from the way I've explained it, it's a doomed project, even two or three years from now?

RLP: I don't know. Two or three years from now, if you were to meet again, and if neither of you has found somebody else in the interim...

Harry: You're saying I shouldn't wait.

RLP: You can, if you want to, but I don't think you're going to join a monastery for two years, and come back out when the time is right. You may, but I don't think you will. In any case, this isn't the point.

For anyone who stays in a love affair that's not working, we have to ask, "What's the purpose of staying in it?" There's a number of possibilities that occur to me: First, you're in the same circle, you and Debbie. There'd be some loss of face. You've gone after her, but she won't have you.

Harry: People are saying, "When are you going to get married?"

RLP: Right. "When are you going to get married," and so on. So there's some sense of defeat, of not being able to succeed, of having made a real effort and not succeeding.

Harry: Yes, and I also don't want to.... It's going to be tough to throw myself back into the game, the...I don't know.

JG: The market?

Harry: Yeah. The market, or whatever you want to call it.

RLP: Well, the line is forty blocks long for a young Jewish man who wears a clean shirt.

Harry: (Laughter.)

RLP: And who brushes his teeth every day.

Harry: (Laughter.)

RLP: A line forty blocks long of young women, young Jewish women, who will be delighted to meet you and be happy with you *just as you are*.

Harry: Well, so then it comes back to, "but she's so perfect for me, and I'm so perfect for her."

RLP: Then we have to ask ourselves, "In what sense is she so perfect for you?"

JG: What kind of perfection is this?

Harry: (Laughter.) This *grief*. (Laughter.) What kind of perfection is this grief?!

RLP: We have to ask ourselves whether you want to be married at all.

Harry: If this is the kind of life I want, maybe I should stay single. (Laughter.)

RLP: At the moment, I think you do want to stay single. You are also at a time in your life when you want to establish your independence in your own field, in your own business. If I were in your place, anyway, I would want to be able to demonstrate to my father that I'm able to make it on my own.

Harry: Oh, sure.

RLP: And I think it would be such an important ambition for me that I would allow myself to be intimidated by it from time to time. If I want *so* much to show my father that I can make a success on my own, and if that's what I most want, what is it that I don't want? I sure as hell don't want to let my father see that I've made a botch of it on my own. Right?

Harry: Uh-huh.

RLP: That's the negative pole of the ambition, and it's enough to intimidate anybody.

Harry: I'm not so much worried about everything else.

RLP: Right. And if this is such a big deal, and if I *do* make a botch of it, it may be to my advantage to feel -- in my heart, anyway, and to save my self-esteem -- that I made a botch of it because I was caught up in an unhappy love affair that distracted me from it.

Harry: Here I've got the excuse.

RLP: Yes. I've got the perfect explanation for having botched it up.

Harry: That's what I'm saying. I've got a perfect excuse for botching up.

RLP: Sure. How could I possibly concentrate on my work?

And there's more. There's a positive side to it as well, because if I do make a success of it, in spite of the fact that I've got an unhappy love affair, the success is a triumph -- a success in spades!

Harry: Uh-huh.

RLP: So then I've proved that I can do it even when...

Harry: ...the chips are down.

RLP: Right. Even when I'm handicapped. So the distraction with Debbie and the preoccupation with food and so on, is a kind of insurance policy. If I succeed, I'm a tremendous success, and if I fail, who could have succeeded?

Harry: So I've used it, in other words, like a tool.

RLP: More like an insurance policy. With this much trouble, plus a success, it's a triumph; with this much trouble and no success, it's not a failure. It's understandable. Who could possibly have succeeded?

Harry: Uh-huh.

RLP: Either I have a triumph, or I'm exonerated.

Harry: Uh-huh.

RLP: It's a marvelous policy. It pays in either direction. An insurance man once said to me, "There are two things you have to insure against: one is that you'll die too soon; the other is that you'll live too long."

Harry: (Laughter.)

RLP: And you have a similar kind of insurance policy: Either I'll succeed big, or I won't fail at all.

Harry: So I shouldn't.... I mean, my life will go on the same whether I worry about it at all.

RLP: Well, I don't know what you should or shouldn't do. It's only important to see what, so far, you have been doing so that you're free to consider what else you may want to do. I think it's important for you to consider disengaging from this ambition to prove something to your father, at least to some extent.

Harry: Disengage from it?

RLP: From the ambition to show something to your father, to prove something to him.

Harry: Should I not be intimidated by it? You said, "Don't be intimidated by it."

RLP: I only pointed out that you are, and that I don't think it's necessary. I don't think it is worth it to make your life into a project for proving a point to your father. It may be more satisfying for you to find something you enjoy doing, and enjoy your own experience of competence.

Harry: I thought that was what I was trying to do.

RLP: I think the other ambition intrudes on it.

Harry: Oh, sure it does, a little...or some. A lot, maybe.

RLP: Enough to spoil it for you.

Harry: It spoils the job right now.

RLP: The fun.

Harry: Yeah. The fun. Yeah! I've always enjoyed managing, selling -- until I got here. It's certainly not as easy as I thought it was going to be either.

(Long, thoughtful silence.)

JG: Would you like me to go on? O.K. [JG continues.]

After talking about love, we talked about friendship. Harry has friends he grew up with and went to college with who are here. His best friend is Bill, who lives in San Diego. He also has good friends back home, "but if I told them too much it would get back to my parents." Also, they bug him with the question, "When are you going to get married?"

Harry: It's all in relationship to her. My parents and everybody are always asking, "How's she doing?" And that's the.... Hey! That's the defeat!

RLP: Uh-huh. You can define it as a defeat, and then you'd be terribly distressed. Or, you can define it as a choice: "I don't choose to pursue her any longer. She has her own agenda, and she has to work it out on her own."

Harry: Uh-huh.

JG: I asked Harry about what kind of impression he thinks he makes on people when they first meet him and he said, "Well, I talk. I'm talkative." That's about as far as he could go. He said, "I don't have a clear picture of that. I do have an image of myself, though. I'm real insecure. I act much more sure of myself than I feel and sometimes I feel that this, that, and the other thing is wrong with me."

RLP: Isn't this in line with the masculine ideal of decisiveness?

Harry: Uh-huh.

RLP: See, "I act much more sure of myself than I feel," because men, Real Men, are supposed to be clear, decisive, and untroubled about their decisions.

Harry: Uh-huh

RLP: Whereas, as a mortal person, I'm not always so sure. I make choices without being sure. But there's some idea that I'm supposed to -- as a man -- have confidence in my decisions and know what I'm doing. That sounds like Father talking.

Harry: Yeah, sure. (Laughter.)

RLP: There's a right way and a wrong way, and you should know the right way, and so on.

JG: When he said, "Sometimes I feel that this, that, and the other are wrong with me," he said, "That could be a little paranoid, but when I look back at my history, maybe there's some evidence that there is something wrong with me."

RLP: That's a haunting idea. I have something to say about that. Is that the end of your record?

JG: No.

RLP: Well, let me just say this briefly. There's something wrong with everyone. Every human body has anomalies of structure. And no two human beings have the same organic strengths and weaknesses. When we make an issue of it, we turn our ordinary imperfections into a syndrome.

I want to write a paper on this subject some day. The difficulty is in trying to capture a tone of voice and a mood in the title of the paper, which I plan to call, "The *Something Wrong* Syndrome." This requires an upper case "S" and an upper case "W" and the words have to be italicized, to suggest the haunting quality of introspection and self-doubt involved in the syndrome.

In fact, there is something wrong with everyone, but we usually refer to it in "lower case" terms, and without the italics. Most of the time we don't focus on our deficiencies, or on what they may prevent us from achieving. Instead, we focus on what we *can* do with what we've got, and count on the contributions of others to assist us when necessary, or even to correct us when that is required. The *Something Wrong* syndrome stalls us, and keeps us busy in a search for imperfections, as if we had to be faultless before we could proceed with anything. That's not possible.

Harry: Yeah. Well, you're saying it's another excuse.

RLP: Something like that. But not a very good one.

Harry: (Laughter.)

JG: Back to the record, all right? I asked Harry what his friends value in him. I asked, "If I called Bill and asked him what there is about you that he values, what would he say?" Harry said, "He'd say I'm a good friend. We do a lot for each other. When a person needs something, Bill or I, we help each other." Harry added that he thinks of himself as a loyal friend. He doesn't run out on his friends when the going gets rough or something goes wrong.

In the work area, I asked if there's anything he brings to his work that he's aware of as troublesome. He said, "Yeah. If only I wouldn't run away from it. If only I'd stand there and do it. I get side-tracked." Then he said, "If there's something that I really want to do, I do it."

RLP: Like the rest of us.

Harry: (Laughter.)

JG: He said, "I felt Dad really threw a lot on me, and I feel bitter about that. Finally, I would just say to Dad, 'You do it!' I don't stick to things. There are things that I let go." Then he added, "There was just too much for one person to do. Dad had brought the business out of a swamp -- the place was going broke, and he rebuilt it. He could have bought out the rest of the family and he didn't. Now he has nothing to leave his kids except his share of the business, and he's bitter about this. I would scream at him when I was in the company and we weren't getting along. My brother has a different attitude. He says to Dad, 'O.K., we'll do it your way,' and just smiles."

RLP: A second born.

JG: Harry also said, "My dad feels terrible about what's happened. A number of times he came home crying." When he and Father got along, though, they went sailing together. Harry's father is a great sailor, and they have a big sloop. But Father felt that Harry should learn to sail it. Harry said, "He felt he had to push me to take the boat out. He nagged me, and I resisted and I kept putting off doing it." This, even though Harry wanted to do it, and felt able to do it, and wanted to take his father out.

RLP: You took each other too seriously, the two of you. You're too impressed with each other!

Harry: (Laughter.)

RLP: He's very impressed with you. Therefore, he's frantic to tell you everything he knows, and to see that you learn everything. With your brother he's more relaxed. He's not so impressed with him -- and Brother isn't so impressed with Father, either. He says to Father, "Fine. O.K. We'll do it your way." Then he goes and does what he wants anyhow. That's my guess.

Harry: Well, he does what Dad tells him to -- with the job. In his personal life, though, he doesn't do anything Dad tells him to.

RLP: No. It doesn't matter to him.

Harry: That's right. He doesn't listen. He just walks out, leaves. He says, "Screw it!"

RLP: Sure, but you and your father are too impressed with each other. Each of you is trying to impress the other, in turn, that you also know something. Father is so impressed by you, he's afraid that you won't be impressed by him.

Harry: Uh-huh.

RLP: You're so impressed by Father, you're afraid that Father won't be impressed by you. Do you recognize what I'm saying?

Harry: Yeah. Yes. I see what you're saying. It's a form of rivalry.

RLP: No. It's not a form of rivalry. It's a form of affection. You really admire your father.

Harry: Oh, yeah!

RLP: For what he did for that company, and for his whole family... taking that company out of the swamp that his father had left it in. You admire his loyalty to the other members of the family. Am I right or wrong?

Harry: Well, that was stupidity for the most part. He really feels that it was.

RLP: That may be, but it's not what you feel.

Harry: No. But, yeah. I admire his morality and his motives. I have a lot of respect for the way he thinks.

RLP: The fact that they abused him is not to *his* discredit.

Harry: Oh, I see what you're saying. Sure I do, I admire him.

RLP: You admire him. And what do you want in turn? You want him also to admire you. It's the same for him. He admires you. You're his first-born son. He sees wonderful things in you. You can do anything. When he sees hesitation on your part, he says, "Come on! You can do it!"

Harry: (Laughter.) Yeah. You're probably right. Yeah.

RLP: Yes. It is right. Otherwise, he wouldn't be so frantic. Part of your difficulty is that you have what you want!

JG: He wouldn't even bother to fight with you, to get into power struggles with you, unless he thought of you as a worthy adversary.

Harry: (Laughter.) Yeah!

RLP: Now, Harry, we have to draw this to a close. Let me give you my impressions. We'll type them up and send them to you, and you'll make use of them however you want to make use of them. Before I state them, though, I want to ask you how it feels for you to have had this conversation with us? We only met today, and here we've gotten to talk about all kinds of personal things.

Harry: It's good. It feels good. It's interesting. I'm hoping I've gotten something that I'm going to turn into some positive stimulus for myself, for how I see things. There are things I want to sit down and think about now.

RLP: Good. Let's see if I can come up with some impressions that will be useful to you.

> [Note: At this point RLP made the following statement, in Harry's presence. JG wrote the statement down, pausing from time to time to enter into further conversation with RLP about a choice of words, or a detail which had been forgotten, etc.]

SUMMARY OF IMPRESSIONS DERIVED FROM THE INITIAL INTERVIEW

Harry presents himself at what to him is the "magic" age of thirty: The time in a man's life when he should be able to demonstrate his success, consummate a good marriage, and be the head of a family. He should no longer be acting like a young fellow in his twenties, unsure of himself, unsure of his goals, and unmarried.

He has, therefore, set out to do what he should do: Get a wife, start a family, get his own career independent of the family business, and demonstrate to his father that he is entitled to respect as a man amongst men.

Unfortunately, it has not yet clearly occurred to him that he requires the cooperation of an enthusiastic partner to make a marriage and a family. Furthermore, until now he has not seen clearly that the two goals of establishing himself in a career and impressing his father are mutually exclusive.

That is to say, if he wants above all else to impress his father favorably, he must be prepared to act the way Sidney does in the business. If he wants to establish an independent career for himself, he has to do what Father did in his life, namely, set his own goals and pursue his own course, disregarding anyone else's opinion as to the wisdom or desirability of his choices.

[Note: A method for composing the "Summary of Impressions derived from the Initial Interview" is presented in Chapter 12.]

Conclusion

Our intention in presenting the complete discussion between Harry and the two therapists was to demonstrate that a person who appears to have several different concerns can gain a unifying clarity in the space of a single interview. Use of the *IPCW* inquiry format, combined with client and therapists working together in the review process, can lead to an understanding of what the client is doing, what he or she is doing it for, what it costs to keep it going, and what else is open to his or her choice.

The remaining chapters in Part III will guide the reader through the review and interpretations of the family constellation data, revealing how key features of the client's childhood experience provide a context and background for understanding the person's interpretations of the current situation.

Chapter 6: GENDER GUIDING LINES AND ROLE MODELS

The image of fictional guiding lines was used as an early theoretical construct in the development of Individual Psychology, an image later included among ideas represented by the term life-style. As meridians facilitate navigation across the surface of the earth, so guiding lines provide orientation for individual movement in the social world.

The guiding lines are the evaluations and expectations that a child employs in forming a schema of apperception. This schema, formed early in life and unique to the individual, provides the axiomatic foundation from which the reasoning of the private logic proceeds.

Since subsequent impressions are filtered through this schema, the biases of the preverbal and early verbal period carry through, with more or less modification, into adulthood. As Adler put it, these impressions or guiding lines are "attached to the individual as a pattern, permitting him to express his self-consistent personality in any situation without much reflection" (p. 219). Among the most important and ineluctable of the early impressions is the picture the child forms of what it means to be a man or to be a woman; what it means to be one of these among others of the same and of the other sex; and, what being a man or being a woman means with respect to the struggle to overcome inferiorities.

Success in life depends, in part, upon our ability to solve the problems connected with sexuality. Each of us is born a member of one sex or the other. In either case, we encounter the problems of sexuality in a particular cultural context of meanings. Reproductive love and the securing of children in the supportive bonds of family life are tasks set for two persons (Adler, 1982, p. 124). Therefore, to succeed in these tasks, even to be able to address them at all, requires that we develop a readiness for cooperation with a member of the other sex. We cannot depend on fixed action patterns, as the other animals appear to do, for the solution of the problems associated with these tasks. Instead, we have to rely on the symbols and images we ourselves create, using our own ideas about what it means to be male or female to govern our sex-related attitudes, convictions, expectations, and operations.

At each stage of our development throughout childhood and adolescence we operate as if we were asking and rehearsing trial answers to questions such as, "What does my gender require of me, what does it promise me, and what am I going to do about it in order to secure a place (or avoid a place) with a partner of the other sex?"

When gender definition is conveyed to us through images of masculine and feminine that are both desirable to us and useful in our social world, we feel at ease in our sexuality, and in our relations with other members of our sex as well as of the other sex.

If these images are mistaken, particularly with respect to the demand for cooperation, and if they exaggerate either the requirements or the promises of our gender's social role, we may experience trouble in our dealings with members of our own sex and the other sex. Then all our capacities for sexual functioning, for connecting with a partner in love, and for success as one of two cooperating parents, will be undermined.

In our present historical circumstances cultural images of the differences between the sexes (and of the proper biological roles that each has to perform to ensure the future of the species) remain distorted by an autocratic tradition of inequality. Images of masculine and feminine are therefore often unattractive (in that they point backward to standards that are no longer acceptable) or unclear (in that they point forward to standards that are not yet culturally defined). Many individuals are burdened with hesitation in their confusion about what it means to be persons of their sex, and about what may be required of them to engage intimately (and happily) with a person of the other sex.

Adler understood the importance of these questions in their effects on basic feelings of dignity. His awareness of the damaging effect of a social and symbolic system defining the sexes in terms of inequality, led him to formulate the concept of "the masculine protest." Since American English has largely lost the original meaning of protest, this has become a less and less useful phrase, easily mistaken for an objection or a complaint. These meanings can be included in the protestation, which is, however, properly understood as an assertion or a claim. As Griffith and Powers (1984) put it:

> The masculine protest can be understood as an assertion or claim for the perceived male position of dignity and status with its perceived prerogatives and power. Adler posited that the girl or woman senses her socially inferior position to the boy or man and strives to feel equal. Her goal: Treat me like a man! In the event, she only feels *equal* to the man she perceives as superior to her if she senses herself to be ("equally") *superior* to the man. Adler also saw the boy and man who perceive themselves to be inferior to other men (or,

> worse, to girls and women) protesting: Treat me like a Real Man! (pp. 32-33)

To understand a life-style, and especially to search out and identify the errors standing in the way of successful adaptation, it is, therefore, of central importance to understand the person's governing images or guiding lines relating to gender. We are also alert to gender exemplars the individual has chosen either to emulate (positive role models) or to attend to as cautionary examples (negative role models).

As a general rule, the more disturbed and misfitted the individual is by reason of a faulty style, the more we can expect that person to interpret sexuality (and all gender-related imagery) in oppositional terms. Adler therefore recommended that the very phrase, "the opposite sex," be abandoned, for encouraging as it does a continuation of such ideas, and called for use of the phrase, "the other sex," instead. More and more often we can see a direct correlation between the extent of dysfunctional movement and the intensity of ideas of inequality between the sexes. As Adler put it:

> In the [private] sense of the patient, but not in the general [common] sense, memories, impulses, and actions are always arranged according to a classification of *inferior=below=feminine* versus *powerful=above=masculine* (p. 249).

Dreikurs used Adler's general concept of guiding lines to identify a person's governing images of masculine and feminine, and what it means to the person to be a man or a woman. In our continuing exploration of the importance of these images, we have discovered that it is greatly to our advantage to maintain a distinction between gender guiding lines and role models as theoretical constructs.

Gender Guiding Lines

We understand the gender guiding lines to be:

1. Largely *outside* the person's conscious awareness;

2. patterns for the person's *expectations* regarding gender;

3. experienced as if presenting a *destiny*; and

4. shaped in conformity with images of mother and father, who serve as the *norms* for what a real man and a real woman are.

According to this understanding, children form their pictures of what it means to be a man or a woman by experiencing, and assigning meanings to, the differences between mother and father. When we were children, mother and father established the norms for what it is to be a man or to be a woman. Without having to think about it, we compared other men to father, other women to mother, and found that the others deviated in one or more particulars from these norms, either by going beyond expectations dictated by the guiding lines, or by falling short of them. It is as if we were noting, "All men are like my father or unlike my father; all women are like my mother or unlike my mother."

This process takes place against a background of cultural norms and values. It therefore requires little, if any, conscious awareness. The assumptions formed by a child in the early years of life regarding his or her own sex and the other sex continue throughout life, largely unexamined, to the extent that they remain effective for the individual (however troublesome or offensive they may appear from the points of view of others).

These assumptions become the child's expectations concerning gender. Contrived in the universal striving to overcome feelings of inferiority, the guiding lines point the way to a vision of the future, in which weak, insecure, and dependent children can picture themselves enjoying the strong, secure, and independent status of adults. Bringing an image of future competence into the frame of reference of the present phenomenological field, the guiding line serves as a compensatory mechanism, as a source of encouragement, and as a template for training and self-training.

Children shape images of themselves as adults along the guiding lines, which they come to regard as if tracing a *destiny*. As the capacities for critical discrimination grow, and the guiding lines are seen to encompass unattractive, unwelcome, or repugnant features, the sense of destiny may reveal itself in an uneasiness, as if the child were thinking, "When I grow up I'm going to be like that (referring to qualities of the same-sex parent), unless I do something about it."

Even in situations where one (or both) of the parents is absent, the child forms an image of the missing parent(s). A parent may be absent owing to death, divorce, abandonment, confinement to an institution, or other circumstances. A child will seize upon scraps of available information (such as a photograph, overheard bits of conversation among relatives, or personal possessions of the missing parent) and organize the impressions gained from these against the "whole cloth" of creative imagination. The resulting picture serves as the gender guiding line for that parent.

Case example. Margie's parents divorced when she was two years old. She retained no memories of her natural father. Her mother remarried shortly after the divorce, and Margie grew up with an affectionate stepfather whom she called Father, the only father she had any sense of ever having known. Stepfather was quiet, unobtrusive, a steady person who was a hard worker and a good provider." Margie did not see her natural father, nor was he in touch with her in any way until she was in her thirties.

At twenty-two, Margie married a man whom she described as "flashy, impulsive, passionate, and exciting." In short, he was in every way as different from her stepfather as could be imagined. In an exploration of gender guiding lines she said, "I don't know how I could have ever married a man like Tommy." We asked if she knew anything about her natural father. She said that all she really knew was what she had overheard in a conversation between Mother and Grandmother in which they were talking about his gambling habit and his fast-living style on one occasion when she was about eight or nine years old. She had been intrigued by this. Then, there were several occasions when she knew that he was visiting in town, because there had been conversations between mother and other people as to when "Ralph" was expected to arrive. She remembered comments such as, "I sure hope I get to see Ralph when he's here! Boy, is he a character!" Mother and Grandmother were abuzz at these times, and people Margie did not even know would speak to her mother on the street, saying, "I hear Ralph's going to be in town. He'll put on a show!"

Margie never saw her father during these visits. Secretly, however, she wove an image of what this dashing, entertaining man was like, and mooned over it, thinking how grand it would be if he would come and sweep her away from the life she was leading, which, in comparison with her fantasy, was humdrum and colorless. As she told the story, she began to smile with recognition, and, displaying a pronounced blush, said, "Now I understand why I chose Tommy!" She had come to see how he had met her expectations for what a "real man" was.

Role Models

We distinguish role models from the gender guiding lines, and understand them to be:

1. Largely *in* conscious awareness throughout childhood and adolescence;

2. patterns for the person's *imitations*, independent of gender;

3. experienced as if providing an escape from destiny by way of *choice*; and

4. shaped in conformity with images of men and women who represent possibilities for *deviation from the norms*.

Children, ineluctably and increasingly aware of the importance of gender, must attend to and study both its positive and negative possibilities. We encountered many men and women other than our parents in the early years of our development. Grandparents and other relatives, teachers, preachers, bus drivers, letter carriers, neighbors, and the parents of other children all played their parts in our world. Some of these people took on a special importance in our eyes as illustrating something important about human possibilities, and therefore about gender possibilities. We hoped or wished to be like some of them; we wanted to avoid being like some others.

Expectations characterize the guiding lines; the parallel terms for the role models are imitation and rejection. We want our lives to be like those we admire, and we study them in imitation. These are our positive role models. We deliberately strive to copy those aspects of their personalities and histories that appeal to us. In the same way, we set out deliberately to avoid being like people we regard as reprehensible, offensive, or unattractive. These are our negative role models, and we study them in an effort to reject the possibility of anything entering our behavior that may remind us of them.

In the Life-Style Assessment, we ask clients to tell us about any adults other than the parents who were important to them when they were growing up. Usually there are two or three who come to mind.

Case example. Edith described her mother as a perfectionistic, fault-finding woman whom Edith could never please no matter how hard she tried. Mother seemed to her to complain about everything, and not to enjoy life, except with respect to new clothes, and especially when she was able to dress for a social occasion: Since she had a striking face and figure, she could do this very well indeed, and was much admired by Father (and others) for her style and flair. Mother's sister, on the other hand, was a happy and accepting person. "She'd just let me be me. She liked me and was always glad to see me. We spent a lot of time together, and she'd always be cooking up a storm -- good things. Mother wasn't interested in that at all. Aunt Carolyn was fun! I wanted to be like her, not like my mother."

When a child finds the behavior of the same sex parent to be *unattractive* to her, as Edith did, she will regard that parent as a negative role model, and set herself the task of avoiding any imitation of it. She will look for positive role models as encouraging examples of what else is open to her as a girl who will grow up to be a woman. Edith's Aunt Carolyn was one of these for her.

Typically, however, such a person will feel some sense of uneasiness resulting from the struggle she is having to free herself from the gender expectations dictated by the guiding line set by the parent of the same sex. In Edith's case she safeguarded in an exaggerated way against criticizing anyone or complaining against anything for fear of becoming a faultfinding woman like her mother. She had come to find it hard to let others know where she stood, for fear of appearing critical. She could also feel tormented by her sense of being critical of people who are critical, and, in a kind of psychic hall of mirrors, found herself trying to be perfectly free of perfectionism!

Edith was also a woman of striking good looks, like her mother, and this likeness felt to her to be another danger, which she fought against by a studied avoidance of anything fashionable. Even this did not keep her safe, however; the studied character of her avoidance resulted in her having a stylishness of her own that people found attractive. Finally, in deliberate imitation of Aunt Carolyn she had studied and mastered the culinary arts, and continued to enjoy "cooking up a storm" -- except on those occasions when something went wrong with a recipe: "You see," she'd say to herself or to anyone else who would listen, "I'm just like my mother when it comes to cooking."

The sense of dissonance and uneasiness increases for the child who not only decides not to be like the same-sex parent, but who also sets out to imitate the parent of the other sex. In such a case there is a conflict between one's gender and the chosen role model, and the person's experience of gender identity may be clouded by a suspicion of inauthenticity. It is as if the person were asking, "If I am like my mother, what kind of a man am I? Am I a real man?" Or, "If I am like my father, what kind of a woman am I? Am I a real woman?"

Case example. Frank reported that his father was a bully and a show-off. He beat the children, and was always getting into fights and being suspended from work. He abused Mother as well. This ended when, at sixteen years of age, Frank intervened in a fight between Mother and Father. He knocked his father down and said, "Don't ever hit her again, or I'll throw you out." Father knew he was beaten, and timidly acquiesced. Frank was pleased to have ended the violence between Mother and Father, but was uneasy over the humiliation he had inflicted on his father through his own "brutality."

Frank had always seen his mother as a kind, fair-minded person who worked hard and did what she could to maintain peace in the family. He admired her. He grew up thinking, "I don't want to be like my father. I want to be like Mother, a person of character."

As an adult, Frank is soft-spoken and low-keyed. He is a hard worker and a family man. He is also uneasy about what kind of man he could possibly be, and troubled by fears that he may be "feminine." He won't fight to get his own way, even by arguing with his wife. He says, "At work I let people walk all over me, and at home the kids just run wild when I'm alone with them." He is preoccupied with a fear that, "Really, down deep, I may be a homosexual." He asks, "What's wrong with me?"

Frank's adult functioning is constricted by the safeguard he has erected against the "destiny" of emerging as a brute, which could occur at any time he so much as expressed himself in a forceful tone. He would then be "revealing himself" in the image defined by his masculine guiding line, and would be seen as the "real man" of his imagination.

People can experience another difficulty of this kind when a positive role model is recommended to the child by a parent, who offers it as a standard of personal value. In a typical example, the parent of the other sex says (or, more likely, implies) to the child, "Don't be like *your* mother; be like *my* mother" (father to daughter), or "Don't be like *your* father; be like *my* father" (mother to son).

Case example. Judy saw her mother as a good-hearted and well-intentioned person, but "confused. She just couldn't get organized. She seemed to be in a private world. It was a daily problem. For example, she never could get dinner together and ready on time. Dad would come home on a tight schedule (and he didn't demand very much from her, as it appeared to me), and dinner wouldn't be ready. This didn't happen once; it happened night, after night, after night. She was late to every appointment she ever had. God, how they'd argue and fight over this. And it was hopeless! He couldn't count on her for *anything*. It was so different at my grandmother's (his mother's) house. Everything was so orderly there. Dad was always comparing my mother to his mother, and my mother always came out on the short end of the stick. I don't know why he stayed with her. Well...she was the prettiest woman in our town, and she was so vain! I guess that had a lot to do with it. Anyway, I never wanted to be like my mother. So I'm a capable, orderly person -- but I don't know how "feminine" I am, or whether I'd get the attention of a real man like my father. Mother was such a bubblebrain, but she had him! I'm so down to earth and practical that it scares me."

There would be no reason for Judy's worried appraisal of her everyday sensible and practical approach to things unless she had a basic idea that a "real" woman (that is to say, a woman capable of attracting and holding a "real" man) pays the price for her advantages in a loss of dignity: incompetent, self-absorbed, and flighty, like Mother.

Judy was so safeguarded against being a "bubblebrain" that she was rigid, lacking spontaneity and lightness in her approach to life. She was following the role model presented by Grandmother to compensate against the danger of feminine inferiority represented in the guiding line she saw set by her own mother. All compensation tends toward overcompensation, and she had lost sight of her own femininity (and her grandmother's), experiencing a *dissonance* between her gender guiding line (which had its appeal, even to her) and her role model, to which she felt (so to speak) "honor bound," as a way of maintaining her self-esteem. Until she explored these issues in therapy she was uneasy in her self-appraisal of her attractiveness and sexuality, as if she believed, "I'm not truly feminine."

The sense of expectation that flows from the gender guiding lines dictates attitudes toward one's own, and toward the other, sex. Those who conform to our hidden gender guiding lines, even though we may not like them, remain recognizable to us as "the genuine articles," either as men or as women.

We sometimes express our gender guiding lines by stumbling over them, even though, typically, we remain unaware of what we express in our unguarded outbursts. For example, when a man (or a woman) says, "Women are like that!" or when a woman (and sometimes a man) says, "Isn't that just like a man!" some basic assumptions about gender are being expressed. These expectations for one's own and the other sex predicate the norms of personal movement in relation to both sexes.

Case example. Jim grew up in a household in which Mother was manic-depressive. His sister was a sickly child, and one of his aunts, who lived nearby, was an alcoholic. He had concluded: "You can't count on a woman; either they're screwy or they're sick. In either case, the men have to take care of them." His feminine guiding line, established by his mother's wild flights alternating with silent withdrawals, was reinforced by the periodic illness of his sister and his aunt's episodic bouts of intoxication: Whatever else is true about them, women are not to be trusted.

Jim's picture of Father, by contrast, was all positive. He saw Father as steady in temperament, tolerant, and unfailingly reliable as a caretaker and provider. Jim loved Father, and was able to count on him for a secure sense of having a place in the world. Father never defaulted. He endured.

Father provided Jim with a noble masculine guiding line and, since Jim wanted nothing else so much as to be like Father, Jim had self-consciously chosen Father as a positive role model as well. Here there was a clear case of *consonance* between the destiny of the guiding line and the open desire to pursue the role model. Ordinarily, in such a case, we can expect the result to be a comfortable adaptation to adult sexuality.

In Jim's case the life of a man seemed to be a tremendous challenge and a heroic burden. He had grown up admiring his loyal and reliable father, and at the same time wondering, "Do I have what it takes to be like that?" He set out to prove that he did, in order to "succeed" in the task of being a "real" man.

Not surprisingly, the only women who managed to catch and hold his attention were those who appeared to require a caretaker. When he came to see us, it was at the end of four years in a relationship with a woman who couldn't hold a job because of all kinds of somatic symptoms, who had constant money troubles, and who couldn't maintain friendships because of her hair-trigger temper. Her first husband had abandoned her, and she was raising a son who (understandably) adored Jim. Jim found it impossible to break it off with her (and her son) in spite of her endless complaints, demands, and fits of temper. After all, his motto was, "Men don't give up!" If he were to give up on her, he wondered, "What kind of man would I be?" His heroic picture of what is required of a man had kept him in a destructive relationship with a woman who was prepared to exploit him.

As with all preparations for life, the gender guiding lines can be traced to efforts at orientation begun in early childhood. As with all human phenomena, this does not require us to conclude that they were irremediably fixed in childhood. Their fluidity remains especially obvious through adolescence, when they are still subject to dramatic modification on the basis of new experiences and information.

Case example. Mark told us that until he was eleven years old he had seen his father as flawless. Father doted on his wife and children. A successful businessman, he was well respected in the community, gregarious, and an athlete who enjoyed a Saturday afternoon soccer game. When Mark was eleven he learned accidentally that Father was involved in a long-standing affair with his secretary. Mark's world seemed to collapse. From that point on he thought, "No matter how men look and act, the hidden truth is that they can betray everything important in life." Mark saw his mother as a good and kind woman, an encouraging person, and fun to be around. He saw her as the victim of his father's misbehavior. He hated his father for what he had done to "this good woman."

How did these ideas express themselves in the movement of Mark's adult life? His first sexual affair was with a married woman, and his next liaison went on over the course of several years, during which his partner deceived him with other men numerous times. His private logic was: Since I am a man, I cannot be counted on to be faithful to a woman. I must therefore not allow myself to become involved with a good woman whom I would ultimately betray. Therefore, I must find a woman who is worse than I am, and who will keep me safe against the shame of being a betrayer by being the one who will betray me.

Further Examples

The Case of Catherine. Catherine saw Father as cheerful, confident, and competent. He was also playful and uncritical. He was at home in the world, presenting himself as a friendly person. She saw Mother as fretful, concerned with propriety, ill at ease amongst others, and dependent upon Father to make everything in life both work and work out. Catherine's gender guiding lines, therefore, presented men as competent, the enablers of life; and women as dependent upon the men for whatever the men chose to do or not to do for them. Women were basically misfitted to do anything but to look nice, and to be fretful if things did not go as they would have liked, according to Catherine's view. The only power she clearly saw as belonging to women was that of moral judgment. Catherine, believing that everything is up to the men, has been waiting for a man to make life for her. Until then, she concerns herself with her appearance, with biding her time, and with being critical of others.

Until these issues were explored, Catherine had not seen herself as an actor who, by what she does and does not do, has an effect upon those around her.

The Case of Matthew. Matthew saw Father as encouraging, outgoing, and practical; Mother was righteous, quarrelsome, and suffering. No matter how hard Matthew and Father tried to please Mother, they were never able to succeed. It seemed that all their efforts only served to increase Mother's sense that life had been unfair to her, and to invite her further complaints against one and all for how much she had been, and still was being, mistreated.

Matthew expects a woman to suffer, and that it will be his manly duty to make it up to her for what she has suffered. The only way to avoid this position is not to get involved with a woman; or, failing that, to keep one's distance and to protect one's privacy. Matthew has a job that takes him on the road all week, away from the suffering woman to whom he has been married for the past fifteen unhappy years.

The Case of Joe. Joe saw Father as a hard worker, a man who could overpower others by a tyrannical style of demands and expectations which no one could satisfy and no one could meet. He saw Mother as caring and cautious, and as encouraging the children to better themselves as a way of escaping Father's domination. Joe has a good alliance with his wife, but has trouble with members of his own sex. He expects it to be "a jungle out there" in the world of men, especially those men who are in senior positions to his in the business world. He believes that they will demand too much, that their expectations will be too high, and that, since there will be no way for him to please them, his only hope is to escape them. Joe had changed jobs many times before he decided to explore this issue in therapy.

The Case of Julie. Julie saw Father as wonderful. He worked hard, was reliable, and was uncomplaining. Although he did not encourage her, he never hampered Julie in what she wanted to do. Father was practical, and led a life of routine.

Julie saw Mother as restless, complaining, and determined to do whatever it was she wanted to do, even if it was beyond the family's means, and even if Father objected. Mother was frivolous and selfish, according to Julie. As an adult, Julie believes herself to be tempted to be self-centered, and is determined not to yield to this temptation.

She does not experience herself as having anything to offer to a man. In her view men are wonderful, and women are a drag on them. She cannot go out with "good" men, therefore, since she believes that she would only mess things up for them and hurt them. Instead, she dates a series of unsuitable partners who get bored with her and leave her.

She works very well with men in the business setting, but expressed her bias against her own sex when she said that she never gets along with the women there, and that, "They just do whatever they want to do without any thought of anyone else. It's infuriating!"

The Case of Rafael. Rafael grew up in a Puerto Rican neighborhood that was close-knit and full of his relatives. He was the only child of his parents, whose ambition to have a large family had been thwarted: When Rafael was two years old Father had suffered an injury that left him invalided for life. Mother became the breadwinner and the caretaker at that time, and Rafael grew up feeling sorry for her. She was a good woman, and she deserved better.

Members of the extended family made a pet of Rafael, who spent as much time with them as possible. At home, Father became increasingly tyrannical and embittered, managing to rule both Mother and Rafael from his bed by means of temper outbursts, insults, and accusations. Mother acquiesced as if to her fate; Rafael obeyed while maintaining his defiance. He came to hate his father.

The other men in his life did not offer attractive models: One of his grandfathers was known as a "drifter" who moved from town to town, leaving Grandmother to care for the household as best she could. He would return periodically, to be nursed back to health, after which he would leave again. The other grandfather, while a steady and kindly man, was a "dreamer," interested in woodworking, in nature, music, and (according to Mother) "things that don't matter," and both Mother and Grandmother dismissed him as foolish and inconsequential. The two uncles Rafael knew best couldn't hold jobs. It seemed to Rafael that there was no good way to be a man. Besides this, he liked his position as a little boy, fussed over and enjoyed. He made a homosexual adaptation, as if to proclaim: I would rather identify with the female side. Men are defaulters, either troublesome or silly. Women, on the other hand, hold the world together with responsible caretaking and practical skills. I don't *want* to grow up at all, but if I must, I will take the female part, which at least has some dignity attached to it.

He came to see us complaining that his lover, a self-anointed person of importance in the theater, was exploiting him under the guise of helping him in his career. The lover's behavior became more and more bizarre in the following weeks, coincidental with Rafael's work with us in a Life-Style Assessment. Rafael felt responsible to take care of his lover as things deteriorated, but was unable to manage the situation as it eventuated in the lover's having a psychotic episode requiring admission to a hospital, leaving Rafael stuck with the lease and the obligation to pay the rent on their apartment.

Conclusion

The basis for the present gender-related attitudes and operations of the client become clear in a review of the client's gender guiding lines and role models. Sometimes it is possible to relate life-style data recorded in the family material to responses to the questions in the Initial Interview, "What makes a man a 'masculine' man to you? What makes a woman a 'feminine' woman?" Correlations between descriptions of the mother's and father's (and the various role models') attractive and unattractive features, and these qualities as sketched out by the client in the first session, provide dramatic confirmation of the self-consistent character of the individual's attitudes and values.

Following upon this review of gender-related values, we will direct our attention toward an examination of the atmosphere created by the parents (and others in the household), the values they communicated, and the conclusions reached by the child concerning interpersonal relations and a personal code of behavior. These topics are explored next, in Chapter 7, "Family Atmosphere and Family Values."

Chapter 7: FAMILY ATMOSPHERE AND FAMILY VALUES

Family atmosphere and family values are terms we use to describe qualities of the social environment (field) in which the creative child worked out a style of living. Our goal is to awaken the client's awareness of how the present style (now called into question, and subject to reexamination) was once a solution to the problem of successful adaptation in a particular childhood situation. Here, as elsewhere in the psycho-clarity process, we are striving for an appreciation of context that will facilitate understanding, believing that errors that are understood will be no longer necessary.

By family atmosphere we mean the quality of emotional and affectional exchanges between family members, and the resulting quality of the social field in which the child develops a style of personal interaction.

By family values we mean matters of importance both to mother and to father (not, therefore, gender-limited in their application), with reference to which the child develops a personal code of values.

Family Atmosphere

Of all the terms we use in Life-Style Assessment, family atmosphere belongs most clearly to the art of interpretation; it does not pretend to a place in any science of measurement. Following Dreikurs, we use this phrase to evoke a sense of the "climate" of the client's childhood household.

A meteorological metaphor can bring an old frame of reference into a fresh light and perspective, making it more accessible to understanding and reevaluation. Homely and vivid imagery will be the most useful for this purpose. For example, everyone is familiar with what is meant by a "warm " greeting, a "cold" formality, or a "heated" argument. In the same way, everyone knows what to expect in "stormy" relationships, a "suffocating" situation, or a "climate" of friendliness.

The use of such terms to refer to the family atmosphere highlights the way family members were characteristically disposed to relate to one another. The relationship between mother and father was, of course, primary in this. Other adults resident in the household either reinforced the pattern established by the parents' relationship, or offered examples of contrasting possibilities.

We rely upon picturesque language in Life-Style Assessment because we need devices to reawaken the client's creative imagination. Bear in mind that we want the peculiarities of a style of living to be recognized as intrinsic to an adaptation originally worked out in a situation in which they worked well enough to seem appropriate. However narrow and unsuited for successful engagement with life in the wider community now, they can be acknowledged as having been effective in adapting to the climatic conditions of the client's childhood world.

A loud and quarrelsome family life, full of outbursts, insults, and tears, may have established the background for a style that is closed and cautious, as if "buttoned up" against the unpredictable fierceness of the weather. For another person, coming out of the same family (or another family with a similar atmosphere) the alternating scenes of conflict and brooding may have provided a training ground for theatricality, with rehearsals of intense feelings over a wide spectrum. Such histrionic styles were often worked out apart from clear thinking, perhaps even as a substitute for rational processes, since in such households systematic, deliberate, and consciously cooperative problem solving was usually at a minimum. Rationality leads to agreements, and those who want victories are not interested in agreements.

A "calm" atmosphere may characterize a house in which attitudes and exchanges are pleasant, "balmy," and conducive to secure feelings and playfulness. In another house the use of this word to describe the atmosphere may refer to a "calm before a storm," full of electricity and apprehension. A child growing up in an atmosphere of the second kind may develop a suspicious but patient style of studied composure in any situation in which there is no evident agitation or disruption, as if to say, "There's nothing I can do until the storm breaks and I'm able to see which way the wind is going to blow." Another child may practice a surly, forbidding style, as if to say, "If we're in for a storm, watch my thunder!"

Remember that these meteorological metaphors are useful only when they are useful to the client, and when they fit the information presented by the client in the inquiries. Moreover, the fit should be comfortable, not forced. Just because analogies drawn from descriptions of the weather are often the most dramatic and powerful does not mean that they are the only ones that can be used. Often there are more suitable ways to convey the characteristic feeling of a given household. For example, in "The Summary of the Family Constellation" in "The Case of Janice," reported in Chapter 11, we said, "Janice grew up...in a family in which the atmosphere was constraining, as if the parents were concerned to hold the energies of each of the children in check."

To identify the family atmosphere with a few key words or phrases, take into consideration what the client has told you about the relationship between the parents during the course of the life-style inquiry. The questions about other significant adults and the family milieu may also provide clues. This information is elicited in Items 1 through 13 under the heading "Special Diagnosis," pages 10-12 in the *IPCW*. For an example of the sources of family atmosphere information, see these items in "The Case of Dan," reported in Chapter 4. For examples of the way we include references to family atmosphere in the course of our summaries of family constellation, see Chapter 13. In the list below, also, we offer an assortment of words and phrases we have used in various cases:

[The client] grew up in an atmosphere that was:

"clouded over by Mother's fearfulness and sensitivity, and relieved by the occasional breakthrough of sunniness provided by Father's exuberance, gregariousness, and affection."

"close, warm, still, and at the same time, isolating, as in a hothouse."

"generally warm and conducive to the growth of self-confidence."

"tense and volcanic, though never threatening the possibility of breakup or loss, and therefore endurable."

"invigorating and warm, with each of the children feeling well cared for and able to develop without constraints."

"balanced between Mother's smothering warmth and Father's forbidding coolness."

"somber and discouraging, with Father playing the part of rainmaker with his squelches, and Mother maintaining a damp and covert rebellion against Father's rule."

"was one of relentless striving, as if under a steely grey sky."

"turbulent, as if the family was situated on a storm front of conflicting currents of hot temper and icy disdain."

Family Values

At the beginning of this chapter we defined family values as having to do with matters of importance to both mother and father. It would be impossible to compile a complete list of such values as one might encounter them in work with clients. Even so, we can offer a partial list of those we commonly encounter in order to illustrate the variety of issues, each one important to someone, that parents sometimes strive to transmit to their children, and sometimes convey without striving, by those actions that speak so much more loudly than words:

Education
Religious observance
Not drawing attention to oneself
Honesty
Loyalty to family
Order
Hospitality
Deference to adults, teachers, "betters"
Obedience
Independence of thought and action
Doing your best
Being first
Perseverance
Thrift
Distrust of outsiders
Hard work
Manners
Not complaining
Bettering oneself
Being the boss
Propriety
Service to others
Fair play
Doing one's duty
Perfectionism
Not taking things seriously
Trusting to luck
Competence

Keep in mind that family values are defined as matters of importance to *both* parents. Otherwise, values held by either parent apart from the other should be considered as helping to define the gender guiding lines (Chapter 6).

The family values refer to standards that are held up before all the children, with the implication (or explicit statement) that, "These are the things that are important in this family, whatever others may think or do in other families."

This means that family values operate as imperatives. None of the children can ignore them; on the contrary, we see each child taking up a position toward them, whether in support or in defiance, either overtly or covertly. They are the issues that all the children in the family had to deal with in the formation of their life-styles.

We identify these values with the help of Items 2 and 7 under "Special Diagnosis" in the *IPCW* and the data recorded there on the values of the parents. Where these are alike for each, we assume that we have a family value. Sometimes, however, the situation is not so clearly stated because the client is in fact unclear about the values of one or both of the parents. Then we may gain more information by seeing how the children of the family, where there are more than one, lined up with respect to various issues. For example, if in a family of three children two of them now hold graduate degrees and the third one dropped out of high school, we may assume that education was a family value: Two of the children accepted and deferred to it; the third one defied it.

The fact that a client reports what each of the children did in respect to any particular issue must of itself suggest to us that this was a matter of general importance, and therefore a family value. As an example, one client said, "George was president of his graduating class the same year Susan was editor of the yearbook. Marilyn was on the School Council all through high school. When I came along, and just wanted to hang out with my friends, nobody knew what to do with me." We identified community involvement as a family value.

To sum up, we ask explicitly for information about what was important to each parent and, in the section of the *IPCW* concerning the children (pp. 13 and 14), we ask not only for a description of the activities of each child and how each distinguished himself or herself from the others, but also the extent to which each of them accepted, rejected, or modified the family's standards and values. These entries should be excellent resources for the therapist in helping the client toward understanding the family values and the position the client took with respect to them. Chapter 13, "The Family Constellation," provides further examples of the usefulness of this material.

Conclusion

Children are born into a world that is already inhabited, and into families that already have histories. In these families they encounter standards for a quality of interaction with others in the family atmosphere, and standards for distinguishing between what is important and what is not in the family values. This is the basis for the folk wisdom that says, "The fruit doesn't fall too far from the tree." Even so, we look to find the individual variant, and to see how the child's creative power made use of these givens.

In the next chapter we move from considering the person's place as studied against the background of the entire family system to give our attention to the subsystem of relationships between the siblings. Our task there is to understand the various meanings children attached to the birth-order positions they held in their families, and the various attitudes they adopted with respect to those meanings.

Chapter 8: PSYCHOLOGICAL BIRTH-ORDER VANTAGE

We use the term vantage instead of position (more common in discussions of birth order) to emphasize the distinction between psychological birth order and ordinal position. We want to consider how each child's situation in the family provides a unique perspective from which to view self, others, and the world. Thinking in terms of perspective rather than position helps the interpreter understand the particular use this one person made of a particular place in a particular family.

This terminology also helps to avoid an implication of causal determinism in birth order. "You are bound to do [whatever]; you're a first born," is an example of typological errors that obscure the genius of Individual Psychology, "the task of [which] is to comprehend the individual variant," as Adler said (p. 180). We pursue this task by the original Gestalt method of locating figure against ground. When the discipline of this method is ignored in simplistic efforts to fix cause and effect, the importance of birth order is obscured, and dismissed by serious investigators as on a level with astrology or numerology.

To make use of the information provided by an exploration of birth order, we must see it as indicating probabilities to be tested against the particularities of a given family constellation. These probabilities then contribute to a frame of reference for interpretive guess work that is both useful and encouraging.

Variables

A complete understanding of birth-order vantage takes the following variables into account: age and sex differences among the siblings; the health of siblings; whether a sibling died, was confined to an institution, or otherwise defaulted; and mother's unrealized pregnancies, whether through abortion, miscarriage, or stillbirth.

Age Differences. These are significant for the way in which the children grouped themselves. In large families there may be several groups of children. Most clients know at once what you mean if you ask, "How did the children group themselves?" or, "How many groups were there among the children?" Here is how Grace, the third of five, answered:

> Jim and Burt were a pair. They were the big boys. Then I came along, followed by George and Catherine, the little kids.

Grace may mean that she took her position as first of the three "little kids"; or, as the older of the two girls, with George in a class by himself as the baby boy; or, as middle child between the older boys and the "little kids." There may have been other possibilities open to her as well; only Grace could tell us which position she claimed as her own. The importance of the question is to establish the client's vantage, as the client saw it.

Where children were born close together in age, we are also alert to cases of the younger overrunning the older, taking a position of leadership usually claimed as a prerogative of the older child. Such an exchange of places is usually experienced negatively by both of them. Although the older may be relieved to be out of the spotlight of leadership, and the younger may be pleased to be the pacesetter, the older most often feels defeated and demoralized by the displacement as well, and the younger resents having to take the risks of the untested lead.

Sex Differences. Children are alert to any discrepancy of value based on gender. In some families children of both sexes know themselves to be valued equally by the parents; in other families one sex has greater value than the other. These attitudes affect the ways parents interact with their children, and the ways in which the children interact with one another. Sons are still often assigned a higher value than daughters. The cultural heritage of pyramidal forms of social organization based on conquest and subjugation persists. Disturbances experienced in the souls of children when they confront the challenges of the emerging democratic era, its demands for cooperation, and its insistence on equal respect, can be profound and destructive. Girls do not move cheerfully toward positions of submission and subordination; boys do not move courageously when they believe they must sustain positions of domination.

In a time of social change, when autocratic forms are challenged by the democratic critique, but when new democratic forms have not yet been established clearly and firmly in their stead, there are many variations in the experiences of inequality among children. Here is one male client's report:

> My sister was a princess. Everyone doted on her and I felt ignored. Men in our family weren't worth much, even to themselves. Women could do no wrong. I decided to make

> the most of a bad position: I was a little monster and they couldn't do anything with me!

In some traditional families the genders are sharply distinguished in role expectations, but an attitude of respect for the equal dignity of each is maintained. In a family of this kind there can be both a first-born son and a first-born daughter, each of whom exercises a role of leadership in a separate domain. "Separate, but equal" is a doctrine increasingly difficult to maintain in a democratic era, however. Here is a female client's report:

> There were the boys, and there were the girls. We each did our own things. We were a large family; we even had separate sittings at supper. The boys were fed first, of course, and then the girls. I hated that.

The Health of Siblings. A sick or invalid child affects birth-order vantage, altering the field in which the children are moving to make their places. Even a mildly ill child can train for (and be trained by the others for) the position of invalid. One of the siblings may seize the chance to play little mother to this child, thereby ensuring a place of importance both with the sickly child and with the parents. It is then in the little mother's interest to have the sickly child stay sick, and the caretaker trains the one cared for to play the part of invalid. Another child in this family may see an opening to the place of Father's "tough little guy," as if to make it up to Father for his distress over the sickly one.

The Defaulting of a Sibling. When illness overtakes a healthy child who then dies or is handicapped, the whole constellation changes and each child's vantage is altered. If a first born dies after establishing a position of leadership, the second born may be thrust into first place, expected to assume the lead, and feel out of place in any position of success or eminence through the rest of life, as if forever improvising without the guidance of the missing pacesetter.

The death of a sibling can be regarded as a form of defaulting, and resented. Even a sibling who died before a child was born can play a part in that child's imagination. One woman described her childhood image of her older sister, whom she had never seen: A neat and clean girl, with spotless white shoes and stockings, sitting on one of a pair of straight chairs on a cloud, next to her grandmother, who sat in the other chair. This picture of "my sister, who art in heaven" was onerous to the living child, who could never stay as clean and neat and properly seated, or so free from the danger of scolding or criticism.

Siblings may also be viewed as defaulting through withdrawal into addiction, psychosis, or even general ineptitude, adding to the parents' burden, and so to the distress of those who want to move along their own lines of ambition without having to be concerned for the parents.

Mother's Unrealized Pregnancies. A child's training and self-training is affected by an awareness of other, unrealized pregnancies. The parents may view a child, whose birth was preceded by a series of miscarriages or stillbirths, as "God's gift." Such a child may grow up feeling invincible, supported in the idea of having a special immunity to trouble by the parents' being always in awe of his or her accomplishments.

Another possibility is that the parents treat the living child as so precious that it must be protected from any danger, as if the least difficulty could be disastrous. Such a child's convictions, deformed by the limits placed upon the exploration of experience, may be that "life is too much for me, too dangerous; unless I have the protection of others, I must be cautious." Also, such a child may be especially pampered, and believe that the world should be in his or her service.

With these special considerations in mind, we may, without too much remaining danger of mistaking them for determinants, review some of the probabilities connected with the various birth-order vantages.

The Vantage of the First Born

The perspective common to these children is upward, forward, toward the adult world and its standards, and away from the world of the other children, except when sharing the concerns of the adults over them.

Remember that a first born was, for a time, an only child. First borns often retain some of the characteristics of onliness, including loneliness. Such persons have a sometimes poignant sense of personal uniqueness. They may practice self-reliance as if sensing it to be a necessity, as people do who are accustomed to being left alone to solve problems. They may be less at ease with members of their own age cohort than younger children are, sometimes feeling prepared only for places among the elders of any group to which they belong.

Adler noted (p. 378) that first borns tend to be conservative in outlook, because they are nostalgic about the lost golden age of their only child status, from which they were dethroned by the birth of a younger sibling. Adler thought that this fictional overvaluing of the past brought with it a greater respect for tradition, concern for law and order, and caution in assessing innovations. It is true that most first borns experienced themselves as very important persons in their "good old days." Indeed, they often were. They made wives and husbands into mothers and fathers, and (when they were also the first grandchildren) promoted the parents of their parents into grandparents, another important social role. More photographs were taken of them than were taken of their younger siblings, and their families kept more complete records of their first steps, first words, and first teeth.

Later-born children often complain about this, unaware as they are of the negative features of such a special status. A great deal can be expected of first-born children. For example, a younger sister was called The Baby at a much later age than that at which her first-born sister had become The Big Girl. This title came with "all the rights and privileges thereunto appertaining," but with some matching burdens as well. Many first borns become perfectionists in the effort to meet the challenges of parental expectation (and later, to do what they believe is required of them if they are to have a place among others). They are often constricted by righteousness, unable to see how they are of any value unless they are doing something wonderful or (even more important) admirable.

The sense of obligation to do only things that are outstanding leads to hesitation, stalling, and a dread of engaging in anything. After all, whatever anyone does can always be improved upon. A style of procrastination (sometimes disguised as preparation) may burden first borns. They experience anxiety (an expectation of defeat or humiliation) in the presence of opportunities they first define as obligations and then feel unable to refuse. Achievement, leadership, an interest in exploration, and the first-born vantage all go together when these children are encouraged, appreciated for what they can do, and respected for how they choose to do it, without the burdens of unrealistic expectations.

Adler was a second born, and described first borns with more than a hint of the asperity, impatience, and failure to sympathize many second borns feel toward their older siblings. His observations about first-born characteristics should therefore be read with some care. All of Adler's comments on the various sibling positions are, in fact, suspect as general rules; they should be studied only to show how he framed his hypotheses for reaching an understanding of the unique variant, and to sharpen awareness of the differences in phenomenological field made likely by different birth-order vantages. The study of Individual Psychology can contribute greatly to clinical sensitivity; it is not a substitute for it.

The Vantage of the First Born and Only

First borns who never have siblings are never dethroned. To be spared the presence of, and possible competition with siblings is also to be unfamiliar with the skills required to dicker and negotiate with them in the give and take, rough and tumble of childhood politics. Their major common complaint about their childhood situations has to do with loneliness. Even those who deny any consciousness of this loneliness often reveal it in their remembrances of wanting impatiently to be grown up, and so, to be like the other members of their families. Another revelation of it is in their commonly stated ambition to have more than one child.

The advantages of being at the center of the parents' worlds belong to the only child. Never to have to yield any part of that, or to share it with other children, can be a source of confidence. However, this central place can also have the disadvantage of carrying with it a sense of burden. "The hopes and fears of all the years" of their parents' ambitions, difficulties, and decline are laid on them. They know that if they fail, the parents have no other children to compensate. It is consequently not surprising to find a consistent theme in their styles expressed in the thought, "It's all up to me." This idea is experienced with increasing uneasiness as their parents move into old age. They have no sibling to confer with over what to do about "Mom's failing memory," or "Dad's insistence that he can drive, when everyone knows that he can barely see." Because they often exaggerate the meaning of the common human sense of uniqueness, regarding it as a kind of impenetrable privacy, they find it difficult to discuss these and other worries even with a devoted spouse. They too easily assume, "I must be the only one who thinks and feels this way."

During childhood the exaggerated sense of being different can be painful to them in dealings with other children. Having spent their early years with adults, and therefore apart from peer level problem solving, they often entered the world of the neighborhood and school without training for getting along by going along, and may have felt lost among the others. The bright side of this experience is that they understood adults better than the others did, and so were better able to fit into the organizational regimen of the school. They were better able to figure out what the adults wanted, and were also better able, or at least more readily disposed, to deliver it. The dark side is a frequently reported sense of having been a misfit or "oddball," of always having to guess about what was going on among peers and, when the guesses were wrong, of being embarrassed by their *faux pas*.

Many who grew up as only children have come to expect and resent a common assumption of others that they must have been spoiled by their parents. In fact, the pampered only child is a rarity in our clinical experience. Those who grew up sharing the world with siblings may believe that their only-child chums were spoiled because they saw them as having more things of their own. The objects of their envy see things differently, however. Here is one man's report:

> Yes, I was the first one and sometimes the only one in the neighborhood who had a ten-speed, or an electric train, or a Monopoly set, and so forth. And, yes, I had a room of my own; in fact, I had the whole third floor, complete with bathroom, all to myself! BUT, the key words are "all to myself." What good were those things to me when I had no one to play with? I got furious when people told me I was spoiled. I *always* did what I was told, studied hard, took care of myself, and was a good kid. Is that spoiled?

An only child can have a place in the triumvirate with Father and Mother, but only as the one at the awkward disadvantage of not knowing as much as the others. In this trio, the only child may experience a pseudo-sibling relationship with the same-sex parent, as if mother and daughter were the two girls in Father's life, or father and son the two boys in Mother's life. Such a child may train and be trained in second-born operations and expectations to some extent.

Encouraged only children are characteristically self-reliant and competent. They enjoy working alone in solitary problem solving in which they mull things over for long periods and then announce solutions. They are people who had to figure things out alone in the course of growing up, without much consultation or assistance; the necessity was mother to the invention of a style whereby this might be done.

The Vantage of the Second Born

Central in the awareness of the second-born child is the presence of another child. It is as if the second born knows from the beginning that, "someone more or less like me is here, a pacesetter scouting out the territory of life, discovering what it holds and what it requires." The second born hears the first born using the language, sees the first born relating to father and mother, and watches the first born go out into the neighborhood and the school, as if in an exploration of territories beyond immediate reach. Before they feel ready to meet the challenges themselves, second borns are listening to the first borns' reports on how it is "out there" in a world for which they are still (most often impatiently) preparing.

If the first born is of the other sex, the second may take the vantage of another first, the eldest of my sex. Then, if the children see a friendly relationship between the parents, we can expect them also to be friendly (or at least polite) to each other, to avoid direct competition, and to find separate and distinct spheres of successful activities.

When the second born is of the same sex as the first, the children are more likely to make other choices. Number one may regard number two as an interloper, and attempt to thwart the challenger's advance. One way to achieve this is to keep number two in the position of baby, either by belittling the younger child, ordering it about, or (more subtly) conspiring to pamper, protect, and serve the younger so that the second born comes to feel dependent upon the first.

Success is not guaranteed to any of these strategies. Nothing a first born does to meet the challenge of rivalry can avoid the possibility of spurring the rival onward. Held back, second borns struggle all the harder to advance; ruled, they are all the more likely to rebel.

Even to say this much, however, is to risk obscuring a sense of the variety of ways that can be taken by a child, perhaps especially a second-born child. If first borns are more concerned about the world of adult rules and standards, and if second borns are at pains to distinguish themselves from the firsts, we can expect a greater degree of openly displayed creativity and spontaneity in their styles. Conformity and innovation do not mix easily in the same person. To gain the attention and enlist the active interest of a first born we say, "We don't find anyone who is able to do this task in accordance with the specifications." To a second born, the challenge lies in hearing, "Until now, we have found only one way to do this satisfactorily."

The Vantage of the Middle Child

While the advent of a third child alters the objective position of the second born to that of middle child, the second born may hold fast to the vantage of the second-born child and never become a psychological middle child. When the second does shift to the vantage of the middle, however, a new range of possibilities presents itself to the child.

If, until now, numbers one and two have been engaged in a struggle for preeminence, the newly deposed and hitherto baby of the family may feel forced to fight a war on two fronts, alternately contending with the first born for the honors of leadership, and with the new baby for the exemptions and protections of littleness.

Or, if the parents are pressuring the older child to excel, and fretfully fussing over the younger one, the middle child may be aware of being the only one free of the burdens of parental management.

In either case these children often feel squeezed, and have to evaluate the feeling. An active child may feel squeezed into an awareness of inequity, forming a guiding ambition to contend against injustice that will shape the choice of vocation. A less active counterpart may see the need to struggle for justice as in itself unfair, and adopt the posture of a victim. Sometimes the squeeze feels like buoyancy, pushing the child up and out to a greater sense of freedom. It may also be felt as pressing the child down and out toward the threat of insignificance, against which the person fights throughout life. The squeeze can also be described as buttressing, with the middle child reporting enjoyment in having a supporting role played on either side, and shining as the star of the show, or "the rose between two thorns."

The variety of these possibilities probably helps to account for the middle child's so frequently exhibiting an exquisite capacity for empathy. These children know how it feels to be under the heel of someone ahead of them, and what it is like to have someone of less experience relying on them for care and guidance. They know what it is to look up to others, what it means to look down on them, and how it feels to be on the receiving end either way.

In subtle ways at first, and in more and more practiced ways as they grow older and the other family members are separated and scattered, the middle borns tend to operate as the central switchboards of their families, through whom the others stay in touch. Remembering birthdays and anniversaries, they remind those who (counting on the middle child to remind them) are likely to forget. When there is an estrangement in the family, or where delicacy may prevent one from speaking to another, this person receives a call, responsive to the plea to negotiate a settlement or to convey a difficult message.

The Vantage of the Third Born

"The enemy of my enemy is my friend," according to the adage. The alliances typical between third-born and first-born children tend to bear it out. Siblings can be expected to compete to some extent, but the more intense forms of competition are most often between first and second borns. In the experience of many third borns, consequently, this conflict was there from the beginning. One result of this derives from the fact, noted above, that the middle child is not only fighting against being held back, but also against relinquishing the advantages of baby without a fight. First and third can come to see something attractive in each other, having as they do a common enemy. In the case of the third, admiration of the first is demonstrated by imitation ("the sincerest form of flattery"), understandably adding to the first's enjoyment of the third.

A second consequence follows out of the apparent endlessness of the fighting between first and second. With no sign that either of them is going to emerge as winner, neither appears to be gaining anything from the struggle. "Therefore," many sensible third borns conclude, "there must be a better way." They may decide that nothing is worth fighting about, that charm is more effective than force, and that it is wiser to beg forgiveness after doing what you wanted to do than to ask permission beforehand and risk refusal or opposition.

Feedback confirms the wisdom of the choices: (a) The first born accepts the admiring third as a protege, as if to say, "I got off on the wrong foot with the second born. I'm going to get it right this time, and stay ahead by being the mentor who teaches this one how to get ahead." (b) Charming is disarming, and the parents, already relaxed by it, relax further to see the little one being so well tutored.

The Vantage of the Baby

"Babies are made, not born," Dreikurs said. Any child is vulnerable to babying. A first born, strongly favored, not necessarily by both parents, may be pampered, and demand and get special service. This is also true for any other child in the family, especially one for whom parents and siblings feel sorry, for any reason. Such a child can exploit their pity, as if challenging them to "make it up to me for what I suffer."

If this is a posture more readily assumed by younger children, it is because it is facilitated by co-conspirators among the older ones, who may imagine it to be to their advantage to shut a baby out of competition by keeping it babied. This is done by translations of baby talk; constant fussing and care; overprotection against the possibility of any hurt; and, most effectively, by providing services that make it unnecessary for a child to explore and learn, so thwarting its development. Add a stream of warnings and cautions, degrading in their reminders of special status ("You're not big enough, smart enough, strong enough, responsible enough, etc."), and the babying may be complete.

Many children who trained and were trained to be babies exploit the position throughout their adult lives, as if to say, "You wanted a baby? You got a baby!" As families grow smaller there are fewer cases of the bachelor uncle or maiden aunt still at home with parents, but there are still many examples of the relative who never learned to drive and has to have a ride to any event, or who cannot hold a job, or who "goes to pieces" when there is any hint of being left alone to handle responsibilities or of being counted upon by others.

The Vantage of the Youngest

The baby is not always the youngest, and a youngest will not always remain a baby. Where children are encouraged and their individuality is respected, the experience of the youngest child can be rich in opportunity. Older siblings may offer themselves as coaches of the youngest's efforts, or as champions of the child's aspirations. The youngest can also study each of the older children for examples of successful and/or unsuccessful strategies, finding a variety of useful role models, both positive and negative. The unique privilege they enjoy among their siblings of never being dethroned is a further source of confidence for these children. Never dividing their attention by looking backward to see who may be overtaking them, they are free to focus all their energies on what lies ahead.

It is not for nothing that so many sacred stories, legends, and folk tales celebrate the triumphs of the youngest child, as illustrated by the Biblical story of Joseph and his brothers. (Granted, Benjamin was younger than Joseph, but only in birth-order position; in vantage he was an only child.)

Often encouraged toward success, the youngest may also feel spurred to it. There is some obstacle to dignity in a situation in which older siblings often refer to matters of which one has no knowledge and demonstrate competencies beyond one's present ability. More common, and more onerous, is the readiness of the older children to regard one's contributions with a kind of delight hard to distinguish from amusement. A youngest child may feel the need to struggle to be taken seriously.

One woman, the youngest of eight accomplished children, reported the reaction of her siblings to the news that she had earned her doctor's degree. "It was funny," she said. "They were very nice, and seemed sincere in their congratulations. But I kept picking up something in their tone that said, 'Look who got a Ph.D.! Isn't that cute?'"

The Vantage of the Later Borns

In a large family, later-born children form their own groups, including a first; second or middle; third and youngest, or baby. A fourth child can take part as baby; or (paired with number three) as the younger of two; or as ally of number two (especially where number one has appropriated number three); or as "odd one out" between an older group of three and a younger group (in which case he or she may develop some characteristics of only children). Innumerable other combinations depending on age, sex, and other factors are also possible.

Case Examples

The following brief sketches illustrate some of the ways children found vantages for themselves among the others in their families. Additional cases are cited in Chapter 13.

First Borns

Mary is a first-born daughter, with a brother two years older. She was Father's favorite, and enhanced her special place as the only girl by satisfying Mother's demands as to household chores, homework, and practicing the piano; and by satisfying Father's wishes that she be happy with him and enjoy him. Mary's brother was ahead of her only in that he was older.

Paul is a first-born son with a sister five years younger, and two brothers, six and seven years younger than he. He was in a class by himself, with the other three children in a class of their own. As the first, and the only child for five years, Paul had ample time to establish his kingdom. None of the other children threatened his position. He kept his distance from them, and saw to it that they kept their distance from him by his solitary habits of reading and tinkering, and by playing the part of "the one who knows all."

Sam is the first born of six. He stayed ahead of his brothers and sisters by setting an example of rectitude and restraint, never failing to do what was expected of him. As the family increased in size, Sam turned his attention to the wider world of the neighborhood and school, where he took a leadership position among his peers.

Lucille is the first of two sisters. She made a place with Mother by being "Little Mother," thereby also insuring that her sister remained The Baby.

Second Borns

Bill is the second of two boys, psychologically a first-born and only child, owing to his brother's congenital incapacity to make a place for himself. Bill experienced himself as one who could do no wrong in the eyes of his parents, who were delighted with their healthy boy, providing him with every advantage and encouragement.

Martha is the second born of twins, whose brother, Mark, is eight minutes older. Psychologically she is the baby girl, with an older brother who took the position of the first-born son. Their parents had been told they would not be able to have children. They were therefore thrilled to have one of each. They counted on their son for achievement, and they spoiled Martha, giving her whatever she wanted. Growing up as the center of attention, Martha didn't have to do anything except "be." She didn't make a place: She was handed a place.

Al is the second born, whose older sister was "Miss Goodie-Goodie Two Shoes." He found a place in the family by being the naughty boy, given first to teasing, jokes, tricks, and being cute; and later, in the neighborhood and the school, to an escalation of these "darling" games into troublemaking of all kinds. Mother and Father didn't know what to do with him, took pride in his being "all boy," and hesitated to "squelch" his mischievous inventiveness.

Shirley is the second of two girls. She distinguished herself from her older sister by developing her artistic capacities, followed the family values in education and religion, and found a place among her peers by practicing ways of offering them amusement and entertainment.

Middle Children

Florence is the second-born child, with an older brother and a younger sister, psychologically the middle child of the family. She took advantage of the middle position by being the family peacemaker and negotiator. In the neighborhood, and later in the school, she turned this ability to further good effect by making many friends and by involving herself in school politics.

Bill is the second born, psychologically the middle child, with an older and a younger brother. He felt squeezed by the other boys, who were close in age to him. Jake, two years older, was the achiever in the family; Paul, two years younger and the last of the children, was Jake's protege and the family's "junior achiever." Bill made his place by being the most active of the boys and a daredevil in the neighborhood and school. He was outstanding in sports, being well-coordinated and able to run fast, exceeding the accomplishments of his brothers in this area. He further distinguished himself by doing poorly in academics.

Third Borns

Karen is the third born in a family in which a stillbirth and two miscarriages preceded her arrival. Her brother is seven years older, and her sister six years older. When Karen was five years old Mother gave birth to twin girls. Of the five surviving children, Karen is the sickly one. Mother had overprotected her, believing that she might not survive a severe illness in her first year of life. Karen had taken a place as the homebody, involved in Mother's activities, and now shared with her in caring for the twins after their arrival. *Psychologically Karen is a middle child,* between the older two children and the twins.

Joe is the third-born child, with a sister four years older and a brother three years older, each of whom took first-born positions. He is psychologically the second born of the two boys. He made his place in the family by being the non-competitive, charming, and friendly child. While he wouldn't let anyone push him around, he was not aggressive. He was popular with all the family members, counted on to keep the peace and to keep his word.

Peggy is the third born of three girls, psychologically the baby of the family. The others fussed over her and taught her to be cute. She was Father's favorite and, since Father ruled, Peggy was the Princess. The other girls mimicked Father's attitudes and behavior, and also pampered Peggy, as a way of retaining their own alliances with Father and inducing Peggy to accept an inconsequential position.

Conclusion

A birth-order position includes advantages and disadvantages. There are no "good" or "bad" positions that in themselves could have made us happy or unhappy in the situations into which we were born. In our ordinal positions we created the vantages from which we considered the world; our birth order was part of what we saw from our vantage.

Awareness of psychological vantage established by evaluation of birth order offers counselor and client opportunity to reconsider how training and self-training rehearsed an attitude from that vantage. We learned how to move among others in our original families, where we formed our basic impressions of how we fit in, how we stand out, and what is required of us to do either. It can be liberating to reflect on what we made of our positions there; to turn this around, or to imagine that positions made us as we are, is to miss the point.

In the next chapter, we examine heredity and environment in an investigation of the sense children make of their other possibilities and opportunities.

Chapter 9: GENETIC POSSIBILITY AND ENVIRONMENTAL OPPORTUNITY

In *A Religious History of the American People*, Sydney E. Ahlstrom reports on a quarrel about the idea of original sin that divided the congregation of North Church in Hartford, Connecticut, from 1833 until 1847, when the minister, Horace Bushnell, published a book memorializing the dispute under the name of the "Nature-Nurture" controversy (1972, pp. 610-611). Like other theological arguments of its kind this one was not so much settled as forgotten. The original antagonists died, and the issue that had been at stake between them seemed to die as well.

It should be a matter of some interest therefore to see that this debate, which took place in a local nineteenth-century New England church, has (at least in name) for some reason survived or been revived. Contenders in the new Nature-Nurture controversy appeal to the majesty of "Science" instead of Scripture, but with the same kind of confidence that they enjoy the support of an absolute authority.

Inspired by the provocative and original studies done by Nikolaas Tinbergen and Konrad Lorenz on fixed action patterns in animal behavior, the Nature partisans in this new form of the old quarrel have been further stimulated by the work of Edmund O. Wilson, Robin Fox, Lionel Tiger, and others in the vanguard of what is called sociobiology. As the name implies, this involves extrapolations from animal studies in speculations on how the forms of human social customs may have been fixed during our phylogenetic history.

In the current round of the debate, the Naturists hold that genetic determinants shape the forms of culture; the Nurturists answer that the operations of culture are sovereign in molding genetic material. By extension to personality theory, one extreme argues that everything regarded as distinctive of persons was encoded in their genes; the other extreme retorts that a person is nothing other than a learned pattern of observable interaction with the world.

There is clearly an irresistible charm to this argument. However, since it pits the proponents of two sets of equally unverifiable speculations against each other in an intractable way, and since the matter is never settled (and the argument is never dropped), we are entitled to suspect that something unstated is reflected in the two positions. Dreikurs maintained that the hidden debate was a contest between two radically opposed political visions of the ideal social order (neither of which is sympathetic to democracy): On the one side are latter-day supporters of the old aristocratic ideal, summed up in the phrase, "blood will tell." On the other are proponents of one of the utopian egalitarian ideals, with a model of the person as a *tabula rasa* of infinite possibility, infinitely malleable.

From the standpoint of Individual Psychology the argument rests upon a fundamental misunderstanding, and is therefore meaningless. So are efforts to work out positions between its polar extremes. For example, "Heredity *times* environment equals personality," one university professor of human development put it to one of the present authors. He might just as well have said, "None of us knows how to account for the uniqueness of personality." Adler distinguished Individual Psychology from any such efforts (1963, p. 1):

> We proceed quite differently from other psychologists who would like to apply almost mathematical values and who, when their calculations do not come out, try to find causes in heredity, a dark area which can accommodate almost anything.

In fact nothing can be seen to *form* personalities. On the contrary, the very term, personality, refers to someone who is *giving form* to experience. We want to examine an individual's style of movement in the use of genetic possibility and environmental opportunity. A life-style rests on opinions, on evaluations of a genetic endowment in a historical situation, and on the meanings a human being has assigned to them in the course of seeking a successful adaptation (or, at the least, in trying to secure against failure to adapt). When Adler identified the field of study of Individual Psychology as located in "the relationship of the individual to the problems of the outside world," therefore, he went on to say:

> The Individual Psychologist must observe how a particular individual relates himself to the outside world. This outside world includes the individual's own body, his bodily functions, and the functions of his mind. He does not relate himself to the outside world in a predetermined manner as is often assumed. He relates himself always according to his own interpretation of himself and of his present problem. His limits are not only the common human limits, but also the limits which he has set himself. It is neither heredity nor environment which determines his relationship to the outside. Heredity only endows him with certain abilities. Environment only gives him certain impressions. These abilities and impressions, and the manner in which he "experiences" them

> -- that is to say, the interpretation he makes of these experiences -- are the bricks which he uses in his own "creative" way in building up his attitude toward life. It is his individual way of using these bricks, or in other words his attitude toward life, which determines this relationship to the outside world (pp. 205-206).

We must attend both to the physical material of human life and to the social world apart from which it cannot flourish, and could not arise. To avoid errors we do well to consider Adler's image of the bricks: Bricks do not determine the kind of structures we build out of them. Their availability cannot account for the emergence of Georgian architecture in the eighteenth century. Artists and artisans decide these questions. Individual Psychology inquires into genetic endowment and environmental opportunity, therefore, as archeology may inquire into the quality of baked clay and the skills required in bricklaying. The purpose there is to guess at how architects in a given historical situation might have experienced the limits of structural possibilities, and how they achieved whatever seemed possible to them in the light of their understanding. Our purpose here is to guess at how children, in their creativity, have assessed the limits of biological possibilities, and how, by their lights, they accomplish what they believe is open to them within the compass of their assessments.

Genetic Possibility

> The style of life, in our experience, is developed in earliest childhood. In this the innate state of the body has the greatest influence. In his initial movements and functions, the child experiences the validity of his bodily organs. He experiences it but is far from having words or concepts for it. Since the way in which the environment approaches the child differs in each case, what the child feels about his capacities [as such] remains permanently unknown. With great caution, on the basis of statistical probability, we may conclude that where an organ inferiority is present, the child has the experience of being overburdened at the beginning of his life. How the child attempts to cope with this overburdening can only be discovered from his movements and trials. Here every causal consideration is in vain. Here the creative power of the child becomes effective. He strives within the incalculable realm of his possibilities. From trial and error a training results for the child and a general way towards a goal of perfection which appears to offer him fulfillment (Adler, pp. 186-187).

According to most accounts Adler's interest in psychiatry began to develop almost as soon as he had established himself in the practice of medicine. His office was close to Vienna's *Prater* (a kind of amusement park, zoo, and circus combination), and he had acrobats and other performers among his patients. People who earned their livings as exemplars of physical fitness confided their medical histories and weaknesses to him. Adler used the familiar medical concept of compensation (referring to the overdevelopment of one organ or organ part to make up for damage or loss of function in another) as an organizing idea for understanding his new clientele. It was a short step from an organ to the whole organism; thus it was possible to consider how an acrobat could be compensating for specific constitutional limitations by overall development and training of agility.

Adler's personal history provided a context for his ideas about felt weakness and the compensatory quest for strength. He could remember lying ill in childhood and hearing a physician tell his parents that there was nothing to be done to save his life. He remembered that his father had refused to give up, dismissed the pessimist, and called in another physician, who was willing to continue treatment. He also remembered the unwelcome sense of constriction he took from his bandaged legs as he endured a treatment for rickets. The meanings he gave to these experiences were expressed in his later observation on overcoming: "To be a human being means to possess a feeling of inferiority which constantly presses toward its own conquest" (p. 116).

We can see how Individual Psychology originated in the personal and professional interests Adler took in the various psychical compensations individuals erect against organic inferiorities. The implications he saw in general efforts to resist limits and overcome shortcomings led him at last to locate the only true compensation for personal weakness and insignificance in a fully developed sense of our participation with others in shaping the common life (*Gemeinschaftsgefühl*). Individual Psychology did not abandon its original ideas in the course of its development. It still attends to any sense of smallness, incompleteness, or disadvantage in a person's self-awareness; it still notes the value of those images of strength, triumph, and perfection with which we console ourselves, and by which we inspire ourselves to persevere.

Our earliest awareness of ourselves arises while we still have much of the long period of infancy and childhood ahead of us, and are barely at the beginning of our physical and mental development. To know oneself is, at first, to know that one still has a long way to go. That we are responsive to stories of successes in overcoming difficulty may be owing to this common feature of our individual subjectivities. From ancient times, our pedagogy has treasured the story of Demosthenes, the stammerer honored for his oratory. In modern times, Scott Hamilton's story offered the same kind of encouragement. A congenital disorder of the pancreas, Schwachmann's Syndrome, marred his early childhood development, leaving the growth of his body irremediably stunted. It did not, however, crush his spirit as he perfected the skills that made him an Olympic Champion in figure skating.

These stories mean, even to those whose development and constitution are normal, that courage overcomes handicaps, that attitude can defy limitations. Courage is the readiness to act on the useful side of life, to contribute what we can to the solution of the problems we encounter in our situation as it is. In courage we press on with whatever we have at our disposal to face whatever challenges we meet. The courageous child says, "I am strong enough now for what is required of me, and I will be stronger still in time." The discouraged child changes this to, "I am never sure that I can be as strong as I must be." The conclusion for the former is, "Therefore, I will do what I can, toward the goal of success." For the latter it is, "I must do whatever I can to guard myself against defeat."

The Right Reverend Angus Dun died in retirement after a long life, his distinguished career having culminated in his position as Bishop of Washington, D.C. As a forerunner of the Civil Rights movement, he had used his position (and the pulpit of the National Cathedral) to challenge the consciences of political leaders on the demand for equal justice and for the removal of racist barriers to its attainment. (For these efforts his opponents had dubbed him "Black Angus," an attempt at a slur which he had accepted as an honor.)

After noting his many contributions, newspaper obituaries described some of the circumstances of his childhood: He had been born with a defect of the hip, which kept him from full participation in boyhood activities. The sting of this handicap was ameliorated by his knowledge that the condition could be surgically repaired after his growth had reached a certain point. At thirteen years of age he underwent the promised surgery, but while still in recovery he was stricken with poliomyelitis. After the fever had passed his mother came to his bedside and proposed an agreement to him. She asked that, whatever else might happen, they would agree never to talk about things he could not do, but only about the things he could do.

With this challenge she stimulated her son's courage. The story is an illustration of the principle of encouragement upon which so much in life (and in any therapeutic process) depends. If encouragement is lacking, a child's native sense of smallness can become an alien feeling of inadequacy. Dun's mother showed a confidence in him that called up his confidence in himself. Had she pitied him instead, he could have concluded, "Since I am so weak, I cannot count on myself. Therefore I must make sure that the people I do count on are always aware of how much I need them."

To inquire into the issue of "Genetic Endowment" is therefore to seek out the foundations of an individual's sense of "having what it takes." Certain probabilities do, of course, exist with respect to various conditions. Ugliness is not an advantage, for example. The loss of tonus in the facial muscles (which so often accompanies and expresses the experience of being rebuffed) further exacerbates its effects. The face of a bewildered and frightened child may give others the impression of someone wanting to withdraw. This may provoke a counterwithdrawal by them, leaving the child confirmed in the sense of being excluded.

Children who suffer faulty hearing (an impairment of which they can have no direct awareness) often come to think of themselves as slow-witted; others seem to be quicker to catch on to jokes and better able to follow along in exchanges of banter. It is a short step from this to suspicions that the others are deliberately keeping things from me, and not a much longer step to paranoid convictions that they don't want me to hear because they are talking about (and against) me.

Meanings assigned to body size and form however, or to any genetic patterns, are value judgments of such a personal kind that every probability can be defied by the single case, and the investigator can be startled by what is disclosed.

We will all sympathize with a complaint about a bodily injury or anomaly experienced in childhood as a deformity. It is easy for most of us to understand what is meant (or implied) by statements such as, "I was (too) fat," "I was (too) skinny," "I was (too) short," "I was (too) tall." It may be harder for some of us to see what is meant by, "I was too smart." ("It led the adults to expect more of me, and kept me from being accepted by the other kids.") It may be hardest of all for us to understand the complaint, "I was forever being told how beautiful I was." ("No one was ever interested in my mind, only my body because everyone *knows* that 'beautiful' means 'beautiful but dumb'!")

In any case, it is never wise to assume that you know how a child must have felt about any particular feature of the genetic endowment. Private sense is by definition elusive. It is important to be alert to things which we would not have expected, and to maintain respect for the unique ingenuity of this one person's continuing way of working out a successful adaptation. In Adler's words:

> It goes without saying that the inheritance, primarily of physical attributes but also of specifically human potentialities, is not subject to any doubt whatsoever. But what matters ultimately is what the child, the individual, does with the equipment he inherits. This is his own creative achievement. It is certainly human chromosomes, the individual's physical endowment, his endocrine glands, and his blood con-

> stituents, which enable him to move, to function, and to look like a human being. But how and for what purpose or objective he molds and shapes these various formative factors becomes manifest only through the millions of variations in individual styles of life (pp. 206-207).

Below are four brief statements by different clients, provided in answer to Item 32 in the *IPCW*, which inquires into childhood bodily development (p. 16). These examples are followed by "The Case of Maria," whose childhood can serve as a paradigm for the positive uses of adversity.

Shortness of Stature. This man was the baby of the family, much younger than the youngest of his siblings. He stated:

> I was short for my age. I had a sense of defenselessness as a child because of it. This improved somewhat when I reached puberty and kept up more with my peers. Taller guys, though, always seemed to be better accepted. It felt like a burden to me to have to *do* something to be accepted.

For this man, shortness of stature served as a rationalization for his feelings of vulnerability, to which he expected others to respond with caretaking. He had trained for this, first in his family of origin among the much older siblings, and later in life with friends and lovers. His failure to form a lasting attachment with someone of the other sex was ascribed by him to his disadvantages. He judged life to be too hard, and believed that he shouldn't be expected to make his place by way of making contributions. To have to *do* something to be accepted was a burden, out of line with the expectation that he could gain a place by *being* something (short) or *feeling* something (defenseless).

Physical Strength, Coordination, Speed. The younger of two children, a woman with an accomplished older brother (the favorite of both parents) said:

> I always felt good about my body. I was agile, and learned how to do things quickly. My good coordination was always commented on by people. I liked tumbling, and I could throw a ball well. I was a very good runner. I learned pretty early that I could excel over my brother in these things. I was always challenging him and showing him up. He hated it that I ran faster than he did.

This woman's physical ability was acknowledged and encouraged early in life, and she developed herself along the line of this effectiveness. She realized that in this realm she had an advantage over her brother, and could win a place with her parents in spite of their favoring him. She competed successfully in several sports as she grew older. As an adult she continued to press her advantage, seeking out men she could defeat, both on the playing field and in professional life. She came to see us, wondering why she had failed to make a match with a man worthy of her respect.

Ethnic Identification. A later-born son in a large family reported:

> I didn't have any problems with my body. I was about average in my abilities and could hold my own. But, you could tell which side of my parents' mixed marriage I came from! My mother and father had no trouble with this, but my Mom's family, being white, didn't have much to do with us. I didn't like my relatives on her side. They seemed to look down on my dad, and I didn't like that. I was the only one of the kids who was really Black, and so it was easier for me to identify with Dad. That suited me. I think he's a great guy.

Here a positive evaluation of dark skin color was made by the boy in defiance of the norms of his mother's family and the larger white community. His solidarity with his admired father compensated for any disapproval or difficulty he might encounter as a consequence of being Black. He regarded what someone else might have considered to be a detriment to be a mark of distinction in his family and elsewhere. He and his wife came to see us because she complained of his lack of sympathy. She was struggling to make a place for herself in a male-dominated profession, against her uneasiness about the incompetence of women as defined by her feminine guiding line. Her self-doubts were unintelligible to him. He had not allowed prejudices to stop him, and he responded to her concerns with pep talks that sounded to her like criticism, and left her feeling worse.

Weight. A woman with two younger sisters said:

> I was born fat. No, really, I was always a chubby little kid, not fat, but somewhat overweight. I hated it. My Mom cared a lot about the way we looked, and she was always on my case about my weight, always trying to get me on a diet, commenting on everything I put in my mouth. Mealtimes were awful. And my sisters got into it too. They'd tell her if they saw me eating stuff I wasn't supposed to have, like candy bars, that sort of thing.

Food issues are often the *stated* topic of power struggles between mothers and daughters, though the *subtext* is typically a fight over who is in charge of the daughter's life (i.e., body). When such a fight is not resolved quickly, the daughter can develop a full-blown practice of obesity or anorexia nervosa, with or without bulemia. In the case cited, the client's genetic disposition enabled her to put on weight and to maintain it. She made use of this capacity to fight her mother's control, as if to say, "You may dictate to me about everything else in my life, but you cannot control what I put into my mouth, what goes down, or whether it stays down." She said that she hated the extra weight and, of course, she did. It was the high price she had to pay in personal unhappiness in order to defeat her mother. She was in her forties when she decided to make choices for her life unrelated to what her mother might or might not think about them.

The Case of Maria

Maria was the second of five children of the second marriage for each of her parents. The first of these children was a boy, as was the third, and Father had two much older sons from his previous marriage. She was therefore Father's first, and for some time only, daughter. Mother had one child from her former marriage, a pampered daughter, eight years older than Maria.

Maria was asthmatic, knew that her parents did not expect her to live, and did not expect herself to live. She perceived herself as frail and sickly all through childhood. Now she is the mother of four grown children, and still regards herself as vulnerable to illness unless she takes every sensible health precaution available to her (good diet, exercise, adequate sleep, etc.).

Maria had ample opportunity to make a place for herself as the pampered pet of her father, and to set a course for a life as a neurotic invalid, demanding special attention and service from others.

However, her hidden reasoning about herself as a child was that, since she was soon to die, every day was a bonus in which to discover how much she could do. Recognizing the special place she had with Father, she did her best to demonstrate to him, in return, that she was a responsible and reliable daughter, even if she was doomed to an unavoidably early death. Her older half-sister's self-indulgent style did not meet Father's approval, and Maria felt all the better able to contrast her more sensible and practical approach to her sister's frivolities in cementing her place with him.

The older sister also assisted her by refusing to cater to her crying, and by persisting in teasing her, possibly out of resentment at being displaced as a babied pet. Maria got angry with her in response to the unrelenting teasing, and unexpectedly won her sister's respect by standing up to her.

Maria's own children are all strongly independent and self-reliant. Believing that she would not live to see them grow up, she stressed the importance of their being able to care for themselves.

Maria has a senior management position in a large corporation, and entrusts a great deal of initiative to her subordinates, who "always know exactly where things stand, and what has to be done," whenever she is required to be away from her office.

So far, we have the story of Maria's courageous and successful rebuff to the threat to her life she experienced in childhood. What, then, brought her into psychotherapy? She had been married twice. Both alliances ended in divorce. She said of her husbands that they offended her by acting as if they should be able to control her, which she found intolerable. Her father had never done anything like that; he was happy just to have her alive.

Environmental Opportunities

> Individual Psychology has been misunderstood to be an environmentalistic theory, tracing the entire psychological structure of a person to environmental influences. To examine this misunderstanding more closely, one would have to ask: Who seeks, who answers, who utilizes the impressions from the environment? Is man a dictaphone or a machine? There must be something else at play (Adler, p. 207).

In the course of family counseling, parents often complain that a child takes advantage of the parents' generosity, good nature, preoccupation with maintaining a tidy house, or whatever. In response, we say that bright people always take advantage of their advantages.

Life-Style Assessment can be thought of as an ethological study of the human being in relation to the human habitat. Any consideration we give to the importance of the environment in which an individual grew up, therefore, must avoid crude assumptions of cause and effect. At the same time, we must maintain an awareness of probabilities. There is a real difference between growing up in the only Catholic family in a rural county otherwise populated entirely by Protestants, and being part of an urban family in a neighborhood in which everyone was Catholic and belonged to the same parish church.

There is also a likelihood that familiarity with the court system will be as common among the poor as academic degrees are among the affluent. No such probability can be relied upon to be true in the single case, however. To assume the inevitability of dysfunction among the poor is (for the poor) to indulge in self-pity, and (for everyone else) to condescend; to be surprised by the occurrence of dysfunction among the privileged is (for the privileged) to indulge in self-righteousness, and (for everyone else) to fawn.

Remember figure and ground, and the context in which uniqueness is recognized. The understanding of the individual variant is our goal. We must not lose sight of the creative power of any child to defy the statistical odds, or to make a fresh and positive meaning of a situation that is unpromising -- not to mention the power of a child to make of a good situation with every objective advantage a lifeless and negative meaning that becomes the ground for resentment and complaint.

The Case of Paul

Paul grew up in a poor ethnic neighborhood that had lost its coherence to urban development and economic hardship. Mother had a part-time job in a manufacturing plant. Father worked only occasionally, and when he did work was regularly fired for drinking. Paul remembers having to take care of his father when he had been drinking, and being embarrassed by having to go get Father and bring him home from a nearby bar.

Paul spent as much time as possible with his maternal grandmother, a widow whose husband had died in an industrial accident years before. She made do on a tiny pension. His other grandmother was dead, and the paternal grandfather had abandoned the family when Paul's father was a child. Other family members had scattered.

He describes the parental relationship as violent. He has no memory of any affection between the parents. "He'd drink, and she'd bitch at him, and he'd hit her. I was terrified of him, and I felt sorry for her."

He was aware that a few blocks away there was a nice neighborhood where the houses were well-maintained and the children well-dressed. "They wouldn't have anything to do with us. Most of them went to parochial school, and we couldn't afford to go." Paul went to church in the parish with his mother, but attended the overcrowded, rundown public school.

He says that he made up his mind, "almost as soon as I can remember, that I was going to get out of there if it was the last thing I ever did. It was so depressing. Even my grandmother's situation, which was better than most! There she was, this little old lady, and she didn't have anything. I knew I'd make money some day and take care of her and my Mom -- and I did."

Paul came to see us because he was depressed. "I don't find life interesting any more. I work hard, but what does it get me? I've got lots of money, but I don't enjoy it any more."

It turned out that Paul had made taking care of women his life's work. He had a beautiful house in the suburbs, complete with a gorgeous wife and two well-groomed daughters in private schools. He pampered all of them and, since they felt both entitled to what he provided and condescended to by him, they responded with demands and anger, and he felt unappreciated.

He had overcome a background of poverty, alcoholism, and brutality. He had also developed some mistaken ideas, especially about money and relationships of intimacy, which he reconsidered in the psycho-clarity process.

The Case of Carolyn

Carolyn entered therapy when she was a thirty-two-year-old woman with two children. Her nine-year marriage to Stephen had come to an end the month before, when he announced that he had fallen in love with an associate in his law practice and wanted to marry her. He had moved out, and Carolyn knew his mind was closed to the possibility of reconciliation.

Carolyn came from a prominent family, known for its business interests, money, accomplishment, and good works over three generations. When her mother had become pregnant with Carolyn, it was a shock to the parents, who thought their childbearing years were over. They had one son who was fifteen when Carolyn was born. Like most parents of their generation, they decided to make the best of it, and were delighted with their little daughter.

The family lived in a wealthy suburb of the large city where Father had his office. He traveled often, and had many civic responsibilities. Mother was equally busy in her own domain. She served on the boards of several charities and was the hostess at frequent social events. Both parents played tennis and golf, enjoyed their friends, and, when possible, took trips together.

Carolyn described her family life as taking place "in a goldfish bowl." The pressure to be proper and to do the right thing was experienced as "immense" by her. When the family was together she saw her father as "gregarious and affectionate" and her mother as "motherly, almost grandmotherly." She said that her brother adored her: "He treated me like a little doll. When my parents entertained, he'd trot me out and show me off. They'd say, 'Isn't she cute!' and he'd whisk me away again. It was fun." Carolyn and her brother were cared for by a staff of indulgent servants. She said, "I really had pretty much whatever I wanted, as long as I was good. They picked up after me, took me places, and bought me things."

Carolyn went to boarding schools and camps, and often felt misfitted. She complained, "I never felt comfortable with children my age. I don't know what was the matter with them. We never seemed to have anything in common. I ended up pretty much staying to myself in school." She found her refuge in academics. She was brainy, got top grades, and wanted to be a scholar. She went to Vassar College, where she graduated with highest honors, then to Harvard to get her Ph.D. It was there she met Stephen, who was in law school. "He was my first love. We had a mutual interest in the Elizabethan period. I was studying Shakespeare, and he was studying the Common Law. We got married in graduate school. I think that my parents were relieved that I had found someone."

She said that their marital problems began soon after they completed school. "We moved here, bought a house, and he began his practice. It wasn't long before he began spending a lot of time downtown. I knew he was establishing himself, but I resented his not spending more time with me. I just felt that it was more important to be together, since money was not a problem, but he was involved in the practice, and quickly got into a lot of civic things, like my father.

"Then, before any of that got resolved, we had the two children, one right after the other, and I got frantic. I couldn't do anything. Stephen got really mad at me. I remember one time he said, 'We aren't playing house, for God's sake!' I was hurt by that, really hurt. *I* knew we weren't playing house! He didn't see how hard it was for me." Carolyn thought the solution was to hire help, but after going through a number of bad experiences, with much complaining, Stephen finally put his foot down. Carolyn reported, "He didn't want them around, intruding on his privacy and causing problems. He said he'd rather do it himself. And he did. He shopped, cooked, everything! I ended up staying out of the way." There was a running battle between them during this period over his desire to have the family move downtown, closer to his work. "I said, 'Absolutely not!' Can you imagine? What kind of life would that be for children?"

Carolyn had known many advantages in her growing up years. They included money, position, good health care, an excellent education, cultural opportunities, a family that doted on her, and the example of socially concerned people. With all of this, she had failed in the tasks that confront us all: Friendship, work, and love. The first clue to her lack of preparation for life was shown in her report of her inability to make friends among her peers. Second was in her failure to find something useful to engage in while Stephen was establishing himself in his life work. Third, she failed when she found herself in the position of being responsible for others, namely her children. When things did not go her way, she retreated, with complaints and resentment. The loss of her marriage was one of the outcomes.

What had gone wrong? She had made a mistaken conclusion about herself and about life. She believed that she *required* the services, support, and attention of others in order to live, and that aside from these she did not know how to proceed. Her belief was that it was up to the others to take care of things generally, and to take care of her in particular. When they failed to do so she felt, for all the wealth of her background, impoverished.

Conclusion

In this chapter we emphasized the significance of the child's own evaluation of childhood circumstance relating to questions of heredity and environment. We have suggested that the art of guessing depends on a use of probability as a framework in which one is often surprised. We have cautioned against the uselessness (and danger) of causal and stereotyped thinking. Nothing believed to influence the individual can be assumed to be true unless the individual asserts it. In matters of life-style interpretation, the client is sovereign.

In Chapter 2, among topics suggested for examination in a Life-Style Assessment, we listed "other particularities," including (but not limited to) the ethnic, religious, social, and economic situation of the child. In the next chapter we continue our review of family material in considering these particularities in the framework of the child's training and self-training (especially in the neighborhood and school) for life outside the family, and for meeting the challenge of adolescence.

Chapter 10. PARTICULARITIES OF THE CHILDHOOD EXPERIENCE AND THE CHALLENGE OF ADOLESCENCE

Throughout the life-style inquiry, there are many opportunities to note and record information on particular ethnic, socioeconomic, and other matters characterizing a client's childhood experience, especially while taking the descriptions of mother and father and inquiring into the histories of the grandparents and other members of the extended family. Also, if there are other details of importance to the client, the *IPCW* provides a further opportunity to identify them by specifically asking for such information in Item 13 (p. 12), "Family Milieu."

In Chapter 4, we recounted the entire inquiry in "The Case of Dan." In this chapter we will return to that material in order to draw attention to the particularities of Dan's childhood situation discovered there. We will also review "The Case of Eugene" as an example of the way this information permeates the discussion of the family, rather than standing apart as discrete subject matter.

Remember as we review these cases that we are not so much interested in the facts of Dan's or Eugene's childhood milieu as we are in the *meanings* they gave to them and the *uses* they made of them. We cannot repeat often enough that, "We are influenced not by facts but by our opinion of facts" (Adler, p. 192).

Adler (p. 205) taught a "psychology of use" (*Gebrauchpsychologie*), distinguishing it from a "psychology of possession" (*Besitzpsychologie*) to emphasize his teleological analysis of psychological phenomena. Individual Psychology studies the particularities of a childhood situation to learn how the person either turned them to advantage, or shifted responsibility to them as rationale or alibi for failures or setbacks.

Particularities in "The Case of Dan"

1. Ethnic Origin. Dan reported that his parents were both of English ancestry, adding that Mother "said her people were of 'better stock' than the Allens because they'd been here since colonial times, and the Allens hadn't come over until 1885." Later he said, "I can't be all that

sure about Dad's family; he *says* they're English, but Mother's *is* English, through and through."

2. Religious Practice. Dan said, "I was steeped in the Episcopal Church. Sang in the choir and so forth, although it dawned on me as I got older that we were a little out of our league there, in terms of class. But it was part of Mother's thing. She always referred to us as 'Anglicans'! My father didn't go, by the way -- another bone of contention between them, and another opportunity for her to lord it over him."

3. Social Situation. "Mother was very ambitious for me.... She was determined that I wasn't going to be deprived of the opportunities that came with higher education." Mother also wanted a higher station in life for her sons: "She demanded that I look spotless, well-groomed, and that I was perfectly behaved." Her response to the accident in which Dan broke two of his permanent teeth was to be "terribly upset" in her concern for his appearance, not his well-being: "You'll be disfigured for life!" Finally, we know that she didn't want Dan to play with the neighborhood children, whom she considered "too tough."

4. Economic Status. While they were "better off" than the others in their neighborhood, this was a poor, working-class area. Mother complained that there was not enough money, blaming this on Father's gambling. As compared with others, though, "our house and yard looked nicer, we ate better, and I was better dressed," which tells us either that Mother was a good manager of what was available, or there was more available than she recognized as ample, because of the extent of her ambitions.

Discussion. We concluded that in Dan's family, where Mother was the dominant figure, Dan felt obliged to follow her lead in claiming the socially preferred background, and to honor her social ambitions and goals. Mother aspired to see her boys "rise above" their beginnings: They should get a good education, learn and maintain propriety (good manners, good clothes, good teeth, good "Anglican" training), in order to "better" themselves and escape into the middle class, as she had been unable to do.

How did these values and attitudes serve Dan when he went out into the neighborhood and school to make a place for himself among others? We can see that in the neighborhood Dan took the position of being "better than" the other children, and that this carried over into the school, where he studied and was bright enough to be taken out of the neighborhood group and "elevated" to a higher "track," again showing himself to be "better than" others. There was, however, an ironic price to be paid: Having located himself in this vertical frame of reference he found himself out of his element and felt "ill at ease." His speech gave him away as unacceptable, and he was publicly identified as "not as good as" the others.

About his dealings with the other sex, Dan said, "When I hit puberty I ran into trouble with girls." He didn't date until he was eighteen, and his first intercourse was when he was twenty-five. His caution in this related first to his apprehension regarding the power of women (his feminine guiding line), and second to his education in propriety (sex was not "right") and appearances ("I was unattractive"). Finally, he was also "terrified" of getting someone pregnant, and thereby derailing himself from the completion of his education and the route up and out, in keeping with the ambitions he had accepted as his own. With his view of women as knowing better, Dan was vulnerable to being caught up in the life of one of them, which is not the same thing as being a man who makes a life with a woman.

About working, Dan said that he "didn't have a clue" about what to do when he grew up (there were not many options available to his imagination from the world of work of the men in his family and neighborhood). He was drawn to the idea of being a railroad engineer, but knew that "it wouldn't have been considered the right job...[since] it was manual labor." The only thing that mattered was, "just do the job," and any job would do, except that it had to be in an office. In avoidance of a decision Dan stayed in graduate school for many years and was finally drawn into the world of the laboratory, where he was able to satisfy the demands of his ambition without actually being in an office.

We can see that Dan, having learned Mother's lesson, felt Mother's distress as a consequence. If the world was divided into two groups, the Better and the Worse, and if being best in the Worse group was not good enough, he would strive for a place in the Better group -- and always wonder whether he was the worst in that one, even at his best.

The Case of Eugene

Eugene grew up as the much youngest of six children in an immigrant Arab-American family. It was an Eastern Christian family that had lost its ties to the Arab-Christian community, with no new religious ties to put in their place in a predominantly Roman Catholic working-class neighborhood in a small town in Ohio. It was a family determined to escape its immigrant status by working for financial success, and the independence that would bring, while at the same time keeping very much to itself. (Eugene's name was chosen by one of his older brothers, who convinced his parents that it was a typically American name.) Father was described as a bully at home and a person who was accommodating to others to the point of servility outside the home.

Mother was described as caring, friendly, and cautious. The parents spoke little English. Father had worked his way up through three jobs during the time of Eugene's growing up, and Mother worked at various part-time jobs whenever it was possible for her to leave the children, who were her first responsibility. Mother's business sense enabled the family, in time, to buy a small grocery store and establish itself. Eugene saw Mother as "the brains" of the family and Father as "the brawn." Being the last of the children, Eugene benefited most from the family's growing financial success and considered himself to be spoiled "materially, but not in terms of permissiveness. Father saw to that."

Socially, the family had a place among the few Arab relatives who lived nearby, but had a "low social standing" otherwise. Eugene said, "I was aware that my family was somehow different, and that we weren't seen as 'real' Americans. This was a problem for me. I was ashamed that my parents spoke so little English, and that we weren't invited into other people's homes. It's interesting that *they* came to our house when we lived in back of the store (that is, my father's cronies did, especially on Sundays when the taverns were closed and they wanted to mooch a drink), but we never went to theirs. This bothered me. I definitely had the feeling that we were below other people socially, but I also had the feeling that this would change when we had money, because that was what people were interested in." Ethnicity, religion, and social standing all paled in comparison to the goal of economic security. All their other difficulties would be overcome if only the family gained financial independence through their hard work, and kept a "clean record," which meant avoiding anything that might come to the attention of anyone in authority: "Our motto should have been, 'Caution: Don't Make Waves!'"

In the neighborhood Eugene was a follower. "I went along with what the other kids wanted to do. I was fast and strong, so I was picked for teams, though I was never a star or anything like that. I was an average kid; I had a reputation for being a really nice kid." So, even though he felt defined as "different" from the others, he made his place among them by his strategy, based on the family values, of "going along" and working hard (in this case, at playing ball, in both senses of the phrase).

At school he was bright enough. His only handicap was his belief that his parents represented a handicap. "I didn't want them involved in anything at school, because of their poor English, so I was very careful not to do anything that would result in their being called in." In this way he imitated his parents, avoiding the attention of the authorities by keeping a "clean record" of his own in his own world of the school. (Eugene was the first of the four children to attend college, and the first to graduate. He went on to become a businessman -- like his mother, but in real estate.)

Consider now how he made use of his training and self-training for meeting the challenges of adolescence: Adjusting to puberty, learning how to be intimate with someone of the other sex, and meeting the economic demand of work.

"I was very bashful with girls. I felt I just wasn't good-looking enough to ask them out. Whatever I learned about sex, I learned on the playground from the other boys. Also, one of my older brothers tried to fill me in, but that was pretty useless, and in fact a little scary. Actually, in those years, the girls and the boys were quite separate. Maybe it was the era, maybe it was the town where I grew up, but we just weren't together very much. All through my junior and senior high school years, I never went out on a date. That seems incredible to me now!" He had his first sexual experience in high school when he "went along" with a friend to pick up a girl who "had a bad reputation"; he and his friend both had intercourse with her. He said, "It scared hell out of me. I didn't know what would happen. I wasn't too pleased with what I had done." He said that later on, "My wife courted me, or I might never have gotten married!" Considering Eugene's place as the much youngest child in his family, it is not surprising that he did not take the initiative in establishing an intimate bond with a woman, instead allowing himself to be chosen by her. As he put it, "I always went along with what the others wanted to do."

About his choice of career, Eugene reported, "I always wanted to be rich, but I didn't know how to do it. My career just kind of grew. My mother wanted me to be a doctor, but I didn't want to go to school that long. I don't know. Looking back, it seems that whatever happened to me just happened, without any particular plan on my part."

In the same way as he experienced himself as being chosen by a woman, Eugene saw himself as "chosen" by various employers, including a person with whom his mother had had some real-estate dealings, so that little by little he had found himself occupied in that field. His uncontentious and ingratiating way of being with others stood him in good stead here, in a world in which salesmanship is essential for success.

Getting along, not making waves, and keeping his eye on whatever opportunities chance put in his way were practiced operations for Eugene, and they worked successfully for him in gaining a wife and gaining wealth. They failed him whenever he was called upon to oppose anyone, be decisive (especially with respect to an unpopular stand), manage and direct the activities of others, or make and carry out plans. Further, the idea of being "different" was anathema to him and so placed a firm limitation on his creativity.

A theme of Eugene's life as the last and (during childhood) the smallest in his family was, "I don't want to be left behind," and his compensation against this danger was "to get ahead, or -- at the very least -- to stay even." The crisis that brought him to consult with us came when his partnership broke up in an acrimonious public dispute, and many of his "best people" left him to go into another firm with his former partner, where they believed they would enjoy (as one of them put it) "an innovative edge."

Particularities of Eugene's Situation

1. Ethnic Origin. Eugene's story features his ethnic difference from others in his community. In working with us he often made reference to his having been a member of the only Arab family in town. He also emphasized that he was part of an immigrant family, and was aware of his first-generation status, of which his "typical American name" was evidence. By contrast, he allowed himself to be embarrassed by his parents' imperfect mastery of English.

2. Religious Practice. The family left its religious life behind in coming to the United States. Their Eastern Orthodox customs differed from the Roman Catholicism which dominated the working-class town in which he grew up. Once or twice a year they would make a pilgrimage to Cleveland for a major liturgical celebration, but this only left Eugene feeling further set apart from others in his own town.

3. Social Situation. The family had "a low social standing" compared to others. Eugene resented the fact that Father's cronies came to their house, but that members of his family were not invited to the houses of other people. This, combined with the "servility" he believed Father to exhibit generally, left Eugene with the idea that the family was not only looked down upon, but was exploited.

4. Economic Status. The parents' example of hard work and its rewards was in front of Eugene at all times, as was the belief that with money comes everything else. He was confident that money "was what people were interested in," and that the family's problems would be solved when it was established financially.

Discussion. Eugene overcame his feelings of being ethnically and religiously different from the others and being "less than" they were by accepting the standards of the community as he understood them, and by taking part. He had learned to cooperate inside the family, where everyone worked hard to achieve financial success and to maintain the family's anonymity in the eyes of any authority, group, or person who might stand in the way of that success. He carried this attitude into the world of neighborhood and school, polishing his skills at "going along" to the extent of making a good marital alliance and a successful business career. Eugene's objective life situation had in it the potential for his coming to feel like an outcast, and for developing his resentments into an antisocial attitude; his subjective sense was, however, that he would be able to move beyond the limits of his immigrant family if only he made enough money, which he set out to do, and did. This did not move him beyond the limits of the cautious life-style he had practiced as a member of his family, however.

Conclusion

We can conclude this chapter on "Other Particularities" with Adler's statement (p. 208):

> Meanings are not determined by situations, but we determine ourselves by the meanings we give to situations.

Next, in Chapter 11, we present the process of review and interpretations of the early recollections, addressing special problems that arise in the course of this task, and providing a complete transcript of the process in "The Case of Janice."

Chapter 11: EARLY RECOLLECTIONS

Memory, like attention, is selective, in keeping with the economy of the mind and the purposes of the individual. Actively to remember everything, even if it were possible, would so clutter and fill attention that it is difficult to imagine how we could endure it. The theoretical problem, therefore, is to account not for the fact that we forget so much (which is the burden of theories of *repression*), but rather for the fact that we remember what we do.

There were numberless events in the course of our childhood years, before we reached the age of eight or nine, to which we attended, and in which we took some interest at the time. In most cases, we are likely to retain images of only a few incidents, perhaps six, perhaps as many as ten, which we can call up and review without conscious effort or any sense of purpose.

Individual Psychology is a theory of *expression*. It assumes that we retain these particular memories in order to maintain an orientation through time, to rehearse our understanding of the fundamental issues of life, and to provide ourselves with reminders of the reliability of our convictions. Cultures maintain continuity by means of myth and liturgy: "As it was in the beginning, is now, and ever shall be, world without end." According to Powers (1973), individuals, similarly, maintain identity by means of early recollections.

To understand this process requires that we recognize it as dynamic, seeing it as an active recollecting in the present moment of recall. Of all our movements, the activity of remembering is the most characteristic. It is in this activity that we reveal the style of our movement in purest form. If hyphenation could make our meaning clearer we would say that in our early re-collections we are re-constituting our world from its beginnings; re-membering the elements of our lives into the one body of our identity; re-calling assertions of meaning out of ourselves against the threats of confusion or despair; and re-viewing ourselves in our situations in our practiced way of looking at things.

To know your early recollections, therefore, is more than to have a familiarity with a collection of interesting anecdotes about your childhood. It is to have access to your basic schema of apperception, and to be able to see how you see yourself, others, and the world. It is to hold the key to the biased apparatus by means of which you are predisposed to perceive only the things that suit your purposes among all of life's possibilities, and to grasp only what confirms your convictions in any of life's information. It is to know how you have "made up your mind," and how you "keep in mind," and are "mindful of," those things that guide your choices and reduce your uncertainties. Finally, it is to know what you expect of yourself and others, and so to be able to predict how you will act in response to those expectations.

In your early recollections we will find your evaluations of yourself, your world, and the course of action open to you, as if in answer to the questions: What kind of a world is this? What kind of a person am I? What must a person such as I do in a world such as this to find a place of security (to fit in) and significance (to stand out)? What are my chances for success in all of this?

These are, if not the eternal questions, then the lifelong ones. We began shaping answers to them in the trials and errors of our earliest efforts. To the extent that these most primitive formulations worked to guide us, they became the bases for our further explorations, and for every further articulation of our personal values. If our lives are no longer satisfactory we will begin to reconsider the answers we have worked out. It will be hard. Our only way of thinking about them is itself a part of the way we have of doing everything, part of the way we have survived until now. Harder still, we cannot speak clearly about our basic convictions because they are not available to us except by implication in the images and stories of our recollections, which feel innocent of purpose or meaning. This is particularly true of our more extreme (and hence, more problematical) biases. Since they would not stand up to the scrutiny of common sense, we must, to maintain them at all, keep them unarticulated, out of the public realm of language. We pay a price for keeping them un-understandable, of course: They must remain un-understood by us.

Basic convictions, especially to the extent that they are biased and private, are best maintained and expressed through metaphor, and best illustrated by the seemingly unassailable certainties of private experience. After all, most of us feel safe in believing that almost anything can happen once. Some of us are even willing to believe that our lives are special, and actively to remember unique things that happened to us, perhaps things that the rest of us would believe could not have happened, not even once. One client told us of his boyhood experience of levitation, as he walked alone through an open field. No one could have guessed by looking at him (and no one with whom he conducted his prosperous business did guess) that he was raging against paranoid delusions of being humiliated ("put down"), or that he was dangerously close to doing violent harm.

The skillful gathering, interpretation, and explication of a client's early recollections is a valued art in Individual Psychology. It is regarded by us as pivotal to the psycho-clarity process of understanding life-style, and as close to essential as anything can be to any form of effective psychological intervention.

Adler put it this way:

> Among all psychological expressions, some of the most revealing are the individual's memories. [They] are the reminders he carries about with him of his own limits and of the meaning of circumstances. There are no "chance memories": Out of the incalculable number of impressions which meet an individual, he chooses to remember only those which he feels, however darkly, to have a bearing on his situation. Thus, his memories represent his "Story of My Life"; a story he repeats to himself to warn him or comfort him, to keep him concentrated on his goal, and to prepare him by means of past experiences, so that he will meet the future with an already tested style of action (p. 351).

Early recollections take their place in the Life-Style Assessment in three phases: Gathering and recording (see Chapter 4 for a discussion of this); review and interpretations (the subject of this chapter); and the early recollections summaries (Chapter 14).

In the remainder of this chapter we explain the procedure we use for the review and interpretation of early recollections. We then present a method for interpreting the recollections by attending to five key categories (context, content, gender, movement, and evaluation). Finally, we demonstrate the use of these categories in four examples. The chapter concludes with the complete transcript of the review and interpretations of the early recollections in "The Case of Janice."

Procedure for Review and Interpretation of Early Recollections

After the "Summary of the Family Constellation" has been completed, the next task in the Life-Style Assessment is the review and interpretation of the early recollections. This may follow immediately, or it may be scheduled separately for the next session.

The first therapist reports each early recollection in turn, reading a verbatim record. The second therapist functions as a consultant to the first therapist, inquiring into each instance of recollection reported, and leading a discussion with the client, with the first therapist collaborating. It is the second therapist's task to ascertain what the meaning of the early recollection is to the client; that is, to uncover the personal attitude, evaluation, or conviction expressed in the story. To do this means to extend the imagination in order to experience the memory as if it were one's own, until one sees the situation from the client's vantage. The object of the discussion is to discover how self, others, and the world looked to the client in the moment recalled. When the second therapist succeeds in conveying an understanding of what the situation of the memory means, the client will exhibit some form of the recognition reflex (laughter, grinning, or blushing, with a fixed meeting of the gaze) or will offer some verbal assent ("You've got it," or, "That's it!") after which the first therapist reads the next recollection from the record.

After reviewing each recollection in sequence, a second review follows as a preparation for composing and recording the summaries. The first therapist reminds the second therapist of the sequence of the recollections, of observations and clarifications noted in the first review, the client's age at the time of each incident recalled, and any details that remain puzzling or problematical. At the end of this second review and discussion, the second therapist dictates two summaries of the interpretations based on them, one called "The Pattern of Basic Convictions," and the other "The Interfering Ideas." (See Chapter 14 for more information on the way in which these summaries are to be organized.)

Five Key Categories of Interpretation

For teaching purposes we have identified five categories as of key importance. Do not limit your vision. Empathy will go beyond categories to a sense of the whole world of another's experience; still, it should not fall short of or ignore the following:

1. Context. In the most general sense, the context of any recollection is the world itself, which presents itself as an ambiguous stimulus to which the recollection stands as a record of projective response (Mosak, 1958). (As poet Allen Ginsberg said, "We do not see things as they are, but as we are.") Any recollection could, therefore, be interpreted to some extent by itself, in an academic exercise apart from knowledge of the person recalling it. That would be of no interest to your client.

The investigation of family background, of the situation in which the client first experienced the challenges of life, provides the immediate context. This is why the "Summary of the Family Constellation" is completed before the early recollections are studied.

In the review an even narrower context is established for each of the recollections by considering the age of the client at the time of the reported incident. By attending to this we are alert to the special meaning of recollections associated with (for example) the birth of a younger sibling, a parent's dramatic illness or death, menarche, or some other event of consequence to the client.

2. Content. It may not seem worth mentioning, but it is important to note nonetheless that the recollection belongs to the client. It is not legitimate to interpret a recollection based on what "it must have looked like," or what "any child would have felt in that situation." It is one thing to practice empathy; it is another thing to impose one's own ideas upon a client's experience, or to assume the presence (though hidden) of material required by a pet theory. This is what keeps Freud's Psychoanalysis from being a reliable interpretive schema. Treating memories as "internal screens" (*Deckerinnerungen*), psychoanalysts are free to indulge in speculation about what "must be" behind the screens, shoring up the theory by postulating whatever it expects to find there.

On the other hand, it is equally important to pay attention to every detail included in the recollections. In fact, we could say that there is a law of inverse consequence here: The more extraneous a detail seems to the narrative, the more important it is likely to be to the narrator. For example, the color of an object does not alter the use of the object in a story. That it is mentioned at all suggests a visual interest, perhaps an artistic one. If the color is vivid, or described in terms of temperature (cool blue; hot orange), it may imply a reference to emotional calm, or to excitement.

3. Gender. Some clients include only persons of the same sex among the characters appearing in their recollections. Some reverse this, and tell stories with only members of the other sex present. Some (men and women) relate stories of good men and bad women. Others reverse this, and portray noble women suffering in a world of evil men.

No single issue is more important to social life than that of gender. To be clear about where we stand as men or women, and to be at ease in our gender among other men and women, is central to our ability to develop the social interest, that liberating sense of being co-creators of the world in which we find ourselves. Whatever else the history of the past one hundred years may have taught us, we should be clear about this at least: No one, made to feel of diminished worth in comparison to others because of gender, can be expected to cooperate cheerfully as a member of the human community. Moreover, no one made to feel that his or her value depends upon a position of superiority to the other sex, can be expected to participate in community life without pretenses that threaten to disturb its peace, with insults, outbursts of rage, and other disguises of underlying insecurities and occasional panics.

4. Movement. Life is movement. In reviewing the early recollections, therefore, it is essential to see who moves, and how, in what direction, and with what effect. This gives the paradigm for the way in which

the client is prepared to move, and expects others to move. We consider these five issues in examining movement:

i) *Effectiveness/Ineffectiveness:* What are the results of my actions? Are they positive or negative? Are men more effective than women? How? Vice versa? How? Are men and women effective in differing ways? How are these distinguished? Does suffering overwhelm power? Are others effective with me, while I am ineffective with them?

ii) *Relative position:* Are some people above others? Does movement proceed from above to below? Is a vertical dimension prominent in the memories? In certain of them? What is the consequence, as seen in movement?

iii) *Degree of activity and initiative:* Is the client physically active and able to initiate activities with others? Is movement limited to looking, listening, or resisting? Is the client passive while others act? A victim of others? Of luck, fate, or destiny? Or, a beneficiary of these, as in "a charmed life"?

iv) *Extent of participation and cooperation:* Does the client act alone, or with others? Against others? Openly or in secret? As leader, follower, or in what role amongst others?

v) *Sensory appropriation of experience:* Is there one dominant mode? Visual? (Possible detachment, or artistic or design interest.) Auditory? (Poetry, music.) Tactile? (Possible "affect hunger" and compensatory efforts to generate sensation.) Olfactory? (Although odors remain important to us, the sense of smell is greatly attenuated in human beings compared to its acuity in other mammals. If an odor is not pronounced we have to get close to the source for it to be apparent to us. References to odor may therefore be indexes to evaluations of closeness or avoidance, depending on the pleasurable-unpleasurable axis of feeling used to describe them. It follows that issues of intimacy can be indicated by memories of odor.) Taste? (Self-indulgence may be reflected in attention to pleasant tastes. Be alert for other evidence that may suggest a sociopathic pattern.)

[A final note on sensory detail: Someone may be inspired to design research projects to test these clinical impressions. Until results are available, use your intuitive sense to explore with the client what a narrowing of attention to one or another sensory modality may imply. Watch also for recollections with an aesthetic continuum of sense data of every kind, sometimes reported as "dizzying," and having about it an affect described as intensely, almost intolerably, beautiful. We see in this the sign of religious temperament, sometimes taking the form of revolutionary commitment.]

5. Evaluation. An inquiry into feelings has become a therapeutic cliche, so much so that a caricature pictures the therapist asking after nothing else, as if an empathic consequence would be the result, and that this were the only outcome required for successful therapy. By contrast, when we ask what the client's feelings were at the precise moment being recalled in an early recollection, we are after specific and important information.

Feelings are the index to evaluation, the key to an understanding of subjectivity, which is part of the proper subject matter of Individual Psychology. To say how I feel about something is to indicate where I stand with respect to it, how I am prepared to respond, with whom I am prepared to sympathize. For this reason some discouraged clients will be reluctant to let you know what they feel. To let anyone know where I stand, or even to take a stand of my own, is to put myself in a position that may be criticized or opposed by others. To escape this danger some clients will avoid responding to the question, "What did you feel at that moment (the most vivid moment recalled in the memory)?" Instead, they will tell you what they thought, and they will be happy to provide a long rationalization of their opinion. It is important to get beyond this if you can.

Sometimes the client cannot understand the question. There is some genuine confusion of meaning in the common usage of the phrases, "I think" and "I feel." For example, "I feel that the national debt is too large." In fact, there can be no such feeling. We should rather say, "I think that the national debt is too large. I feel fearful of the possible consequences." Of course we have no need to be so careful in everyday speech, since our meaning is generally understood by those who agree to use the words as loosely as we do. The client may therefore wonder why you are making an issue over the distinction. You must find a way to persist. The issue is clarity; the psycho-clarity process depends on it.

Even so, you must not get into a quarrel about words. We sometimes get to the point by asking, "What were the sensations in your body?" That usually takes us a long enough step away from cerebration. The trouble with this tack is that (to give examples from client responses) "It's hard to define," or, "It's hard to put into words." Of course. We encourage: "That's O.K. Just describe the way you felt." If things stay blank we may go as far toward prompting as to say, "Well, did it feel good or bad?" Then, whichever of these is chosen, we can go on with, "What kind of good (or bad)?" If this fails, we try, "Well, was it on the warm side or on the cold side?" This can reveal whether the feelings were toward the conjunctive or disjunctive.

Sometimes none of this works to elicit feelings. In such a case an absence can be regarded as presence of another kind. It is possible to be unable to imagine how to take an action, or even make an assertion, without making matters worse than they already are. When this is so, we dampen all affect that might prompt an attempt. Also, one may have as narrowly limited a style as possible, to prevent attachment and the threat of loss, trying to treat all of life as a technical problem, or a spectacle, as if claiming, in playwright Christopher Isherwood's phrase, "I am a camera."

The absence of affect presents a danger to the novice trying to make sense of another person's memories, and tempted to assume what "any child" of that age, in that situation, "must" have felt. This is a grave error, which will leave you with nothing more than an interpretation of your own projections. One woman remembered fleeing her homeland on a boat crowded with refugees, and hearing the sounds of artillery behind them in the hills above the water. "Any child" at four years of age "must" have felt terror and confusion. This woman remembered a tremendous pleasure, with so many members of her family close around her, the beauty of the sun on the water, and the excitement and sense of discovery at taking her first boat trip! But what about the artillery? "Well, I didn't mind that," she replied. "I knew that if it weren't for that we wouldn't have gone on the boat at all!"

Example 1.

> "I was about six years old and there was this gigantic snowfall. I went out into the driveway. I was supposed to shovel it."
>
> Most vivid moment: "Standing there, seeing that huge drift. How could it get that big? How was I ever going to get out of that driveway?"
>
> Feeling: "Jesus! Futility. I was overwhelmed. It was too much!"

1. Context. The client was six, and had started school. Life outside the family presented itself, and presented the client with responsibility.

2. Content. There are two rhetorical questions: "How could it get that big?" and "How was I ever going to get out of that driveway?" The first of these conveys a sense of drama, wonder, excitement, and an exaggeration of the difficulty; this is seen as so huge that the client's problem-solving ability is swamped, and the answer to the second is implied: "I'm not. There's no way that I can solve this."

3. Gender. Since the client is a man, the recollection may be stating, "Look at what a man is up against in this world." There may be a further implication: "Since it looks as if it's too much for me, I must be an inadequate man." Note, too, that he is all alone in facing life's difficulties. That may be the man's lot.

4. Movement.

i) *Effectiveness/Ineffectiveness:* I am ineffective.

ii) *Relative position:* I am small and the world and its difficulties are "huge."

iii) *Degree of activity and initiative:* Since I am in a world filled with insurmountable obstacles from which there is no escape ("How was I ever going to get out of that driveway?"), there is nothing that I can do.

iv) *Extent of participation and cooperation:* A man is on his own. There is no aid; there are no allies. I am one man, alone in a cold world.

v) *Sensory appropriation of experience:* The emphasis is on the visual. I am impressed by what I see, and what I see is bleak, colorless, immense.

5. Evaluation. Life's struggles are as futile as they are inescapable.

Example 2.

> "I was about three. My mother and I were at the beach. I was playing in the sand. There were lots of birds flying out over the water. Suddenly my mother grabbed me up and took me home."
>
> Most vivid moment: "Her scooping me up."
>
> Feeling: "Mad."

1. Context. The client's younger brother was born at about this time, and mother was no longer as free to indulge him. The contrast between his former (and still claimed) freedom, and his being required ("scooped up") to yield to her wishes shows itself here.

2. Content. Most striking here is the statement, "There were lots of birds flying out over the water." This detail, extraneous to the drama of the story, succeeds in providing an imagery by which to highlight the client's "antithetical mode of apperception" (Adler, p. 248). It

contrasts the absolute freedom of the birds, and the constraint he experiences at the hands of a woman (see below). When we asked him about the birds he said, "I always wished I could fly like a bird." We asked him what that would mean to him and he replied, "Freedom."

3. Gender. In this story it appears that a man is at the mercy of the woman in his life, and she decides what is required of him. His interests don't seem to weigh anything in comparison to hers, and her determination and strength are irresistible.

4. Movement.

i) *Effectiveness/Ineffectiveness:* I can be effective when I am working on my own projects, and I am left alone. I am ineffective against the determination of the woman in my life.

ii) *Relative position:* I am no match for the woman in my life, no matter how disposed I am to fight back.

iii) *Degree of activity and initiative:* I can take initiative on my own, when left to myself. Against the woman in my life, I can take no initiative. She has her way with me, and my anger is of no consequence. She is in charge.

iv) *Extent of participation and cooperation:* I can either be on my own, and able to enjoy what I want, or I can have a woman in my life to whom I must submit. There is no cooperation in either case.

v) *Sensory appropriation of experience:* Visual; tactile (playing in the sand).

5. Evaluation. I am in an impotent rage, trying to impress the woman in my life with my desire to have some freedom, without having to give up her caring for me.

Example 3.

"I was about seven. My big brother and I and a bunch of boys were playing basketball in the back of the house. My brother was bigger and taller than I and kept blocking me so that I couldn't get the ball."

Most vivid moment: "My brother with his back to me, keeping me from getting the ball he was dribbling."

Feeling: "Frustrated. Angry."

1. Context. This is the memory of one of the younger boys in a large family. Here he is, at age seven, in the boys' world, with his older sisters not around to protect him, and with his big brother keeping him in his place.

2. Content. We are struck by the image of the brother's back, turned as if to underscore a feeling, familiar to many younger children, of being disregarded, not taken seriously, or insulted.

3. Gender. This is the way it is in the man's world. It's a rough game, a competitive game, and it's hard enough to get into it, much less to get ahead in it, if you're not as big as the others.

4. Movement.

i) *Effectiveness/Ineffectiveness:* I'm not a big enough player to make a success of things. The bigger players block me, and keep me back.

ii) *Relative position:* I'm coming from behind, looking for a break.

iii) *Degree of activity and initiative:* I'm game. I keep trying. I'm full of fight.

iv) *Extent of participation and cooperation:* I'm right in there among the other guys. I'm playing by the rules, but I'm watching for my chance, and I don't expect anyone to hand it to me.

v) *Sensory appropriation of experience:* Kinesthetic and tactile. The rough and tumble.

5. Evaluation. I am up against unfair odds. I am determined to hold my own and to fight for what I want.

Example 4.

> "I was five. It was my birthday. The party was in my grandfather's back yard. There were about ten children there, both boys and girls. I remember the present my grandfather gave to me, because it was just what I wanted: A buggy for my doll. It was the most beautiful thing I had ever seen. Just as I was running over to get it, one of the boys fell into the fish pond. It was about nine feet deep. They pulled him out and he was covered with tadpoles. They were in his hair, on his clothes."

Most vivid moment: "There were really two: The first was when my grandfather brought out the doll buggy."

Feeling: "Overwhelmed with joy!"

"The second was seeing that boy covered with tadpoles."

Feeling: "Amused. It was hilarious!"

1. Context. This client's other recollections showed women as competent and caring. Now we have a contrasting memory telling us about men. This is presented to us at a time in the client's life when she was experiencing marital difficulties, and complained that her husband was "insensitive to [her] needs." (He complained that she criticized him and put him down.)

2. Content. Two pictures of men are produced, as if simultaneously, showing (1) that a man can be complete and mature, can know just what it takes to make life beautiful for a woman, and can be counted on to do it without having to be told; (2) that other men are inept, get in over their heads and have to be rescued, and appear ridiculous in their incompleteness and immaturity (among the other tadpoles).

3. Gender. Men either provide for or amuse me. As a woman, I can be delighted with what they provide or entertained by what they do.

4. Movement.

i) *Effectiveness/Ineffectiveness:* As the star, I am a centerpiece for the men to fuss over, provide for, or amuse.

ii) *Relative position:* I am at the center of it all, in the happy position of having a worthy man demonstrate that he can please me by giving me "just what I want(ed)"; and of having a raw, unformed man demonstrate that he is not yet equal to anything more than amusing me.

iii) *Degree of activity and initiative:* Others act; I evaluate, and I experience overwhelming joy or hilarious amusement. Nothing touches me to hurt me.

iv) *Extent of participation and cooperation:* I am at the center of the fun as the star of the show. If it weren't for me the fun wouldn't be taking place. I enjoy what the others do.

v) *Sensory appropriation of experience:* Visual. The recollection is cinematic.

5. Evaluation. The "overwhelming joy" and the "hilarious" extent of her being "amused" show her as seeing life as impinging on her in a shower of blessings, for which she is qualified simply by being alive (the celebration of her birthday). Requirements rest on the others, and only those who know what they are doing can fulfill them.

Now that we have said so much about the elements of interpretation, and about the categories into which we attempt to sift the data, we will offer a complete transcript of a session on early recollections as an example of this work. If you find it difficult to compare our interpretations point by point with the preceding categories, this is as it should be. When it comes to the living work of understanding another human being, the "key categories" are not sovereign; the person is. The categories shape our thinking; the work itself shapes the outcome.

The transcript is of the review and interpretations of the early recollections in "The Case of Janice." To establish context, we have included the summary of her family constellation so that you will know what we knew as we entered this interview with Janice. Bear in mind as you read the summary of family material and the subsequent transcript that Janice's presenting complaint was acute anxiety with panic reactions relating to concerns about her twelve-year-old son, a well-behaved, cheerful youngster on the threshold of adolescence, who had never been a "problem child" in any sense of the phrase. She was preoccupied and worried about his activities, and the possible harm that might come to him, to the point of incapacitating herself in a flood of symptoms.

The Case of Janice

SUMMARY OF THE FAMILY CONSTELLATION

Janice grew up as the older of two children and the only girl, psychologically the first-born daughter, in a tradition-bound New England family in which the atmosphere was constraining, as if each of the parents was concerned to hold the energies of the children in check by managing the expression of those energies and channeling them into athletics and family-centered activities.

The family values emphasized self-control, propriety, and privacy (if there was trouble, "no one should know about it"), which alerted the children to the idea that there was little reason to repose confidence in others, or in life.

The masculine guiding line set by Father stressed hard work, caution, and an uneasy pessimism which expressed itself in faultfinding or, when no fault was to be found, in fault-seeking. Father was the unhappy first-born son of his own dominating, cold, and withdrawn father (who confirmed the character of the masculine guiding line for Janice).

The feminine guiding line set by Mother stressed gregariousness, "ladylike" composure (Mother kept her own counsel, and never raised her voice), and "feminine" interests in clothes and appearance. Mother was also, however, athletic and robust, and rejected her own mother's rejection of men.

Ralph, four years younger, made a place for himself as the first-born son who imitated Father in a quiet determination to have his own way, in being self-absorbed, and in being critical of the women.

Janice kept her place by being a better student and by doing her best to meet the parental demand for decorum and restraint.

During childhood she was able to follow the masculine guiding line in terms of withdrawal, isolating herself in the world of books, and consoling herself against the constraints of her situation by picturing the other places, other times, and the lives of other people that her books disclosed to her.

In adolescence her success in following the masculine guiding line became problematic. As a girl who would be a woman, she aspired to enjoying advantages inhering in the kind of position Mother enjoyed: That of a pretty, soft woman, fussed over, protected, and maintained by a powerful man (like the nineteenth century heroines she admired in novels). She succeeded in being like Mother in terms of gregariousness and enjoyment, but never came to see herself as being sufficiently feminine. On the one hand, she fell short by the measure of soft-spokenness and the suppression of anger and resentment; on the other, she deviated through her determination to make an independent life for herself (though not without taking note of the fact that Mother had also arranged to do as she pleased, as long as Father didn't know about it).

Prominent among other images of femininity available to Janice was that of her Aunt Sarah, who was "trapped" in an unhappy marriage to a harsh and unfriendly man.

Through everything in Janice's childhood and adolescence runs a scarlet thread connecting a variety of ideas about control, self-control, domination, and resistance, issues expressed in all the family relationships. Her pattern of finding excitement in numerous "sneaky" ways rehearsed a longing to escape from constraints, to take risks, and to experience the liveliness of life. Even here, however, the effort was secret and muted by her sense that, above all, she had to "stay in control."

At the threshold of adulthood, the question remained: How could she, a woman, stay in control in a world dominated by the men?

REVIEW AND INTERPRETATIONS OF THE EARLY RECOLLECTIONS

[Note: The record of each of Janice's eight early recollections appears here. Each is followed by a verbatim transcript of the discussion that took place among Janice, the first therapist (JG), and the second therapist (RLP).]

No. 1: Age 3. We went on a trip to our summer place in Maine. We had an MG roadster with white upholstery. You could fit in there behind the seats with your pillow. I'm in there. It's night. My parents are talking.

Most vivid moment: Being in there, hearing my parents talk.

Feeling: Safe, good, warm, happy.

Discussion

RLP: It's an interesting first memory, visually. An MG with white upholstery. And I'm tucked away. An MG with white upholstery sounds pretty flashy to me.

Janice: It was hysterical. My mother was able to make Dad give it up after my brother was born. My father could get the flashiest car he wanted before he had children, and it was all right with Mother then. (All laugh.)

RLP: And the feeling is secure?

JG: Safe, good, warm, happy. She's tucked in there, looking out at everything, and listening.

RLP: Were you looking out?

Janice: Yes. You two are a trip! (Laughter.)

RLP: What are you thinking?

Janice: Nothing. (Laughter.) It's just fascinating. You two have never been on this side.

RLP: Oh, yes we have! (All laugh.) There's a sense of having a place of my own, among others. They're doing their thing, and I'm doing mine. I'm in the world of the others, along for the ride, but I have my own place. O.K.

[Note that Janice's participation in the discussion of her first memory is an illustration of the meaning of the memory, and a demonstration of her style of movement in distancing herself from others, here disguised as humor. Even her choice of slang ("You two are a trip!"), and her fictional location of herself on a "side" of the transaction, recapitulate the situation of the memory. We could probably go further, and say that her laughter over her father's penchant for flashy cars should have served as a warning to the therapists to the effect that she was prepared to ridicule ("It was hysterical") and thereby diminish any way, not her own, of looking at things.]

> No. 2: Age 7 or 8. My brother had a snake in a tin can in the kitchen on the floor. In the dark I got up for something. I kicked the can over, then I stepped on the snake. *Then* I remembered the can was there.
>
> Most vivid moment: When I felt that thing under my foot.
>
> Feeling: Fear.

Discussion

RLP: *Then* I remembered! After I kicked the can, after I stepped on the snake, *then* I remembered.

JG: After stepping on the snake. It's certainly a cautionary tale.

RLP: Except it says what I *should* have done. Events go out of control. *I* knock things out of control. I *should* have known about it.

Janice: Good time to remember the can, huh? (All laugh.)

JG: There's an interesting contrast between the first and second memories. In number one, she's going along for the ride, and other people are in charge; in number two, she's in charge -- that is, acting on her own -- and she blunders.

RLP: Yes, here she's taking her own initiative and it doesn't work out. O.K.

> No. 3: Age 8 or 9. The house across the street was very old. They had a cellar that had a mud bottom. There was a storm door. There's water collected in a pool in that basement.
>
> Most vivid moment: I'm standing there in that basement with my girlfriend, staring at the pool.
>
> Feeling: Good, peaceful.

Discussion

RLP: Nothing moves. Just still water.

Janice: Yes.

RLP: What was so good and peaceful?

Janice: Water has always done that for me.

RLP: Tell us what you mean, what comes to mind when you say that.

Janice: Warm, contained.... Umm....

RLP: That's all right. You're doing fine.

Janice: I mean it was just so peaceful in that basement.

RLP: There's something about the contained character of it in that pool.

Janice: I don't necessarily.... I was just thinking about it.... I don't necessarily like things that are endless, you know? I mean when I look out at the ocean.... And you just look out.... And you can't see the other end. I don't necessarily like that.

RLP: All right, we've got three...

Janice: It was dark. It was dark down there, too.

RLP: ...we've got three images of containment and uncontainment now.

JG: And the dark.

Janice: Um-hum. I was always more comfortable in the dark.

JG: In the car, in the kitchen, in the basement.

Janice: Um-hum.

RLP: We've got containment in all three of them, though the snake is uncontained in the second memory.

JG: And she's fearful when it's uncontained.

RLP: Yes. It's the "life force," run amok. Things that are not contained, energies that are not confined. It's scary to you.

Janice: Um-hum.

RLP: O.K.

> No. 4: Age 4 or 5. I went to buy shoes at the department store and to see Santa Claus.
>
> Most vivid moment: Sitting on Santa's lap.
>
> Feeling: I was not real comfortable. I was shy.

Discussion

RLP: What was uncomfortable about it?

Janice: My mother wanted this picture with Santa Claus in it....

RLP: Yeah?

Janice: I didn't necessarily want to do it, I don't think.

RLP: See if you can tell us what you remember about it.

Janice: I didn't know him.

RLP: Yeah?

Janice: I mean I'm not real good at...I don't think I was as a child either, real good at things that I didn't know. It took me a while to get used to things.

RLP: Um-hum.

Janice: And I think a lot of times, when I felt that way initially, I never gave myself the time to get comfortable. Once I get comfortable, I'm fine. It took me a lot of years to discover that, I think. To be able to immediately feel O.K.

RLP: O.K.

> No. 5: Age 6 or 7. It's late. My mother and father were in their bedroom. I woke up -- maybe I had a dream, I don't remember -- and went in to them. They were having intercourse. I thought they were hurting each other. There were two white bodies, like marble.
>
> Most vivid moment: Seeing the whiteness of the two bodies and motion. Father was on top, and Mother was on the bottom.
>
> Feeling: I was frightened.

Discussion

RLP: Did they know you were there?

Janice: I never got up again, I'll tell you! (All laugh.) Yeah. They did, because I...I went in anyway.

RLP: What happened?

Janice: I think they put me back to bed. They must have. They didn't get real bent out of shape.

RLP: What happened? What are you remembering?

Janice: I think.... I think they just stopped and pulled up the sheets and took me in bed until I fell asleep and then put me back in my own room.

RLP: They took you into their bed?

Janice: Um-hum.

RLP: So you...

Janice: Yeah. I would say they did.

RLP: So your interpretation was that they were hurting each other? Or that he was hurting her?

Janice: Yeah. Yes. The latter.

RLP: That he was hurting her.

Janice: Yes.

RLP: What did you make of it?

Janice: God knows!

RLP: You're six or seven years old. What do you know about intercourse? All you see are these two people.

Janice: That's right, and hear the...the sounds bothered me.

RLP: What sounds? What was there about the sounds?

Janice: I don't know...uh...uninhibited, I guess, not things I'd heard before, nothing I could relate to.

RLP: The idea you form is that he was doing harm to her.

Janice: Yeah.

RLP: As if what? Since you didn't know what intercourse was, what did you think he was doing?

Janice: I don't know.... You know, like somebody hurting somebody, like when you see people pinned down.

RLP: A struggle?

Janice: Yeah. Yes. Yeah. Not pleasurable.... I didn't think of it as that at all.

RLP: Somehow uninhibited, unrestricted...

Janice: Yes, but that he was in charge.

RLP: Overwhelming. It looks like a dangerous struggle.

Janice: Yes.

RLP: O.K.

No. 6: Age 8. I'm dressed up for Thanksgiving. I'm out in the front yard of a good friend's house, waiting for my parents to get ready to go to my grandmother's house.

Most vivid moment: Being out on the lawn, having my picture taken.

Feeling: Good.

Discussion

RLP: Who's on the lawn?

Janice: Me and my friend.

RLP: Same age? Two kids, huh?

Janice: Yeah.

RLP: And who's taking your picture?

Janice: My father.

RLP: Help me to see where you are in the memory. He's taking a picture of the two of you?

Janice: Um-hum.

RLP: Where is he?

Janice: We're together -- Judy and I are together. And he's back there.

RLP: Back where?

Janice: Father's over this way, taking our picture. We're here, and he's there [indicates]. He's taking the picture from there. I have a red hat on.

RLP: Um-hmm. You have a red hat on?

Janice: Yeah. And a new wool coat. We were all excited!

RLP: Look at the situation: Here's a man at a distance and the women all dressed up. The men act as if they're interested in how the women look, and the women make the pretense of looking good. But the truth of life -- from the prior memory -- is that the men will overwhelm them.

Janice: Um. Yeah.

RLP: What was the excitement about that day?

Janice: Just Thanksgiving. You know, going to Grandmother's house and all that business. Thanksgiving in our family was always a big deal.

RLP: Um-hum. O.K.

> No. 7: Age 9. There were some people who were friends of the family. They had a Halloween Party in their basement. I went to the party as a ghost. I remember bobbing for apples. I had a great time.
>
> Most vivid moment: Bobbing for apples.
>
> Feeling: Good. I liked it. I didn't catch any, but I liked it anyway.

Discussion

RLP: What was there about it that you liked?

Janice: I want to say, just listening to you say this, that it was because I was the ghost, and I didn't care what anybody thought because nobody could see who I was. It didn't matter whether I caught the apple or not. But I don't know why I want to say that. I really don't.

RLP: Well, is it true, or are you making an adult interpretation? Are you remembering that, or are you speculating about it on the basis of present assumptions that...

Janice: I think that's true, that I was covered up in my sheet and I enjoyed that. And it was...God! It was dark in that basement! (All laugh.) I don't want to say that word, dark, any more! But...I liked scary things.... I still do. We took a trip on city buses last week to visit some relatives. (Laughter.) I loved it! My kids thought I was crazy. I mean, we'd never taken the bus there before, so I didn't know where I was going. I mean, we got lost! We got off at the wrong stop and stuff, and I thought, "This is so exciting!" And my son said, "Mom, you're really enjoying this." And I said, "I love it! I've never done this before!" And I thought of you two then, and what you'd said about excitement, and I thought, "It's true. I really do like excitement."

RLP: O.K.

> No. 8: Age 9. We're climbing trees out in the back of the house next door to ours. The really big deal was to jump from the tree onto the roof. This was the house where two of my brother's friends lived. We climbed the tree, jumped onto the garage roof, and, from there, onto the roof of the house.
>
> Most vivid moment: Hiding on the other side of the roof from

the door to the house. Ted's mom was coming out of the house to hang out the laundry. These were pitched roofs, and we kids were holding on to one side while Ted's mom was coming out of the other. We're hoping she won't see us.

Feeling: Good. I was thinking, "I still didn't get caught!" It was an endurance contest: You didn't know how long you could hold on! Or, when you might fall, and be discovered.

Discussion

RLP: Getting caught...doing what? Taking part in a boy's game? Hiding up above, where the boys are -- the men are, up above the women? Do you have some feeling in your life that you're "hanging on"?

Janice: I don't know. I was just sitting here thinking about that.

RLP: How long can I hang on? Do you have some idea about that?

Janice: I feel like I'm hanging on to get through something.

RLP: Like what?

Janice: I had that feeling when I was in college.

RLP: Do you have it now?

Janice: Not now, but when I first came in here to see you two I had that feeling: "If I don't get myself some place, I won't be able to hang on much longer." I was so anxious then.

RLP: O.K. Let's review the entire record. I want to run through everything again with ages and situations.

JG: O.K.

[Note that the discussion now continues in the "second review" of the recollections, to which we referred on page 188.]

RLP: Now, the first one is in the back of that car. How old was the child?

JG: Three.

RLP: Feeling?

JG: Safe, good, warm, happy.

RLP: All tucked away.

Janice: Um-hum.

RLP: And other people are in charge. Is the car being driven? Is it in motion?

Janice: Um-hum.

RLP: So it's in motion. So I'm being carried along. There's some sense of being safe and sound and tucked away and letting somebody else have charge of life. Let's put it that way. And it's O.K., it's fine. I'm safe where I am, sort of hidden away.

JG: And the next memory is at age seven or eight with the snake in the kitchen.

RLP: The first was three, and then we jump up to seven or eight. She tips over the can and then realizes that there's a snake in it and there's a sense of fear.

Janice: Um-hum!

RLP: And then she steps on the snake. Are you barefooted?

Janice: Yeah!

RLP: And here's this wriggling life under my foot, eh?

Janice: Um-hum.

RLP: It's hard to keep it there.

Janice: Yeah!

JG: The next one's at age eight or nine in the basement, looking at the pool, and it's peaceful.

RLP: Eight or nine. Now as I recall, your first period came when you were nine, didn't it?

Janice: Um-hum.

RLP: There's something about the containment, the stillness of the water. O.K.

JG: The next one is sitting on Santa's lap, back at the age of four or five.

RLP: We go back in age now, to the time when your brother was born, and here I am on Santa's lap. I don't know who he is, but I'm supposed to be sitting here. I'm supposed to be enjoying this?

Janice: Um-hum.

RLP: I don't understand the intrusion of this memory into the record at this point in the sequence. Let me get it again: We have the car, the snake, the water -- all in the dark. Then we suddenly emerge into the light, and here I have to sit on Santa's lap. I don't like it, right?

Janice: Um-hum.

RLP: Who is this person? What am I supposed to do here? What was the feeling you had?

JG: "Not real comfortable; shy."

RLP: It indicates some reluctance to engage with him. It's really the first time there's any kind of social...

JG: No. There's the other girl at the pool....

RLP: Yes, but she and I just stand there, and look at the pool of water. The focus is on the water, isn't it?

JG: Yes. "I'm standing there with my girlfriend, staring at the pool."

RLP: Well. Then we come to the first "contact" memory, and it's with a man. We can look at it that way: A man (Santa) and a struggle. All right. What's the next one?

JG: Mother and Father.

RLP: Well, then it does connect. It's a shift there at that point. There I am made to sit in a man's lap. Here I witness this man overwhelming this woman. It's a scene that's overwhelming. It's in the dark. It's the hidden reality between men and women. As if they were a tableau. As if they were a sculpture. It's as if I were seeing something like the secret of what life is all about. And it's not very pleasant: What it's all about is that men overwhelm women, in some strange way that really isn't very clear, but with signs (the sounds) suggesting that the woman acquiesces by abandoning her inhibitions.

JG: The next one is the Thanksgiving picture on the lawn with the girlfriend.

RLP: Now we get back into the company of the girlfriend immediately, and Father, the man, is at a distance, taking the picture. There's a great deal of excitement, pleasure.

JG: In the company of the girlfriend, the feelings are good in both memories; and they're standing still -- just looking or being looked at. Nothing happens.

RLP: You're in a red hat. The Freudians would love that. You know how they get all lashed up over Red Riding Hood and the menarche. You're in literary publishing; you read *The New York Review of Books*.

Janice: Right. I've read more than enough of that stuff!

RLP: O.K. And the next one?

JG: The next one is the Halloween party as the ghost.

RLP: Just think how much fun the analysts would have with this -- and how far away it would take us if we started doing all kinds of symbolic things with menstruation, and sheets, and bobbing apples!

JG: Well, then, let's just stay Adlerian, and we could say it's all right to fail. I didn't catch the apple, but I liked it anyway. I liked the game. It didn't matter -- to win or lose didn't matter.

RLP: That issue suddenly shows up. I see. Well, winning or losing doesn't matter as long as no one knows who I am. O.K.

Janice: You two guys are something else! (Laughter.)

JG: Well, thanks. (All laugh.) The last one is climbing the tree, and hiding on the other side of the roof.

RLP: Um-hum. Out of sight.

JG: Yes.

RLP: Who was with you in this climbing memory?

Janice: My brother's friends, Ted and John.

RLP: And you're all three hanging on the other side of the roof, and it's Ted's mother who comes out to hang wash?

Janice: Yeah. (Laughter.)

RLP: There're three of you hanging there, being still, so she won't hear you?

Janice: Right.

RLP: Where are you among the three?

Janice: In between Ted and John.

RLP: And the feeling is, what? Excitement or what?

Janice: Excitement. Yeah.

JG: And "good." You still don't get caught. "It was an endurance contest." You didn't know how long you could hold on.

RLP: What is the sense of this memory? In the memory you just stay there, hanging on. I'm enduring to see how long I can hang on -- until what? Either I hang on until then, or what?

Janice: Either she goes in, or...

RLP: Either she goes in, or I lose my grip?

Janice: Yeah. And then, if you fell in the cinders down below, she'd hear you, you know.

RLP: If you'd slide down the roof, there'd be cinders on that side, huh?

Janice: Yeah.

RLP: You'd be giving yourself away?

Janice: Um-hum. You're praying she'll go in so you don't get caught ...'cause you can only hold on so long. And then, she can hear you, you know, your shoes? You know how that old tarpaper was?

RLP: Yeah.

JG: So there's nothing about if I fall I'll get hurt.

Janice: I know I will. I know I'll get hurt.

RLP: But apparently that's not the point, or at least not the worst of it. The point is that you'll "get caught." By her. A woman will see something about you that you don't want her to see.

JG: These are boys, and there's camaraderie, closeness. She's in it together with them.

RLP: Where she shouldn't be. That's the end of the record?

JG: Yes.

RLP: See, the record starts and ends with a kind of hiddenness, a being hidden away. It ends with a different kind of hiddenness from that with which it begins. Was this in the light of day, this last memory?

Janice: Yeah. Um-hum.

RLP: You're still out of sight. How do you know she's still in the yard?

Janice: We see her come out the door.

RLP: How do you know how long she'll be in the yard?

Janice: We don't!

RLP: How will you know when she's gone back in?

Janice: We'll see her go in.

RLP: How will you see her?

Janice: Over the roof.

RLP: Hanging there?

Janice: Yeah. It's like you're hanging like this [indicates].

RLP: Oh. So you're peeking. So you can see her across the top of the roof, but she can't see you.

Janice: You've got it.

RLP: Well, we're on to something important, but I still don't feel that I've "got it" in the sense that I can understand it. There is something about making excitement in your life in some secret way. What is your way of stirring up excitement? And what is your secrecy about? People for whom control is a big issue frequently do it by stirring up emotional storms. It's a form of internal excitement that can't be seen by others.

Janice: What do you mean?

RLP: Some kind of "Whoops!" feeling, something going on beneath a calm exterior. I don't know how you do it. I don't...I don't read this very clearly. What are your thoughts about it? I don't get this very clearly at *all,* in fact. I don't know why I say, "not *very* clearly"!

JG: Since "hiddenness" is one of the themes here, that could explain why they aren't very clear.

RLP: Yeah. The memories are doing the thing they're about. Good point. Let's see: I'm hidden away, carried along. In the very first one, if we were to say it this way, "I'm hidden away, carried along in the stream of events, interested in what's going on...."

JG: She knows what the others are doing: She's looking around, and listening to the parents talk. They don't know what *I'm* doing. And she watches things. "I know more than they know; I'm in on their secrets, but they're not in on mine."

RLP: It's as if I'm a hidden observer, huh? That's one dimension. There's also the dimension of coziness, of safety, behind the seats.

JG: And even safety on the roof. She believes she won't get hurt, and the two boys are with her, one on either side.

RLP: But, there's something there about being careful. In the first one, there's not the danger of being caught; they know I'm back here. It's just that I can listen to them talking. I'm taking in what goes on around me, but no one can see *me.* I'm all tucked away in this little hidey-hole. And the car is in motion: I'm "carried along."

JG: In the second one, about the snake, it seems that she can blunder into something. And then, look what happens if I'm not careful.

RLP: Well, that's one place where she blunders, kicking the can over and stepping on the snake. Then there's the other memory, of blundering upon her parents.

JG: So, "in the dark" may be the common metaphor for not knowing what's going on.

RLP: Yes, at least not knowing enough to act on my own, to be one of the people who makes things happen. In the first memory, I'm all cozy on the pillow, and I'm not acting. The others are in charge. Now the third one is the stillness of the water in the cellar under the house. Just observant, just contemplating, and feeling peaceful.

JG: Both of the memories with the girlfriend are still.

RLP: Water is a classic symbol in mythology, in dreams, and so on. If we were Jungians, what would we make of this?

JG: Water would be the womb.

RLP: And so, by extension, the female principle.

JG: And the snake, the male principle.

RLP: I wonder if we shouldn't take it seriously.

JG: Especially since they're juxtaposed: There's the fear of the snake and the peaceful feeling of the water.

RLP: The male principle here is wild and uncontrollable, and the female principle is serene and bounded. Let's assume there's something to it. What's the use of studying psychology if we don't talk about symbols? (All laugh.) What comes after the water?

JG: Santa Claus.

RLP: Ha! There's the masculine principle embodied in a mythic figure of power and bounty, and I just sit there. I don't know what to do in the face of it.

JG: She just sits there. She...

RLP: What does he do?

Janice: Nothing. What *do* they do? They ask you what you want for Christmas.

RLP: How does he act?

Janice: Not any different than with the other kids.

RLP: Let's be in the memory. How old are you? Three or four? Still a very tiny child.

Janice: In kindergarten.

RLP: A kindergarten child. Now, see through the eyes of the child. See if you can get the memory back. Mother stands back to take a picture. You sit on this strange man's lap.

Janice: I didn't want to go in the first place.

RLP: What are you remembering?

Janice: I usually...this was a department store near where we lived. You walked up the stairs and it was the shoe department. And at Christmastime, Santa was in one part of the shoe department. I liked that department store, but I did not want to go and see Santa Claus.

RLP: All right. Now, what happens? What do you remember?

Janice: Hanging back, dragging back, while she walked me up there. I knew I was going to have to go, whether I wanted to or not.

RLP: Yes?

Janice: And then I felt yucky when I had to get up on his lap.

RLP: How did you do it? How'd you get up there?

Janice: He had to help me.

RLP: How'd he do it?

Janice: He picked me up.

RLP: What was "yucky" about it when he picked you up?

Janice: Oh, I just squirmed to get away! I remember that!

RLP: Tell me everything you see as you squirm. What do you remember?

Janice: He was stronger. I mean, once he'd lifted me up, I landed on his knee, so I couldn't get away.

RLP: And?

Janice: I didn't cry or anything. I knew it wouldn't have done any good. She wanted the picture. (Eyes filling with tears.)

RLP: That's O.K. Just let it come forward. Stay in the memory. So? You land on his knee. You know you can't get away. He holds you there. He's stronger. It doesn't make any difference: There's no need to struggle.... What are you remembering?

Janice: That once I relaxed, I felt O.K.

RLP: It's yielding. It's the yielding. And then, some sense of relief.

Janice: Yes. That's how I've felt. I would say that's the basic part of how I relate to most men. (Tears.)

RLP: Can you tell us about that?

Janice: I don't want to.

RLP: What comes to mind instead?

Janice: You know I was thinking about that back when I was telling you about my mother originally, back a few sessions ago, when you were recording all this stuff. I didn't like seeing him (Father) in the dominant position. That frightened me, I can remember. But I never feel comfortable when I'm involved sexually myself any place but underneath. You know. What do they call that position?

JG: The missionary position.

Janice: Yeah.

JG: Well, that's a hidden position. Other ways, you're exposed.

Janice: (Laughter.) Yeah. I was thinking that. I'm getting into this too much! (Laughter.) I was thinking...

RLP: Well, how much can you get into it? It's your life.

Janice: Yes, I know. But I don't even want to think about it. Anyway...I'm like that. That's a big thing for me. It took a lot of years before I was willing to play around with that at all. Like, I'm vulnerable if I'm on top, you know?

RLP: To what?

Janice: I don't know. To getting hurt. To not being in control.

RLP: How are you in control when you're supine?

Janice: (Laughter.) I don't know. I can't get hurt as much. That's how I feel. I can just curl up and not get hurt as much.

RLP: Just submit, eh?

Janice: Yeah, and not be as actively involved, so then, if it turns out bad, I won't be as involved in the first place, you know what I mean? (Laughter.) I mean, it wasn't my responsibility, because I never got involved at all. Yeah. I'm not responsible.

RLP: No, you're not. You're only enduring. As with Santa Claus. The men subdue the women. When Santa holds you, you don't act.... What was that verb you liked?

JG: Yield.

RLP: Yes. You don't act; you yield. That's the whole thing: The man acts, the woman yields.

Janice: Yes. Somehow that's the whole thing. The man acts, the woman yields.

RLP: And then there's a release of tension. Like "falling off the roof." Do you know what that means?

Janice: Falling off the roof? (Laughs.)

RLP: It's old-fashioned slang. A sort of secret code among the girls, in the old days.

Janice: Yeah. (Long laughter.) It's your period! (More laughter.)

RLP: (With the laughter.) That's right. Give *some* credit to the Freudians! Their fascination with Red Riding Hood isn't *all* misplaced! Your first period came when you were about nine years old. (Quietly.) That's how old you are in the story of being on the roof. Hanging on, among the boys, wondering how much longer you can get away with it. That's the feeling you had when you were in college, and that's the feeling you had when you first came to see us. That's what you said.

Janice: (Now very serious, and calm.) That's true.

RLP: And we know that when you were in college at UMass [University of Massachusetts] you had an experience that was hard for you. You fell in love, and defied your religious training by active sexual involvement with the man. More, you defied the standards of your community by publicly choosing a man of another religion and nationality. When you became pregnant he abandoned you, and you had to accept all the responsibility of the affair without anyone to help you. You gave the child up for adoption, and you have felt the loss of that child ever since. Is all that a fair summary of what you have told us?

Janice: Yes. It's all true.

RLP: And you swore that you'd never let yourself be put into that kind of a position again. And you've played a much more careful part, making your husband "responsible" for what happens, in the privacy of your bed, and in the "big decisions" of your life, while at the same time pursuing your profession, and attaining a position of some eminence in publishing without letting it intrude upon the privacy of your family life. Right?

Janice: You're right on. It's amazing.

RLP: It's only what you have told us. And now, the crisis that brings you to see us is connected to your son (the oldest "known," but not the oldest of your children) who has just turned twelve years old.

Janice: (Crying.) I don't get it. What's the connection?

RLP: What happens to boys when they turn twelve?

Janice: What do you mean? (Laughs.)

RLP: Come on. (Both laugh.) You know better than that! I'll give you a hint: What happens to boys at twelve that happened to you when you were nine?

Janice: (Laughter.) Oh, gosh. You want me to say, "puberty"?

RLP: I don't want you to say anything. I just want you to see what you have allowed us to see. Until now you could "protect" your son from all harm, or at least console yourself with the idea that you might do so, that it wouldn't be beyond you. You could even share the exuberance of his boyhood with him: Your adventure on the buses last week is an example.

Janice: Yeah. That was a blast.

RLP: Exactly. It's exciting to play at staying in childhood, prolonging the carefree fun of it, seeing how long you can "hang on" to it with him. But the game is up. He's becoming a man, and you can't control the energies that are coming up in him now, and that will take him away from you sooner rather than later -- at least if all goes well!

Janice: (Crying.) I know. And I don't want to stop him. I know that's nuts.

RLP: Exactly. That's nuts. To want to keep a growing boy underfoot! That's why you experienced your anxiety the way you did. Life was insisting that you go forward with your son's maturity, and you didn't want to go. You expected it to ask more of you than you could handle. How could you keep up your fiction of passive little woman versus active big man, and still keep an eye on your growing son, and try to control his activities?

Janice: A tall order, huh?

RLP: And how. But an even taller one, a much harder task, was to find a way to maintain your protective, controlling management of your little boy when you knew that was nuts, as you put it. That's why you couldn't put it into words. You knew that your anxiety had something to do with your son; you knew that it was somehow connected to your college experience, or, as you put it, to your guilt; and you knew that it was somehow all snarled up in your private notions about masculine and feminine. All you could feel was the embarrassment of it, as if you, a mere woman were trying to control your son, a more and more powerful man.

Janice: Whew! You two guys are too much. I feel all undressed, and at the same time sort of relieved! I can't get my feelings straight. How did I get into this mess?

JG: We're finding that out: How you learned what you learned, how you rehearsed your way of being the way you are, how it's worked for you until now, and what it costs you to keep it up.

Janice: That's a lot to sort out.

RLP: You can do it. The key is in seeing that it's a way. It's not a necessity. It's a way that you worked out. Apparently the purpose at the center of it was to find a position among others in which you could be innocent, and they would be responsible. To grow up is to learn that there ain't no such place!

Janice: I think I'm getting it.

RLP: O.K. Then let's read these memories as if they were little fables or parables, little stories each of which has a moral, and see if we can get the pattern of their morals into clear statements. Then, if our statements make any sense, we'll see whether it's useful to Janice, whether you can use it to begin reconsidering things. O.K.?

Janice: O.K.

[Note: The second therapist then dictated two summaries, "The Pattern of Basic Convictions" and "The Interfering Ideas," with Janice listening as the first therapist wrote the summaries down for later typing. Note that these summaries appear in Chapter 14 (pp. 270, 275-276), where Janice's early recollections serve to illustrate our discussion of how these final summaries of the Life-Style Assessment process are composed.]

Conclusion

With the conclusion of Chapter 11, we also reach the end of Part III, in which we have addressed the process of reviewing and interpreting family material and early recollections.

The final task in both the Initial Interview and Life-Style Assessment procedures is the presentation of summaries of the material to the client. Part IV, "Summations of Understanding," focuses on methods for the development and composition of these summary statements.

PART IV: SUMMATIONS OF UNDERSTANDING

The [life-style] in its entirety can be kept intact only if the patient succeeds in withdrawing it from his own criticism and understanding.... [We] must grasp the special structure and development of that individual life with such accuracy, and express it with such lucidity, that the patient knows he is plainly understood and recognizes his own mistake.

Alfred Adler (pp. 334-335)

INTRODUCTION TO PART IV

This final section of our text is devoted to the Initial Interview and Life-Style Assessment summaries. The summaries are composed in the client's presence by the second therapist at the conclusion of each review session, as oral statements that the first therapist takes down in a verbatim written record for later transcription. Such oral summations are also possible for therapists working alone, who can record the summary statements on audiotape. It is usually deeply affecting and valuable to the client to hear the summary of all that has gone before spoken aloud, on the spot. In the words of one client, "When I was listening, I was mesmerized. Then I felt profound relief. I don't know.... I just thought, 'My story makes some kind of sense...not only to me, but also to them, to others.'"

The direct presentation of the summaries to the client follows the model taught by Dreikurs, who pioneered the method, and who insisted that anyone could learn how to do it.

Granted Dreikurs's certainty that anyone can learn how to do it, the procedure continues to give pause to many otherwise self-confident clinicians. Their hesitation seems to be based on an impression either that summaries are intuitive, even oracular utterances, issuing out of a depth of inspiration inaccessible to the uninitiated; or that they are spontaneous, following no form, and so requiring no preparation.

Part IV is designed to disabuse readers of this impression by demonstrating that, on the contrary, summaries are disciplined, studied compositions resting upon a structure and employing a method that can be mastered, a method whose content and cogency relies not so much upon oracular wisdom or quick wits as upon attention.

The method presented here for composing summaries depends for its success upon its use by the clinician as a frame of reference borne in mind throughout each review session for assessing information, and for considering how each item fits into the pattern of a coherent, comprehensible whole. Adler is clear about the challenge:

> The foremost task of Individual Psychology is to prove this unity in each individual -- in his thinking, feeling, and act-

> ing, in his so-called conscious and unconscious, in every expression of his personality (p. 175).

We believe that the ability to locate this unity, and to summarize the themes of a self-consistent life-style in a way that is useful and encouraging to the client, is within the scope of every empathic, well-educated, and professional counselor's competence.

The methods we use in our practice and recommend in this text have been refined over many years with many different people. That does not mean that we claim our way to be the only or the right way to "prove [the] unity [of] each individual." Once practiced in the art and science of *Menschenkenntnis* each therapist will develop a technique, a format, and a vocabulary consistent with the unity of his or her own style.

Chapter 12: IMPRESSIONS DERIVED FROM THE INITIAL INTERVIEW

The material in this chapter refers to page nine of the *IPCW*, and is based upon data gathered in the Initial Interview inquiry by the first therapist, and upon whatever further information emerges in the discussion between the client and the two therapists during the review and interpretation of the data.

The text of this chapter is divided into several sections. First is a list of topics to consider in the composition of a summary. Following this is a precis of the "Case of Joan." (See Chapter 5 for a transcript of a complete Initial Interview.) After the precis, the "Summary of Impressions derived from the Initial Interview" is presented and analyzed. This analysis illustrates the application of our topics in a single case; "The Case of Peter" is similarly presented and analyzed. Two additional cases are presented more briefly. (For these the data are presented in precis, followed by the "Summary of Impressions" for each case.)

The topics listed below for possible inclusion in a summary do not appear in an order of priority, nor is the sequence of topics to be regarded as ordained. Priority and sequence are questions of emphasis and style arising from each therapist's clinical judgment and sense of language. Readers should bear in mind that not every summary will address all topics, some of which will be relevant and useful in one case and not in another.

Topics to Consider for a Summary of the Initial Interview

1. The presenting problem
2. Onset and history
3. Exogenous factor(s)
4. Relevance of the big numbers to the client's complaint
5. Childhood rehearsal of place, especially as it may be limiting the client's success in dealing with the current problem

6. Masculine and feminine guiding lines bearing upon the client's faulty perception of self and others (convictions, expectations, ambitions, consequences)

7. The client's resources for meeting the difficulty; examples

8. Reinterpretation of the complaint (the client's role; the roles of others)

9. The task to be addressed

The Case of Joan

Joan is a competent forty-three-year-old sales representative for a company supplying linens to hotels and institutions. She came to the Initial Interview with two issues: First, she was concerned about her deteriorating relationship with her boss; she said he was "picking on" her and criticizing her, in spite of her successes with the company over many years, and that he seemed to have made an alliance recently with another woman staff member, displacing Joan as his favorite. Second, three months before our meeting she had learned that her husband of twenty-three years had "fondled" their oldest daughter, Jennie, aged seventeen. Joan learned about her husband's misbehavior from Jennie's boyfriend when the two young people attempted to elope. The boyfriend stated that he had tried to marry Jennie without the family's knowledge only because he wanted to get Jennie away from her father. A confrontation with the husband ensued. After first denying the activity, and then attempting to blame it on his daughter ("she enticed me"), the husband admitted it and has subsequently been in counseling. "My daughter has forgiven him, but I can't," Joan says. "I cry all the time, and can't feel close to him any more." She feels, further, that she let her daughter down by not realizing what was going on. She feels betrayed both by her husband and by her boss.

SUMMARY OF IMPRESSIONS DERIVED FROM THE INITIAL INTERVIEW

Joan presents herself as a woman who has been waking up out of a long sleep over the last three months, aroused by a sense of having been betrayed by the men in her life. Until now she has seen herself as a weak woman in a world of strong men. Her present confusion arises because she has now begun to see herself as a strong woman in a world in which there are many weak men.

Because until now, owing to her childhood training with a powerful father and an ineffectual mother, she has made the mistake of thinking that her strength could only be real if it were sustained by, approved of, and recognized and rewarded by a man, she has been kept from a clear awareness of it.

Her father, her husband, and her boss have been operating as if they were intimidated by the very idea of the possibility of a competent woman's domination (perhaps because each of them leaned on women and counted on them for comfort and support).

Her disillusionment over her husband's misconduct with their daughter, Jennie, has helped to open her eyes, and the current situation with her boss is helping to open them wider.

She has an enormous advantage in that she is only forty-three years of age, and no matter what happens now, she has already seen worse; and in that, by the time she is forty-five (the age Mother was when Father left Mother), Joan will have had the opportunity to decide what she wants in life, and will have acted to secure it.

Furthermore, she has already made a choice to discover how much she can do as one of the New Women in a New World, and she can take advantage of the other great advantage she enjoys as a result of her long training in cultivating an interest in the interests of others.

With her eyes open, she can see that her elevation of men into the position of superiority is a diminishment of herself as a woman; and further, that it places an intolerable burden on the men in her life, who must struggle to live up to her exaggerated expectations of them, and so are precluded from having an equal, caring relationship with her.

Her task now is to get a clear understanding that ideas of "strength" and "weakness" are fictions, and to see more clearly that her effectiveness is a function of choice (not of strength or gender), of choosing and refusing what she will do in any situation, including what she will think about it and how she will feel about it.

ANALYSIS AND NOTES: *The "Summary of Impressions" in the Case of Joan*

Topic 1. *The presenting problem*

State the problem clearly, using the client's own language wherever it may be appropriate. Joan's presenting problem is stated in paragraph one:

> [Joan has been] aroused by a sense of having been betrayed by the men in her life.... Her present confusion arises because she has now begun to see herself as a strong woman in a world in which there are many weak men.

Topic 2. *Onset and history*

It is helpful to provide a sense of the temporal context in which the client has become aware of the difficulty. Some features of this context may be lifelong; others may reach back only through a brief period to a recent moment of crisis.

Sometimes there is a combination, as represented in the following opening sentence of a summary done for another woman: "Portia presents herself at the end of a period of discouragement going back at least three years, in some ways nine years, and probably in some other ways, fifty-two years." This was a person who had experienced severe setbacks three years before and nine years before, and who had said, during the inquiry, "I've always felt out of place."

About Joan, we state in paragraph one:

> Joan presents herself as a woman who has been waking up out of a long sleep over the last three months.

Topic 3. *Exogenous factor(s)*

These are the factors that arise outside the scope of the person's rehearsed style, and therefore may present a challenge for which the person is unprepared. The resulting crisis is a faltering, a "breakdown" of the style, which is now revealed as ineffective. (If this revelation is sudden enough, and far reaching, a radical loss of orientation can result, and the person may be described as suffering a nervous breakdown, or even a psychotic break.) Here, in paragraph four, we tried to put a positive meaning on Joan's disorientation:

> Her disillusionment over her husband's misconduct with their daughter, Jennie, has helped to open her eyes, and the current situation with her boss is helping to open them wider.

Topic 4. *Relevance of the big numbers to the client's complaint*

During the review and interpretations, the therapists and the client note and consider any relation between the current experience of difficulty and the client's privately held expectations regarding age. We have referred to these temporal features of the individual's phenomenological field as the big numbers. These measures, drawn in years, relate to events or turning points in the lives of the parents. They are attended to indirectly and at low levels of awareness, sometimes even unconsciously, as features of the gender guiding lines. It is important to recognize that meanings given to these numbers are always fictional, even when they may coincide with numbers or ages whose meanings are generally agreed upon in the culture (such as, "Life begins at forty"). In Joan's case there was a clear connection between her expectations regarding her age and her feminine guiding line. Here is how we noted it, in paragraph five:

> She has an enormous advantage in that she is only forty-three years of age, and no matter what happens now, she has already seen worse; and in that, by the time she is forty-five (the age Mother was when Father left Mother), Joan will have had the opportunity to decide what she wants in life, and will have acted to secure it.

Encouragement is the *sine qua non* of all effective psychotherapy or counseling. It has at least as important a place in the work of the initial assessment as it does in any subsequent transactions. We therefore seize every opportunity the client gives us to introduce it at the beginning of our work together. For example, by stating, as we did in the above phrase, that Joan will have her life sorted out as she wants it, and that she will do so by experiencing herself as a chooser and an actor within a short period of time, we have lent support, by rewording it, to an expectation she had confided in us. Then, by recording it as a prediction, we added to its force, and to her confidence in it.

Topic 5. *Childhood rehearsal of place, especially as it may be limiting the client's success in dealing with the current problem*

Topic 6. *Masculine and feminine guiding lines bearing upon the client's faulty perception of self and others (convictions, expectations, ambitions, consequences)*

References to these two topics are intertwined in Joan's summary because her training and self-training were shaped around her deference to the perceived power of the man (her masculine guiding line), and her dismissal of Mother as "ineffectual" (her feminine guiding line).

Her convictions regarding gender therefore appear to be that men are indisputably powerful while women are inherently weak. Her consequent expectation, governing her own movement in life as well as her sense of what she can expect from others of both sexes, is that women are coming from behind and are precluded from catching up to the men, no matter what their talent, brains, and effort; while men are dominant, with or without talent, brains, or effort. So, paragraph one:

> Until now she has seen herself as a weak woman in a world of strong men.

The ambition that flows out of these convictions and expectations was formed at an early age: To be effective, she must be under the protection of a man. So, paragraph two:

> Because until now, owing to her childhood training with a powerful father and an ineffectual mother, she has made the mistake of thinking that her strength could only be real if it were sustained by, approved of, and recognized and rewarded by a man, she has been kept from a clear awareness of it.

In paragraph seven, we draw Joan's attention to the consequences of these convictions, expectations, and ambitions, as to something she is now free to ponder and understand, and in doing so we begin to make it more difficult for her to proceed in innocence, should she persist in her erroneous way of thinking:

> With her eyes open, she can see that her elevation of men into the position of superiority is a diminishment of herself as a woman; and further, that it places an intolerable burden on the men in her life, who must struggle to live up to her exaggerated expectations of them, and so are precluded from having an equal, caring relationship with her.

Topic 7. *The client's resources for meeting the difficulty; examples*

Part of the responsibility of the therapist is to aid the client in recognizing and developing useful resources. In a time of crisis the life-style, which until now has enabled an acceptable degree of successful adaptation, is revealed as being inadequate to the demands of the situation. Clients complain, "I don't know what to do! I can't cope!" Even so, everyone has some resources of courage, intellect, or other capacities which may be hidden from awareness or not clearly understood and valued, especially in a time of disorientation. Two of Joan's resources, which can serve her in her present difficulty, are brought directly to her attention in paragraph six:

> She has already made a choice to discover how much she can do as one of the New Women in a New World, and she can take advantage of the other great advantage she enjoys as a result of her long training in cultivating an interest in the interests of others.

Joan was encouraged by the thought that entering a career and making a success of it were choices she had made, and that the courage with which she had met the challenge of occupation was available to her for meeting the current challenge. She had not appreciated the significance of this accomplishment, not having seen it as an index of courage and determination. Further, she had not experienced her success as a salesperson as demonstrating her "interest in the interests of others," though when it was mentioned she immediately recognized what we meant. She had not valued this in herself, and so had not realized how it might assist her now in offering empathy and friendship to her ashamed and unhappy husband.

Topic 8. *Reinterpretation of the complaint (the client's role; the roles of others)*

It was important for Joan to see her role in the difficulty, as set forth in paragraph seven (her elevation of men, and the consequent burden she placed on them). It was also important for her to consider how the men in her life might be perceiving her (and other women) and how an awareness of those perceptions could help her to understand their movement, especially in displays of power and dominance (father toward mother; husband toward Jennie). "Could it be," we asked, "that these men, who clearly depend on the women to take care of them and their interests, are fearful that unless they act this way they might be subject, at best, to the loss of the women's respect and service; and, at worst, to the power and domination of the more capable women?" This idea is recorded in paragraph three:

> Her father, her husband, and her boss have been operating as if they were intimidated by the very idea of the possibility of a competent woman's domination (perhaps because each of them leaned on women and counted on them for comfort and support).

Topic 9. *The task to be addressed*

Typically the summary closes with a statement of the task needing to be addressed by the client. In paragraph eight we set forth the two major ideas which she will have to reconsider: Her fictions of strength and weakness, and her faulty convictions of being unable to act effectively on her own:

> Her task now is to get a clear understanding that ideas of "strength" and "weakness" are fictions, and to see more clearly that her effectiveness is a function of choice (not of strength or gender), of choosing and refusing what she will do in any situation, including what she will think about it and how she will feel about it.

The Case of Peter

Peter is a brilliant thirty-six-year-old public relations consultant. He came to the office in the aftermath of a divorce, after twelve years of marriage. It had been the first marriage both for him and his wife; they had adopted two children, girls now six and eight years old, after they learned that his wife was unable to conceive. Peter's mother is living and in good health. Father died at the age of thirty-seven when Peter was ten years old. When Peter was eleven years old his older sister had a nervous breakdown, and has been in institutions off and on ever since. Before these difficulties he had been the baby of the family. As he put it, "At ten I became the man of the family, and, at eleven, I had to fill the place of both of the children as far as my mother was concerned." Peter's wife initiated the divorce after disclosing to him that she had been having an affair with his best friend for a year and now wanted to marry the other man. At the time of our first interview, the former wife and former best friend had been married for six months. Peter had been depressed during all of that period, and was seeing a psychiatrist who medicated him. "It was some help, but it didn't get to the trouble, and I don't feel any better." Prior to the start of his wife's affair, Peter had suffered a business failure when another "friend" absconded with the funds of their partnership, leaving Peter with numerous financial obligations which required all of his assets to repay. He has regained his financial position and is now once more a wealthy man. His present employer says that his job is secure "no matter what you have to do to get well." His circle of friendships is limited to married couples, friends from his marriage who "have stuck by me." He is devoted to his children and lets nothing interfere with his visitation rights. After eighteen months of job demands, child care, and commuting to and from his apartment, his place of work, and his children's primary residence, he is overextended, lonely, and exhausted.

SUMMARY OF IMPRESSIONS DERIVED FROM THE INITIAL INTERVIEW

Peter presents himself at a time in his life when the question of his vulnerability to being used and abused is uppermost in his mind. He is dimly aware of an urgency to settle this issue while he still has time, because his father died of heart trouble at the age of thirty-seven, just one year older than Peter's present age, and Peter's heart is troubled.

He knows himself to be devoted to doing whatever is necessary for anyone whom he allows to count upon him, as he did for Mother after Father's death, as he has done for his sister since she was fifteen years old (when she returned to the family after her first stay in the hospital), and as he did for his creditors at the time of his business partner's betrayal. In all these works he is uncomplaining, and it is by these works that he recognizes himself as a Good Man.

He is not clear about his hidden expectation that his goodness will be rewarded by the gratitude and adoration of others, and that he will earn this reward for his fidelity in the face of difficulty. He maintains this expectation in a kind of secret, one-sided contract with life, as if he hoped that by keeping it secret the other side would feel uncoerced in entering into it, seeing his virtue as irresistible, and wanting to do its part in the bargain without knowing that there is a bargain.

His version of the contract goes something like this: If I am good I will get what I deserve. If I demand what I deserve, I will no longer be good. Therefore, I must not demand what I deserve, because then I would no longer deserve it. When I do not get what I deserve, the only thing left open to me is to look around for ways to be even more good, to redouble my efforts, and gently to reproach the others for their failure to keep their part in the bargain by confronting them with my undeserved sadness.

The brilliance and ingenuity so prized by his professional colleagues (brought to bear earlier to solve problems surrounding the collapse of his private business venture) will assist him in solving the riddle of his goodness. He will begin to see that goodness is only good when it can be measured in terms of usefulness, and that it is no longer useful for him to suffer.

He is beginning to realize that he has struck a bad bargain, and may decide to end an interpretation and a way of life that has been destructive for him. He may decide to do that now, beginning to live a life of honest self-assertion at about the same age his father was when Father's life ended.

ANALYSIS AND NOTES: *The "Summary of Impressions" in The Case of Peter*

Topic 1. *The presenting problem*

Peter came to see us because of a depression that had been medicated but not remedied. In the course of the discussion we discovered with Peter that he felt overworked in the service of others and then mistreated by them. We therefore defined the presenting problem as vulnerability (expressed in depression) in paragraph one:

> Peter presents himself at a time in his life when the question of his vulnerability to being used and abused is uppermost in his mind.

Topic 2. *Onset and history*

Peter's story revealed a pattern characterizing his style from age ten, the time when his father died, and coalescing at age eleven when his sister defaulted, only one year after the death of her favored parent. In this period he moved from the position of baby to that of Man, and from one of the children requiring Mother's attention to the central position in Mother's life. From this point on he took up his position as the one who could be counted on. His motto could be, "I stay the course." Paragraph two states:

> He knows himself to be devoted to doing whatever is necessary for anyone whom he allows to count upon him, as he did for Mother after Father's death, as he has done for his sister since she was fifteen years old (when she returned to the family after her first stay in the hospital), and as he did for his creditors at the time of his business partner's betrayal.

Topic 3. *Exogenous factor(s)*

The current crisis in Peter's life has been facing him for about a year. It was occasioned by the end of his marriage, following upon the simultaneous betrayals he suffered at the hands of his wife and his best friend who, six months prior to our first meeting, had married each other. By the time of this Initial Interview, it had become clear to Peter that his former wife's marriage was stable, and that she would not be coming back to him. All hope of his reconstituting his family on its prior foundations had ended. Paragraph one encompasses this awareness in its last phrase, "...and Peter's heart is troubled." (The story of the events needed no further rehearsal.)

Topic 4. *Relevance of the big numbers to the client's complaint*

An awareness of age as it may be believed to reflect recapitulation along the gender guiding lines is worth exploring in any time of crisis as a source of reorientation for a disoriented person. Paragraph one states these connections:

> He is also dimly aware of an urgency to settle this issue [his vulnerability to abuse by others] while he still has time, because his father died of heart trouble at the age of thirty-seven, just one year older than Peter's present age, and Peter's heart is troubled.

Topic 5. *Childhood rehearsal of place, especially as it may be limiting the client's success in dealing with the current problem*

Peter made a place as the Good Baby, Good Child, and Good Man. There are many Good Boys who become Good Men, but he would be the Best of the Good. As in paragraph two:

> In all these works [caring for Mother, Sister, creditors] he is uncomplaining, and it is by these works that he recognizes himself as a Good Man.

In order to maintain the place of the Good Man, Peter cannot consider his part in bringing about the difficulties he faces in his life. Were he to see the overreaching and condescension in his style, he would have to see his un-goodness, losing his Good Man's innocence. And so the deal he has made with life must remain hidden.

Topic 6. *Masculine and feminine guiding lines bearing upon the client's faulty perceptions of self and others (convictions, expectations, ambitions, consequences)*

As we discussed with Peter (and as alluded to in the paragraph above), the task he has set for himself in life is in line with a picture of a man who overcomes difficulties at any cost; the task he has assigned to the others (especially women) is to be grateful and to admire him for these efforts. These ideas are expressed in paragraph three:

> He is not clear about his hidden expectation that his goodness will be rewarded by the gratitude and adoration of others, and that he will earn this reward for his fidelity in the face of difficulty. He maintains this expectation in a kind of secret, one-sided contract with life, as if he hoped that by keeping it secret the other side would feel uncoerced in entering into it, seeing his virtue as irresistible, and wanting to do its part in the bargain without knowing that there is a bargain.

Because roles defined in this way ("I will be good and never falter; you will admire me, and give me whatever I want") are untenable in common-sense social transactions, Peter's privately defined contract has remained un-understood by him; and, since goodness is by definition unassailable, his mischief has remained un-understood by others, even when they have chafed under the arrangement. Until now, the bargain has been inaccessible to critical evaluation, standing unseen in the way of Peter's ability to reorient himself. He could, therefore, only continue doing what he knew how to do.

Topic 7. *The client's resources for meeting the difficulty; examples*

Paragraph five calls upon qualities that are available to Peter in sorting out his (one-sided) bargain with life:

> The brilliance and ingenuity so prized by his professional colleagues (brought to bear earlier to solve problems

surrounding the collapse of his private business venture) will assist him in solving the riddle of his goodness.

Topic 8. *Reinterpretation of the complaint (the client's role; the roles of others)*

The problem he presented was depression; he came to see that the depression was a symptom of what we had discovered together, namely, his tacit (and one-sided, secret) agreement with life, as we state it in paragraph four:

> His version of the contract goes something like this: If I am good I will get what I deserve. If I demand what I deserve, I will no longer be good. Therefore, I must not demand what I deserve, because then I would no longer deserve it. When I do not get what I deserve, the only thing left open to me is to look around for ways to be even more good, to redouble my efforts, and gently to reproach the others for their failure to keep their part in the bargain by confronting them with my undeserved sadness.

During the review and interpretations of the Initial Interview data, Peter and the two therapists discussed the idea that his depressive symptoms seemed to arise, ultimately, from an old conviction that he had been a boy sent (unfairly) to do a man's work. It was (we considered) also possible for him to believe that life had presented him with opportunities to take his place as a man (escaping the position of baby) and that he had readily grasped this challenge.

In paragraph six, we acknowledge his willingness to change the bargain he has made with life:

> He is beginning to realize that he has struck a bad bargain, and may decide to end an interpretation and a way of life that has been destructive for him.

Topic 9. *The task to be addressed*

In paragraphs five and six, we identify his tasks, noted above, and express our confidence that:

> He will begin to see that goodness is only good when it can be measured in terms of usefulness, and that it is no longer useful for him to suffer.

The final paragraph refers once again to his father, in order to encourage him to think of the timeliness of his present opportunity:

> He...may decide to [end the bargain] now, beginning to live a life of honest self assertion at about the same age his father was when Father's life ended.

[Note: We close this chapter with a precis of data and "The Summary of Impressions Derived from the Initial Interview" in "The Case of Lillian" and "The Case of Bill."]

The Case of Lillian

Lillian is twenty-three years old, currently between jobs. Since graduating from college, she has worked for an investment firm and for an arts organization. In neither of these jobs did she "catch fire," though her bosses and colleagues let her know that they liked her work and wanted her to stay. Father is a successful entrepreneur, and mother is a successful sculptor and teacher of sculpture. Her only sibling, a brother two years older, is an architect who has just been asked to join a firm with an international reputation. She was Father's favorite, and was brought up by him to "see the world through rose-colored glasses. He said I could be anything I wanted to be." Lillian has been depressed for two months, since going to her home town for the Christmas holidays. "I saw all my friends, and they wanted to know what I was doing with my life." About her goals, she said, "I want to get out there and work, but part of me says I want it handed to me on a silver platter." She feels that her "circle" wonders why she isn't married, doesn't even have a suitable man in her life, doesn't have a prestigious job, and doesn't even seem to have an "important" group of friends and activities in her new setting. She says that her friends seem to resent and envy her money, looks, and talents. "With all I've got going for me, I should be able to do anything. I should be a saint! But I feel so undeserving. I should do more. I shouldn't have any problems. I've become a recluse. All I do is go to the movies and eat." She says that on the first impression people enjoy her and find her personable. Over time, "They find I'm the least confident of people." Father keeps telling her, "It's going to be fine." She has doubts. "I try really hard, and I can't even remember what it feels like to feel successful."

SUMMARY OF IMPRESSIONS DERIVED FROM THE INITIAL INTERVIEW

Lillian presents herself as a young woman burdened with a combination of grand ambitions mixed with a more limited supply of self-confidence.

As the second child of ambitious parents, and the only girl, she appears to have grown up with a sense of being special, and with a feeling of being less than whatever it is she thinks is expected of her.

Her enjoyment of her advantages is undermined by her exaggerated standards of fairness ("with all I've got going for me, I should be able to do anything"), and her sense of having to do something spectacular in order to justify the encouragement given to her and the support she receives.

Her creativity adds to her burden, since it increases the likelihood of her being seen as special, and therefore increases her sense of obligation to achieve in special ways, to live up, to catch up, and to be up.

The depressive reaction since last December appears to have come at a time of restlessness, when she sensed herself to be out of the line of movement, and in some ways even backtracking to a position of financial dependence on her parents.

Her training as the second born in this family of achievers may have predisposed her to restlessness, overambition, and a feeling of coming from behind in a field of thoroughbreds. This would make her current situation all the more onerous for her, leaving her vulnerable to a kind of pessimism about being able to get on with things soon enough and well enough to "deserve" the confidence of her family and her friends.

All these difficulties can be seen as advantages. Her task is to redefine her exaggerated ambitions, and to understand her "guilt" of being undeserving as an unwillingness to rest with what she has long enough to discover what would happen if she were to get on with what she can do with it.

The Case of Bill

Bill is a man of twenty-eight who has been disoriented in life since an automobile accident two years before disabled him in such a way as to preclude his continuing in his chosen profession as a musician. (He had fallen asleep at the wheel during a long, soul-searching drive he took to ponder whether to defy his father's advice to keep music an avocation while pursuing a career in business more likely to secure an ample income.) He is on leave of absence from his present employer, a real estate development firm, because of continuing physical problems, this time a severe rash. Bill's physicians told him that the rash has no discernible physical basis and suggested that he see a psychologist. Because the accident was disfiguring, Bill also brings up his sense that "I can't give myself to anyone any more. I can't reach out. People won't accept me." He contrasts his present situation with his boyhood: "I was a sunny child; always had a smile on my face. I didn't talk about my problems; just the good stuff." He says, "I don't shove my problems off on others" as an adult. Recently his girlfriend of several years ended the relationship. "I honestly think it was because I couldn't talk about my problems. I kept it all inside. I just couldn't marry her. It wasn't fair to her. I don't know what is going on in my life. How could I ask her to get into such a mess?"

SUMMARY OF IMPRESSIONS DERIVED FROM THE INITIAL INTERVIEW

Bill presents himself at the end of a long period of disorientation which began at the time of his accident. Note: Not *since* the time of his accident, but *at* the time. His sense of himself had, until then, been associated with his musical ability and his successful career in music; and his desire to follow the line of this career in the life of a professional musician seemed to require of him that he abandon his role as the "sunny child" in his family, and to assert his desires in opposition to his father's "good advice"; it therefore appears that he began, at that time, a struggle to reorient himself in a new role.

His consequent sense of disorientation contributed to the recent ending of a long love affair, in that he hesitated to include another person in his uncertainties. His unhappiness in the world of real estate adds to his lack of clarity about the next step in his life.

Until now he has been able to preoccupy himself with his skin disorder, and his search for a medical solution. That he is now willing to reconsider the purpose and function this disorder may serve in his life is already a sign of optimism, and of his courage.

As the baby of his family, Bill enjoyed a place of prominence. All that was required of him was to be a source of joy. The bright side of this assignment was the pleasure he could take in bringing pleasure to others; the dark side was that he felt disallowed from having any desires and preferences of his own, much less any problems or complaints. He had no training, therefore, for the forthright confronting and solving of problems with the cooperation and interest of others. He grew up with an uneasy feeling that if he admitted to any difficulties, his special place would be lost to him.

The maintenance of the rash may make it possible for Bill to delay addressing his current distress over the need to set a career path for himself. It may be that he thinks that "until this problem is solved, I can't get on to anything else," such as the pain of his loneliness or the uncongeniality of his occupational opportunities.

At the age of twenty-eight, Bill is entitled to reconsider his training for solitary problem solving, and to see it as an exaggeration of normal self-reliance and responsibility. Since he took this on at an early age, he will have to learn all over again how to accept the invitation extended by his family and friends, and how to reorient himself around the idea of accepting their love, care, and willingness to struggle by his side. It is Bill's self-imposed solitary confinement that is disfiguring, not his physical "confinement," and he can release himself from it in an acceptance of his solidarity with others.

Conclusion

In Chapter 12 we have discussed topics to consider in the composition of an Initial Interview summary, and have clarified the intent of each of the suggested topics, with illustrations from cases.

In our practice the Initial Interview often serves as a form of brief psychotherapy. A number of clients are satisfied with what we uncover together here, and decide that further therapy would not be appropriate or useful to them at this time in their lives. We recommend at least a single session to follow up on the things discussed in the Initial Interview. Most agree, and come in again the following week. Others do not, though we may hear from some of them again after as much as a year or more has passed. Sometimes it is only after a series of crises (such as the one that led to the Initial Interview) that a person is prepared to enter into the psycho-clarity process on a continuing and disciplined basis of reconsideration.

"An individual's life-style is developed as his own unique manner of coping with life's problems, according to the way he feels and sees them in his particular picture of the world," Adler wrote (1979, p. 111). When the life-style no longer serves to cope, that is, when a person's way of feeling and seeing is no longer clearly related to solving life's problems, the remainder of the Life-Style Assessment may seem more clearly advisable, and we can return to it then.

In the next chapter we turn to that part of Life-Style Assessment in which we develop the "Summary of the Family Constellation."

Chapter 13: SUMMARY OF THE FAMILY CONSTELLATION

Adler (1970, p. 80) used the term "family constellation" to designate the system of relationships in which self-awareness develops. This system includes and is maintained by oneself, one's parents and siblings, and any others living in the household of the family of origin (or otherwise recognized as part of its extension). The term represents the family by analogy to a constellation in astronomy: A group of bodies, each of which moves and has a place in relation to the movement and places of the others.

Following Adler, Dreikurs (1967) wrote:

> A clear formulation of a person's life-style can be obtained through investigation of his family constellation, which is a sociogram of the group at home during his formative years.
>
> This investigation reveals [the individual's] field of early experiences, the circumstances under which he developed his personal perspectives and biases, his concepts and convictions about himself and others, his fundamental attitudes, and his own approaches to life, which are the basis for his character, his personality (p. 87).

The family provides the context for the primary rehearsal of a way of movement among others which is to become the individual's style of living. Just as the individual is not encapsulated in "self-boundedness" (*Ichgebundenheit*, Adler) and cannot be understood in isolation from this context, the family cannot be encapsulated as a system apart from a community of others in a given time and place in history. Therefore, we also consider and include in the family constellation summary those impressions and details of linkages to the world outside the immediate family that were factors in the client's training and self-training. These include the extent of involvement in and interaction with members of the extended family; role models outside the family; experiences in the social life of the neighborhood and the school; and impressions and conclusions relating to the ethnic, religious, social, and economic milieu reported by the client in the inquiry and in the review and interpretations.

Remember that a summary is a summary; that is, according to the *Random House Dictionary*, "a brief statement or restatement of main points, especially at a conclusion to a work." The family constellation summary is a brief statement, incorporating major points. It is not intended to be a biographical account of the client's experience as a child and adolescent; rather, its purpose is to give a fresh expression to the client's subjective sense of those years as they relate to the unique style of movement the client learned in the beginning, and continues to practice in the present.

In short, the family constellation summary facilitates the client's self-understanding, with respect for the way the client created a style of living, and (as with all therapeutic work in Individual Psychology) in a way that is encouraging for the client in the current situation.

In this chapter we present a method for the composition of the "Summary of the Family Constellation" based on the topics listed below, as they are expressed in the sentence stems provided in the following examples of form. Each of these topics is then reviewed in detail, and illustrated with case material excerpted from actual family constellation summaries. The chapter concludes with an analysis of the "Summary of the Family Constellation" in "The Case of Dan" (presented in its entirety in Chapter 4 of this text).

Topics to include in the "Summary of the Family Constellation"

1. Birth order
2. Family atmosphere
3. Family values
4. Masculine guiding line
5. Feminine guiding line
6. The place made by the client in the family
7. The places made by each of the siblings
8. Other images: Role models and alliances
9. The experience of neighborhood and school in childhood and puberty
10. The experience of the sexual challenge in adolescence
11. Major unresolved issues remaining from childhood and adolescence

Method of Composing the Summary of the Family Constellation

These eleven topics, together with suggested phrases for use in composing the summary are listed below. Where information in the sentences is enclosed in brackets, follow the lead provided: Use your own client's information in that space. For example, the first sentence stem, relating to birth order, is, "[The client] grew up as the [ordinal position], psychologically the [psychological vantage]." With client information written in, we have this sentence: "Sharon grew up as the third child in a family of four children, psychologically the baby of the first group of three with a much younger brother."

In the coming pages you will find many examples showing how to use each of the sentence stems we present below.

Topic 1. "[The client] grew up as [ordinal position], psychologically the [psychological vantage]..."

Topic 2. "The family atmosphere was [description]..."

Topic 3. "The family values emphasized by Mother and Father included [state, and elaborate upon these common values]..."

Topic 4. "The masculine guiding line set by Father stressed [state principal features of the masculine guiding line, especially those values not shared by Mother]..."

Topic 5. "The feminine guiding line set by Mother stressed [state principal features of the feminine guiding line, especially those values not shared by Father]..."

Topic 6. "[The client] made a place for himself/herself by [description of how client distinguished self in family: Consider activities, alliances, competitors, relationships with parents, and comparison of client's place to those established by siblings]..."

Topic 7. "[Sibling's name], who was [state age or position relative to the client], made a place for himself/herself by [consider elements in Topic 6]..."

Topic 8. "Other images presented to [the client] were [identify role models] who [description of their significance to the client]. [The client] made an alliance with [identify the person] who was important to [the client] because [describe relationship; include particularly any encouragement provided]..."

Topic 9. "During childhood, [the client's] experience was [describe major features of self-assessment in neighborhood and school, including physical self-image]. Upon reaching puberty, [the client's] experience was [describe positive and negative features, including expectations about growing to adulthood, and what this would mean]..."

Topic 10. "During adolescence, [the client] felt [describe the client's self-assessment] and met [note experience in meeting challenges of self-reliance, sexuality, and direction for life]..."

Topic 11. "The question that confronted [the client] at the threshold of adulthood remained: [Here pose a question that states the theme of the client's lack of preparation for adult success, including the conditions under which the client is prepared to go forward]..."

Topic Review and Illustrations

Topic 1. BIRTH ORDER

1. Name the client;

2. state the ordinal position;

3. state the client's psychological vantage vis-a-vis siblings.

Case examples: First-born only children

- Laura grew up as the first-born child of her parents, in fact and psychologically an only child.

- Matt grew up as the only surviving child after two failed pregnancies; psychologically an only child, and the only son.

- Don grew up as the first-born son and only child of his parents, psychologically the second born of the two men in the family, with Father having the role of the first-born son to a woman who operated as a mother to both "her men."

Case examples: Psychological only children

- Sam grew up as the much younger of two and the only son, psychologically an only child with two mothers.

- Amelia grew up as the first of two children, psychologically an only child with a younger sister who, owing to her incapacity, was inconsequential to Amelia, except as a burden to be endured.

- Theresa grew up as the fourth of seven children, psychologically an only child who experienced herself as the "odd one out" between the older and the younger groups of children.

Case examples: First borns with siblings

- Janice grew up as the the oldest of three girls, psychologically the first-born daughter with two little sisters.

- Charlie grew up as the first of six children, psychologically the first born of the two older boys, all of whose four younger siblings remained in a group of their own.

- Doris grew up as the first of two children, psychologically the first-born daughter with a brother who was a first-born son.

- Ted grew up as the first of eight children, psychologically the first-born son in a class by himself.

- Lisa grew up as the older of twin girls, psychologically the first-born daughter with a younger sister.

Case examples: Psychological first-born children

- Rachel grew up as the younger of two, psychologically the first-born daughter because of her older sister's handicap.

- Marie grew up as the second child among five children, psychologically the first-born daughter with an older brother and three younger siblings.

- Jim grew up as the second of three children, psychologically the first-born son with an older sister who was a first-born daughter, and with whom he shared a baby sister.

Case examples: Second-born children

- Dick grew up as the second of five sons, psychologically the second born with three "kid" brothers and a first-born "big" brother.

- Alice grew up as the second of six children, psychologically the second born of the first two children, who entered the family before its "collapse," who had enjoyed a "golden age" together, and whose shared memories kept them in a class by themselves.

- Jeffrey grew up as the second of two boys, psychologically the second-born son, striving, not so much to catch up as not to fall farther behind.

- Ed grew up as the second of three, psychologically the second-born son with a younger sister.

- Patricia grew up as the second of two girls with three younger siblings, whose psychological vantage as a second born was severely dislocated upon the death of her older sister, which occurred when Patricia was five years old. She was disoriented both by the loss of her pacesetter, and by her felt demand that she assume the responsibility of leadership and example in the "first" position left open by her sister's death.

Case examples: Middle children

- Susie grew up as the second of four children, psychologically the middle child and only girl in a group formed by the first three, all of whom shared the fourth as a baby sister.

- Jim grew up as the second of three children, who eschewed the burdens of a first-born son's position, and was psychologically the middle child and only boy.

- Sheila grew up as the first girl and second child in a family of five children, psychologically the middle child between an older brother and a younger sister.

- Joe grew up as the second son in a family of seven children, psychologically the middle child in the first group of five.

- Louis grew up as the fourth of eight children, psychologically the middle child between one group of three older siblings and a second group of four younger siblings.

- Bob grew up as the third of five children, psychologically the middle child among four boys with a younger sister. This subjective sense of "middleness" was based in part on his awareness that the oldest of the boys was not making a place for himself successfully as the first born, and was being displaced by Bob's next older brother.

- Olivia grew up as the fifth of six children, psychologically the middle child in the second group of three.

Case examples: Third-born children

- Sharon grew up as the third of four children, remaining the third born with two older brothers psychologically, and refusing the position of the older of the two girls.

- Richard grew up as the third of three children, psychologically the third born, allied with his first-born sister in their failed effort to keep his older brother from shining.

- Emily grew up as the third of three girls, psychologically the third born, whose sisters took the positions of first-born daughter and middle child.

- Judy grew up as the only girl with two older brothers, choosing to be a tomboy in alliance with her brothers, and remaining psychologically the third born of the children.

Case examples: Youngest children

- Harold grew up as the last born of six children, psychologically the youngest member of the group.

- David grew up as the third of four children, psychologically the youngest of three boys with a younger sister.

- Anne grew up as the fourth of five girls, psychologically the youngest of the first group of four, all of whom shared a baby sister.

Case examples: Babies

- Warren grew up as the youngest of four children, psychologically the darling baby brother of them all.

- Louise grew up as the younger of two children and the only girl, psychologically the baby of the family.

- Norman grew up as the first of two children and the only boy, psychologically the baby of the family with a younger sister who took the position of first-born daughter and "little mother" to "Mr. Norman," thus removing him from competition.

Topic 2. FAMILY ATMOSPHERE

1. Describe the family atmosphere set by the relationship between the parents (and other adults resident in the childhood household);

2. note any extraordinary changes in the atmosphere and the intervening life events relevant to such changes;

3. note the ethnic character of the family if significant in establishing the atmosphere.

Case examples: Family atmosphere

- The family atmosphere was balmy in that Mother and Father shared the same values, and in that Mother was willing to defer to Father's position as the undisputed leader of the family; it was therefore consistent and predictable in its encouragement of the children in their strivings to achieve whatever they could.

- The family atmosphere was idyllic for a brief period in Paul's early life when the family enjoyed the paradise of their own home. Following the move to the household of the maternal grandparents, the dominant pattern was one of stormy contention, resentment, and complaint, relieved only by humid stretches of disappointment and depression.

- The family atmosphere was tense and explosive, though without any threat of a breakup or a loss of place.

- The family atmosphere in this Irish-American family was undisturbed by conflict but equally unrelieved by any sunniness of warmth or affection.

- The family atmosphere was electrically charged, primarily and positively by Mother's social ambitions; secondarily and negatively by Father's failure to meet Mother's expectations and to support Mother's strivings for herself and her children.

- The family atmosphere in this upwardly mobile, nomadic, "corporate" family was tense with striving, though relieved by maternal efforts to support and encourage those for whom that striving was difficult.

- The family atmosphere in this New American Family of Korean immigrants was "enclosed" against the perceived dangers of life, both physical and social, and had about it an internal storminess of anxiety about money.

- The family atmosphere was both stable and tense until Isabelle was seven years old, when the tension gained the upper hand in the aftermath of Father's loss of employment, the birth of a sickly baby, and Mother's illness.

- The family atmosphere in this Scottish-American household was clear and crisp, dominated by the sense of order, of principle, and of propriety.

- The family atmosphere was poisoned by the tragedy of Father's accident when Rafael was two years old, remaining tainted by Father's subsequent impairment and Mother's fatalistic resignation, self-denial, and self-abnegation in the role of nurse.

- The family atmosphere in this Italian-American family was unfailingly salubrious by reason of the unshakable affection, mutual respect, and confidence which the parents showed to one another, and by reason of the family's solid integration in the life of the church, the neighborhood, and the Italian community.

- The family atmosphere was one of subdued, restrained energy, expressing the tensions of a traditional "inside-outside" family, the inside belonging to Mother and the outside to Father. These tensions were exaggerated by another, less easily understood split: The division between the private life and the public face.

Topic 3. FAMILY VALUES

1. Note family values (that is, those values shared by Mother and Father).

Case examples: Family values

- The family values emphasized by Mother and Father included a genteel antimaterialism; devotion to fair play and equity; and education, not so much for the sake of advancement as for the sake of a kind of moral enrichment.

- The family values emphasized by Mother and Father were: Learning, manners, order, loyalty, and responsibility.

- The family values emphasized by Mother and Father were: Education, interests and activity, and aspirations for self-betterment. This was a family in which being special or appearing special had a negative value.

- The family values emphasized by Mother and Father were: Hard work and congeniality, and a confidence that together these would result in improvement.

- The family values emphasized by Mother and Father were: Appearances, timidity, and a certainty that those outside the family (employers, teachers, neighbors) knew better about what was "right."

- The family values emphasized by Mother and Father were: Energy, an insistence upon conformity both inside and outside the family, hard work, and affection.

- The family values emphasized by Mother and Father were: Orderliness, warmth, concern for others, and the practice of encouragement.

- The family values emphasized by Mother and Father were unconvincing. Each stated the value of honesty, but Tracy was aware of Father's "deal-making" and Mother's secret money cache. Each stated the value of hard work, but Tracy was aware of Father's malingering and Mother's failure to maintain household responsibilities. Each stated the value of kindness, but Tracy was aware of Father's bullying and Mother's harsh judgment.

- The family values emphasized by Mother and Father were those of closeness and harmony. These were exaggerated to the point of constriction, with the consequence of alienating Dean from a sense of participation in the social life of the neighborhood and the school.

- The family values emphasized by Mother and Father included the elevation of the women in the family to imperial positions, with the men playing the roles of courtiers. Mother and Father agreed that Father should dote on Mother and on their daughter, Pam; and that Father's task in life was to ensure that the lives of these two women were comfortable and untroubled by any need to strive.

Topic 4. MASCULINE GUIDING LINE

1. State the masculine guiding line (characteristics, attitudes, interests, and competencies ascribed to Father, and Father's values not shared by Mother);

2. if there were other males in the extended family who impressed the client, state how their examples confirmed, enhanced, or undermined the masculine guiding line.

Case examples: Masculine guiding line

- The masculine guiding line set by Father stressed strength and strictness without being overbearing or tyrannical. Father was a good-humored, caring, protective man who was respectful of women, so that none of the girls in this family of daughters felt that they were less by being females.

- The masculine guiding line set by Father stressed kindness, friendliness, and, because of his history of heart trouble, a determination to enjoy life fully while it lasted. The guiding line was enhanced by the paternal grandfather, the patriarch whose hard work and whose undisputed authority throughout the family held everyone together.

- The masculine guiding line set by Father stressed competence, intelligence, strength, reverence for the religious life, and an unwillingness to be defeated by disappointment or reproach. As little as Tony knew Father, owing to Father's having left the family when Tony was six, he knew of Father's reliability because Father continued to stay in touch with Tony. The guiding line was supported by the uncles, who presented a picture of religious devotion and generosity toward others.

- The masculine guiding line set by Father stressed a cheerful and friendly interest in life and a confidence in his own standards and in his own craft as a journeyman. Father was less interested in appearances than in good relationships and in what he could do. He was also a playful and affectionate man, especially toward his children.

- The masculine guiding line set by Father was marked by intensity, ambition, self-absorption, and impatience with those who did not live according to his specifications. Father could also be petulant and demanding of service, especially of Mother and the girls; the boys were apparently exempted in this regard.

- The masculine guiding line set by Father stressed a restless determination to demonstrate power inside the family, by having temper fits; and to demonstrate acceptability outside the family, by ingratiating himself with others. Father was unconvincing in both efforts, as far as Ray was concerned, since both his power tactics and his "generosity" looked to Ray like weaknesses and posturing.

- The masculine guiding line set by Father stressed a kind of frantic pretense to superiority which expressed itself through sarcasm, fault finding, belittling, and disproportionate rage reactions (which Wayne saw as "crazy") in the face of any frustration. The overriding difficulty of Wayne's life was his father's disturbed and exaggerated notion of masculine superiority, which Father clung to as if it were a man's duty to dominate and to demonstrate his ability to rule, either by force of argument or by brute force.

- The masculine guiding line set by Father stressed kindness, regularity, orderliness, propriety, and a just and loving concern for those in his care.

Topic 5. FEMININE GUIDING LINE

1. State the feminine guiding line (characteristics, attitudes, interests, and competencies ascribed to Mother, and Mother's values not shared by Father);

2. if there were other females in the extended family who impressed the client, state how their examples confirmed, enhanced, or undermined the feminine guiding line.

Case examples: Feminine guiding line

- The feminine guiding line set by Mother stressed a kind of relentless goodness, and a determination to apply her higher standards in so conscientious a way as to make her positions seem unassailable to everyone around her. These positions included a perfectionistic striving toward success and the prestige that would come with success, and the maintenance of those appearances that were the signs of that striving.

- The feminine guiding line set by Mother stressed a hard-working attitude of devotion to the family, and a kind of fretful and anxious excitability in the face of any difficulty or any possibility of her being either disregarded or intruded upon. Mother was also capable of another kind of excitement, expressed in gaiety and in an ability to cheer Father up when he was discouraged.

- The feminine guiding line set by Mother stressed a managerial and tutorial style with an unsentimental determination to do what was right in her eyes for everyone else's own good, whether they liked it or not. In the narrow compass of Mother's life there was no room for self-pity or defeat. Mother did not focus on what it was she could not do, only on what she could do, given the situation, to make the best of it.

- The feminine guiding line set by Mother stressed the subordination of enjoyment to the goal of achievement. Mother was also unhappy with her life as a woman, understood femininity in terms of vulnerability, saw herself in danger of humiliation and insult, and also fought against these perceptions by taking a position of superiority to others. Mother's picture of life was that of a person coming from behind (by reason of her Italian heritage, which she saw as a disadvantage in the "WASP" world she yearned to enter), and it led her into a general discouragement and pessimism.

- The feminine guiding line set by Mother stressed consistency, closeness, and a kind of coercive suffering which was used as a method of control. Mother was a survivor against impossible odds. This made her admirable to Charlie, who felt an obligation to protect her against the threat of any further suffering.

- The feminine guiding line set by Mother stressed fearfulness, weakness, reticence, reclusiveness, and a determination to have her own way and to press other people into her service. Mother was also concerned with appearances and with presenting a brave face to the public world through an air of superiority.

- The feminine guiding line set by Mother stressed an outward pose of submission to the natural course of a woman's life, lived out in caretaking, homemaking, and deference to men; together with an undercurrent of smugness and resentment, as if expressing that, while she would go along, she knew better, and implying a continuous, unspoken grudge against the world.

- The feminine guiding line set by Mother stressed beauty, caring, management, and perfectionism. Mother was selfless in the sense that she pleased everyone, although her hypercritical eye made it impossible for anyone to please her.

Topic 6. THE PLACE MADE BY THE CLIENT IN THE FAMILY

1. Describe how the client made a place in the family;

2. note the relationship of the client's place to each of the parents and siblings;

3. note special alliances and sources of encouragement for the client (or address this separately, under Topic 8);

4. note the client's response to the family- and gender-related values.

Case examples: The place made by the client

The Case of Marsha

Marsha made a place for herself by staying ahead of her younger sister by means of her early accomplishments as a bright, responsive child; by being her Father's companion; and by distinguishing herself athletically in the "tennis set" (which was also Father's set), especially by showing that she could handle herself in the company of adults.

She stayed active, took teasing cheerfully (as Father did), and imitated what she saw to be the strengths of each of her parents: Like Father, she knew how to be loud and overwhelming when it suited her purpose; and, like Mother (though she had decided not to grow up to be complaining and reclusive like Mother), she knew how to insist on getting what she wanted through suffering if all else failed.

For the most part, extreme tactics were not necessary to her, and she thrived on the encouraging interest of Father, Grandfather, and Uncle Terry, as well as on the pleasure with which she saw others outside the family responding to her energetic and outgoing manner.

Marsha's response to the family value of education was therefore problematic for her: She was unwilling to subordinate her energy to the fixed and seemingly arbitrary requirements of the school, and set herself on a course of defiance of its restrictions.

The Case of Diane

Diane made a place for herself as "Daddy's little girl," played to him, capitalized on his willingness to teach, and did her best to do well in school and to be religious and "good," all of which were important to Father.

She did not compete directly with her older brother, perhaps sensing that there was no point in trying to upstage someone who wanted so much to be the Star, and learned to be more self-reliant as a way of dealing with feeling excluded from Mother's company (owing to Mother's focus on the brother).

Diane knew that as a tomboy she could do and enjoy all the things that a boy could do. She could not forget, however, that she was not a Real Boy. She was a girl who would be a woman and who, like Mother, would follow the natural course of a woman's destiny. At the same time, she wanted to be valued by a man for those qualities she saw in Father that Mother appeared to her to lack: Independence, knowledge, and competence.

In this way she pictured herself succeeding to the position of a woman who could be a fit companion to a man like Father, and her ambition was encouraged and sustained by the examples of her Aunt Ann and Uncle Bill, whom she saw as having achieved a relationship of mutual respect.

Diane's response to the family value of male dominance was therefore to resolve to be a fit ally to a man by being as much like Father and as interested in him and his interests as she could be.

The Case of Ralph

Ralph made a place for himself in a number of ways. First, he found the place *assigned* to him by virtue of being an illegitimate child, which had both positive and negative connotations: Positive, in that he was fussed over by Grandmother as the Only Child of Grandmother's only child; negative, in that his advent had been an embarrassment and difficulty for the family. Second, he was sickly and required a great deal of attention from his caretakers without his having to insist upon it. Third, he was bright, quick to learn, and quick to adapt himself to the requirements of family life with Mother and his grandparents. Both Ralph and Mother deferred to the grandparents' attitudes and practices, thereby ensuring harmony in the household and security in the world. Ralph took advantage of Grandmother's encouragement to get ahead by doing well in school and by forming good friendships.

The Case of Joyce

Joyce made a place for herself with the only person in her world who could be relied upon: Mother. Mother's "on-again, off-again" affairs and marriages conveyed to Joyce that it wasn't worthwhile to make an effort to form an attachment with a man. As a consequence she failed to form any close alliances with the men in Mother's life, keeping her attention focused on Mother. She took advantage of Mother's uncertainty and feelings of regret and disappointment, exploited Mother's propensity to feel sorry for her, and so kept Mother in her service. She imitated Mother's competence in the world outside the home, where Mother was a successful professional woman. She also imitated Mother's incompetence in close personal relationships, rehearsing the posture of a person whose life will only "work out" if Lady Luck smiles on her, so failing to cultivate the awareness of her own effectiveness.

The Case of Ed

Ed made a place for himself by following the masculine guiding line set by Father and confirmed by Father's younger brother, Erin, who lived in the household: Hard work, intense involvement in his own interests, and a kind of rough determination to rule, expressed by Ed in readiness to beat up on anyone who disturbed his sense of how things should be. Also like Father, he was active and made do with very little in the way of close friendships or close family relationships. The maternal grandparents offered some relief from the rigors of Ed's childhood, Grandfather being an openhearted and openhanded person, and Grandmother being a caring and embracing person.

Because of his restless ambition to do what he could do, and his consequent lack of interest in reflecting upon, pondering, or even attending to matters that were outside or beyond his immediate reach, he began to form a picture of himself as, at best, shallow, and, at worst, dumb. Even so, as the only child of preoccupied parents, Ed understood the family value of independence and action, and set his sights on getting up and out.

The Case of Randy

Randy made a place for himself by being "the little one," alternately overprotected and left on his own by the others. His primary alliance was with his older sister, Lucy, who took him under her wing. Randy had everything he needed inside his family, where he could be little without being bullied or threatened, the center of attention whenever Lucy was around, and free to pursue his own interests whenever he wished. Outside the family it was different, though he was able to make a special place in school by getting along well with his teachers and excelling in academics.

Randy was overly impressed by Father's perceived power, compared to which he saw himself as being relatively ineffective. He determined to make up for this by accomplishments that would take him beyond Father's modest attainments in the world of business. Like Lucy, Mother doted on Randy, comforted him and supported him, and Randy developed a sense that he would be unable to succeed in life without the protection of a devoted woman.

The Case of Bertha

Bertha made a place for herself by being tough like her brothers, and principled like her father. She admired Mother's beauty, but knew that she looked like Father's side of the family, and so felt that she could not rely upon good looks to get her way as Mother did. She learned to stick to her guns, go after what she wanted with a kind of relentless determination, and to avoid anything that appeared unattainable to her, including the relief of humor and fun, and the comfort to be found in giving and receiving affection.

Topic 7. THE PLACES MADE BY EACH OF THE SIBLINGS

1. Describe how each of the siblings made a place for himself or herself in the family;

2. note the relationship of each place to that established by the client.

Case examples: The places made by each of the siblings

- Bart's older brother, Alex, made a place for himself as Mother's boy and, because of Father's frequent travels, formed a special alliance with Mother, from which Bart felt excluded. Alex also followed the masculine guiding line in being gregarious and in wanting to be powerful, dominant, and knowledgeable.

- Ted's younger brother, Hank, made a place for himself by accepting Father's values, by pursuing stated goals, and by imitating Father's mannerisms, especially in his way of joking. Ted felt relieved that Father's attention was focused on Hank, and learned to stay out of Father's way in his alliance with Mother, who was more easygoing.

- Denise's older sister, Gail, had established a place for herself by becoming Mother's indispensable helper in raising the younger children. This model looked too hard to Denise, who decided to take the position of the inept one who could not be relied upon, and of whom, therefore, less was asked.

- The third child, Larry, made a place for himself by being the Only Boy. His advent was a startling revelation to Helen, serving as her first intimation that she had a native handicap in her gender that could not be overcome.

- Margaret made a place for herself by being "offhand," mischievous, socially at ease, and less concerned than Marilyn to stick with things. Marilyn, as the older of the twins, did what was expected of her and met her obligations, wondering how Margaret "got away with it."

- Charlene had made a place for herself by imitating Mother's propriety and by practicing the religiosity of Mother's side of the family. In this way she affronted Father and kept him busy with her by "cultivating" his disapproval. Trudy, aware of this difficulty between Charlene and Father, was all the better able to win him over by taking his part and by otherwise being his ally in the family.

- Frank had made a place for himself as the Good Boy from whom trouble was not expected, and therefore from whom trouble was not tolerated. By the time of Jim's arrival in the family, Frank was well-rehearsed in this position, leaving Jim a clear field in which to be as troublesome as he pleased, and to be defiant of the parental efforts to subdue him.

- Ellen made a place for herself outside the family circle, which was tightly drawn around Debbie. Ellen became a loner, fighting Mother and Father over what seemed to Debbie to be curious and irrelevant issues, a judgment which had the effect of elevating Debbie's position all the more as the logical, reasonable, and cooperative one of the two girls.

- Betty made a place for herself as the Baby, competed with no one, and invited everyone to be affectionate toward her by taking advantage of her advantageous position among the others. Harold made a protege of Betty, thereby hoping to share some of the spotlight.

- Herb made a place for himself by capitalizing on his physical agility, developing his athletic skills, being willing to stay in second place to Michael, and cultivating Mother's empathic and sensitive way of relating to others. This enabled Michael to pursue and excel in the world of academics and to maintain his first-born position without strife.

- Nancy operated with third-born charm, and avoided the appearance of striving for any position other than the one she had as everybody's favorite. Margie enjoyed Nancy and made use of her popularity to gain a place in the wider world of the school.

- Leo made a place for himself by imitating and perfecting Ralph's tactic of staying out of the way, withdrawing into himself, and becoming inaccessible, while Ralph continued striving to escape the pressures laid upon him by Mother and Father by finding activities outside the home in areas that would be above reproach (Boy Scouts, church), and not likely therefore to invite the interference of the parents.

Topic 8. OTHER IMAGES: ROLE MODELS AND ALLIANCES

1. Identify role models (both positive and negative) who were important to the client, and describe the images of possibility or danger they provided;

2. note other alliances made by the client and the contributions they made to the client's development, particularly in terms of any sources of encouragement.

Case examples: Other images: Role models and alliances

- Other images presented to Dolores included the relationship between her Aunt Mary and Uncle Hugh. Through their cooperation and mutual support in caring for their severely handicapped daughter (Dolores's cousin) they encouraged her to see another possibility for the way in which men and women could establish their relationships, in solidarity and respect.

- Other images presented to Jerry were those of Grandfather Thomas and Coach Hammond. Grandfather Thomas was a generous-spirited man who took an interest in Jerry's interests, as well as an interest in the wider community outside the family, providing Jerry with an example of public service to which he aspired. Jerry made an alliance with Coach Hammond, with whom he shared his athletic ambitions, and from whom he received support and encouragement.

- Sandy made an alliance with an older neighbor, Mrs. Grayson, and with her Uncle Jack, both of whom enjoyed her sense of humor and high spirits.

- Another image of manhood was presented to Hank by his Uncle Ron, Father's younger brother. Ron was the "black sheep" of the family, whose periodic appearances, whose rude and aggressive attitudes, and whose self-aggrandizing behavior underscored the dangers of veering off the straight and narrow path.

- Other images presented to Pete included his two grandfathers and his Uncle Dwayne, who were all more relaxed about life than Father, and who demonstrated that a man could be *both* good *and* joyous in life. His alliance with his older cousin, Cynthia, provided him with a rehearsal for give and take with the other sex that would prove valuable to him in his adolescent encounters with girls, a preparation he otherwise lacked as an only child.

- Another image of how a woman could be was presented by Ruth's Grandmother Roth, who was the center of the extended family and the one whom everyone loved. Ruth aspired to inherit Grandmother's mantle, and set out to demonstrate that she was worthy.

- Lee made an alliance with his grammar school teacher, Mrs. Harris, who recognized and encouraged his artistic talent and inspired him to believe in what he could do.

- The images presented to Patrick by his scout master and the parish priest, of men who were both trustworthy and kind, helped him in his struggle against his pessimistic self-estimate as the son of Patrick, Senior, who seemed to Patrick to be both unreliable and selfish.

- The image presented by Father's friend, Danny, seemed to George to be the picture of what he did not want to be as a man. Danny's loud voice, demanding ways, and obsession with money and "making deals" were unattractive to him.

Topic 9. THE EXPERIENCE OF NEIGHBORHOOD AND SCHOOL IN CHILDHOOD AND PUBERTY

1. Describe the client's assessment of childhood experience in neighborhood and school, if this is not incorporated under previous topics;

2. describe the client's assessment of the experiences associated with the onset of puberty.

Case examples: Neighborhood and school experience

- During childhood, Ted defined himself as more passive because he was smaller, weaker, less sure of himself in the rough and tumble of the neighborhood and school than the other boys and girls seemed to be. He maintained his courage by harboring a secret picture of himself as a tall, strong, confident grown-up, and made a project of looking forward to achieving that reality simply by surviving.

- During childhood, Sally managed to escape Mother's management by capitalizing on her social talents. Mother took pride in Sally's many friends and activities and in her success in the world of the school. Sally therefore met the challenge of puberty with a sense of accomplishment and relief: She was now a woman, and the number of her days under Mother's scrutiny were dwindling.

- During childhood, Judy found her place among the neighborhood boys, playing ball, exploring the woods, and riding bikes. She felt less comfortable in the world of the girls and women. The onset of menstruation was, therefore, an unwelcome event, demonstrating to her that whatever else she might do in life she was doomed to be a woman.

- During childhood, Fred explored to the fullest extent possible the pleasures of his active mind and healthy body, welcoming the changes that came at puberty as signs of his becoming a man able to take his place as a man among men.

- During childhood, Ned's place as both the baby and the problem child combined to cause trouble for him among the children in the neighborhood and the school, where he found the others impatient with his demands and intolerant of his obstructiveness. He found relief from these un-understood difficulties only at home, where his mother pampered him and his father left him alone. His love of arithmetic indicates an early desire to find an area of life in which he could figure things out for himself and solve problems on his own. But he was still undecided about whether to go forward in the direction of an adult world that didn't look all that attractive to him, or to entrench himself in the posture of the mischievous child.

- During childhood, as the youngest of the boys, Tim admired Father and his much older brothers, and dreamt of a heroic future in which he would excel in masculine achievement and masculine protection of others. At the same time he felt unsure of his qualifications for greatness, especially in his confrontations with the taunts and insults of the other children in the neighborhood. School served as a deliverance. His intellectual ability flowered there and he decided that his way to greatness would be by way of great books. This allowed him to form a more realistic (in the sense of more attainable) picture of what would be required of him as a man.

Topic 10. THE EXPERIENCE OF THE SEXUAL CHALLENGE IN ADOLESCENCE

1. Describe the client's sexual awareness and experience in adolescence;

2. describe the circumstances and the client's evaluation of sexual initiation.

Case examples: Adolescence

- During adolescence, Carl experienced the kind of victimization, heartbreak, and bitterness that he had seen as characterizing his father's life; and in the wake of his abandonment by the first love of his life felt more and more destined to live out the masculine guiding line set by Father.

- During adolescence, Ann's knowledge of her cousin Beth's pregnancy, her learning the family secret about her Aunt's abandonment by her husband (who had run away with another woman), *and* her awareness of the special status of the men in her family and extended family, led her to conclude that women were vulnerable to men's desires and decisions, and that men were granted a status in the world to which she could never aspire.

- During adolescence, Lori had many boyfriends, was the center of a socially desirable circle, and enjoyed her femininity. With the admiration and support of her father and brothers she was never undermined by feelings of inferiority or subordination, and looked forward to taking her place with a man as an equal contributor to their common life.

- During adolescence, Becky consoled herself with her girlfriends, feeling that she could not hold her own among the boys. What dates she had were arranged by others, were awkward, and were not repeated. She yearned for the kind of position enjoyed by Mother who was cared for and catered to; however, she also wanted to follow the masculine guiding line of independence set by Father and reinforced by the other men in the family.

- During adolescence, Elsie enjoyed being a girl and looked forward to being a woman with a man, provided that the man were a protector and encourager like Father. Her sexual initiation with the man who would be her husband was a welcome event therefore, marking in her mind her emergence as a woman who would enjoy being a woman.

- During adolescence, Bill had a restless ambition to get on with it. With the exception of the encouragement that one of his high school teachers gave him in his sophomore year, and his subsequent decision to make use of his remaining years in school, the changes that occurred in Bill's adolescence were changes in the scope of his movement away from the parental home, resistance to any entanglement with the other sex, and, finally, escape into the armed forces.

- During adolescence, a number of ideas about masculinity and femininity combined in Len's thinking: The first derived from his parents' reminders that they hadn't wanted more children and that, when Mother got pregnant with Len, they had hoped that at least the baby would be a girl. The second was that, since (unlike his brother) he had not been circumcised, there was "something wrong" with him. Third was his idea that the task of dealing as a man with a woman was a doomed endeavor: Women were unreliable, unpredictable, untrustworthy, and irrational. Finally, there was his idea that a man's life was hard, and that a woman's life was comparatively easy, exempted as it was from the rigors of economic struggle outside the home. These things conspired in Len's thinking to persuade him to train himself away from the masculine role: It was too hard, and he was unqualified (uncircumcised). He began to turn his attention away from the other sex, and toward his own sex.

- During adolescence, everything went smoothly for Don. He knew what he must do: Play by the book. As long as everyone else followed the rules, things would proceed as they should. Because of his energy, his lack of abrasiveness or antagonism, and his good looks, girls were attracted to him; and because of his enjoyment of them he had no trouble making friends with them and winning over the one he wanted. His trouble came later when his girlfriend, now his wife, wanted to play by a new set of rules, and he was unable to write a new book.

Topic 11. MAJOR UNRESOLVED ISSUES REMAINING FROM CHILDHOOD AND ADOLESCENCE

1. Identify and explicate any issues remaining to be resolved by the client at the threshold of adult life, including the conditions under which the client is prepared to go forward.

Case examples: Unresolved issues

- The question confronting Christopher at the threshold of adulthood remained: How could he combine a sure thing with the main chance? On the one hand, he would keep things under control without becoming rigid, inflexible, or odd (like Mother); on the other hand, he would play at gambling in the markets, using his mathematical knowledge of the odds to keep himself from making dumb mistakes (like Father). The consequence of this training in double safeguards seems to have left him in a position in which he suffers from both dangers. When he makes a mistake, he feels stupid; then, when he tries to keep himself from making further mistakes, he paralyzes himself, takes no further action at all, and feels odd.

- The question that confrontèd Carla at the threshold of adulthood was: How could she manage the "wild energies" of the women in her family so that she might bind the beauty and the power of a man to her. Should she, like Grandmother, use these energies to overwhelm and tame a man? Or should she, like Mother, tame herself and thereby bind the man to her?

- The question Ken confronted at the threshold of adulthood remained: How could he be a man without having to do what men do, namely, accede to the demands of perfectionistic women who claim a right to have their demands met by reason of their suffering?

- The question confronting Kim at the threshold of adulthood remained: How to be the man her father was and still remain eligible for the position of the woman? How could she succeed in the world of men, the world of hardship and accomplishment, and still succeed in the world of women, the world of comfort and indulgence?

- The question that remained to confront Al at the threshold of adulthood was: How to escape as Father had escaped? He was unable to be like Father, however, in that he was haunted by the opinions of others, as by a nameless threat that undermined his courage and distracted him from finding for himself, in any situation, a clear course by which to proceed toward his own goals and his own fulfillment.

Analysis of a Family Constellation Summary: "The Case of Dan"

Now that we have set forth the topics for a family constellation summary and have illustrated them with excerpts from cases, we can turn to considering how they were applied in a single case. For this we return to "The Case of Dan," presented in Chapter 4. In the material that follows we use Dan's "Summary of the Family Constellation" (pp. 85-87) for a step-by-step analysis, first stating each topic, then illustrating how the topic was addressed in this summary by providing relevant quotations.

Bear in mind that because each life-style is unique, each application of these topics is also unique, adapted to the one situation of this one person, as you will see below.

Topic 1. Birth Order

a) Name the client; b) state the ordinal position; c) state the client's psychological vantage vis-a-vis siblings.

"Dan grew up as the older of two boys, psychologically the first-born son."

Topic 2. Family Atmosphere

a) Describe the family atmosphere set by the relationship between the parents (and other adults resident in the childhood household); b) note any extraordinary changes in the atmosphere and the intervening life events relevant to such changes; c) note the ethnic character of the family if significant in establishing the atmosphere.

"The family atmosphere was one of disturbed security. The security lay in knowing that Father would provide for and protect the family; the disturbance lay in knowing that Mother would, nevertheless, be anxious, unhappy, and dissatisfied."

Topic 3. Family Values

Note family values (that is, those values shared by Mother and Father).

"The family values emphasized by Mother and Father included hard work, caretaking of what one has (house, garden), and religious feeling."

Topic 4. Masculine Guiding Line

a) State the masculine guiding line (characteristics, attitudes, interests, and competencies; values not shared by Mother); b) if there were other males in the extended family who impressed the client, state how their examples confirmed, enhanced, or undermined the masculine guiding line.

"The masculine guiding line set by Father stressed a kind of relaxed cheerfulness and steadiness, together with a balanced temper and a practical intelligence capable of flashes of brilliance. Father was also capable of putting up a show of fighting back, and knew how to pursue his own interests quietly even when opposed (playing the horses). Grandfather confirmed the masculine guiding line in his loyalty to the women in his life. Uncle John enhanced the masculine guiding line through his sense of humor and relative material success."

Topic 5. Feminine Guiding Line

a) State the feminine guiding line (characteristics, attitudes, interests, competencies; values not shared by Father); b) if there were other females in the extended family who impressed the client, state how their examples confirmed, enhanced, or undermined the feminine guiding line.

"The feminine guiding line set by Mother stressed a fretful, ambitious, pessimistic, and temperamentally unpredictable busyness. Mother was better than others, and yearned to be among her betters. Mother's failure to express warmth was confirmed as characteristic of femininity by the attitudes of Dan's Great Aunt and his Aunt Jill, both of whom were cold. Even Aunt Carla, a generous, comfortable woman, kept her distance by 'sending' presents, and by avoiding any alliance with a man."

Topic 6. The Place Made by the Client in the Family

> a) Describe how the client made a place in the family; b) note the relationship of the client's place to each of the parents and siblings; c) note special alliances and sources of encouragement for the client (or address this separately, under Topic 8); d) note the client's response to the family- and gender-related values.

"Dan stayed ahead of Douglas by sharing Father's interests, and by being Mother's chief object of interest. Mother, who saw her life in tragic and heroic terms, was determined to see to it that her sons would succeed in ways that had been foreclosed to her by what she regarded as unfair circumstances.

"It was difficult for Dan to understand Mother's fretfulness about appearances, about striving, about education and moving up and out in the world, and about Father and his alleged inferiorities.

"In the world of the home, Dan apparently imitated Father's way of quietly enduring Mother's agitation, which led to his enduring her fussing over him as well. He also imitated Father's temper outbursts, by means of which he (and Father) were able to gain occasional relief from Mother's pressure. In Father he found a source of acceptance, but no standards by which to measure progress. Mother, who praised him when he met her standards and chastised and withdrew from him when he did not, provided the source of judgment."

Topic 7. The Places Made by Each of the Siblings

> a) Describe how each of the siblings made a place for himself or herself in the family; b) note the relationship of each place to that established by the client.

"Douglas, three years younger, made a place for himself by leaving the first-place position to Dan, uncontested; by staying out of trouble; and by developing an easygoing, friendly attitude toward life. Seeing that Mother's focus on Dan was the source of Dan's troubles, Douglas contrived to stay out of Mother's way, and out of her 'spotlight.'"

Topic 8. Other Images: Role Models and Alliances

> a) Identify role models (both positive and negative) who were important to the client, and describe the images of possibility or danger they provided; b) note other alliances made by the client and the contributions they made to the client's development, particularly in terms of any sources of encouragement.

"Dan found another source of acceptance in his Uncle John, whom he often saw in Father's company. John encouraged Dan, took pleasure in the boy's efforts, recognized his intelligence, and, like Father, did so without judgment."

Topic 9. The Experience of Neighborhood and School in Childhood and Puberty

a) Describe the client's assessment of childhood experience in neighborhood and school, if this is not incorporated under previous topics; b) describe the client's assessment of the experiences associated with the onset of puberty.

"In the world of the neighborhood, he was able to do well enough without striving, buttressed by a sense of being 'a cut above' the others that carried him through his difficulties with them. His good appearances, maintained by Mother, and the good appearance and steadiness of the household, probably sustained him in this idea.

"He managed well enough in the world of the school until adolescence, when everything changed: He now found himself propelled into a new group of peers, and compelled to assess his personal situation against the background of a much wider social world."

Topic 10. The Experience of the Sexual Challenge in Adolescence

a) Describe the client's sexual awareness and experience in adolescence; b) describe the circumstances and the client's evaluation of sexual initiation.

"Dan suddenly saw himself as a very small duck in a very large pond. His uncertainty about his place in the larger world, beginning at this time, continued to express itself in his hesitation to engage with someone of the other sex in caring intimacy, until in his mid-twenties he could make his first effort to do so under the protection of a formal engagement."

Topic 11. Major Unresolved Issues Remaining from Childhood and Adolescence

Identify and explicate any issues remaining to be resolved by the client at the threshold of adult life, including the conditions under which the client is prepared to go forward.

"In adolescence, all of Mother's complaints against Father's lack of ambition, and all of Mother's warnings against Dan's being 'like the Allens,' previously hard for him to understand, came to make a certain kind of sense to him: Appearances in his new world were much more important than he had thought. It was not even enough to look good; he would have to sound good as well, with the proper accent. He came to see that Mother's brand of ambition and striving were essential if he wanted to better himself. (Unlike Father, he could not afford to miss any buses; for him, another might not come along.)

"The question that confronted Dan at the threshold of adult manhood remained: How could he prove himself to be a man unlike the Allen men? To do this, he might suppose, would require that he set out in quest of an unhappy woman, and then demonstrate that he could make her happy by becoming whatever she wanted."

Conclusion

Chapter 13 has presented a method for constructing the family constellation summary, the first of the Life-Style Assessment summaries. In our practice, as we have noted elsewhere throughout the book, this summary is dictated in the presence of the client after a review of the relevant material. Other professional settings will require other ways to compose and present the summaries.

In the next and final chapter we discuss our method for interpreting and summarizing the client's convictions expressed in early recollections.

Chapter 14: THE PATTERN OF BASIC CONVICTIONS AND THE INTERFERING IDEAS

Other Individual Psychologists use other names for the two summaries that conclude the Life-Style Assessment. Dreikurs called The Pattern of Basic Convictions "The Summary of the Early Recollections," which is an accurate way to describe the procedure itself. We prefer our name because we believe that it has more meaning for the client. We use the word pattern in its double sense: As a design to show how each of a person's ideas is related in the whole style of the person's movement; and as a guide by which something is made, as a carpenter's or dress-maker's pattern, and in this case, as the underlying guide for the person's movement.

Similarly, some of our colleagues have used the terms "basic mistakes," "fundamental errors," or "erroneous convictions" for what we call Interfering Ideas. We prefer our name because it presents the client with an awareness of the interfering quality of the trouble these ideas introduce, as an added cost in the business of life. Because it does not hint at anything more dire or durable or "basic" to deal with than ideas, it seems to us to be a more encouraging term. Whatever the nomenclature, these two summaries are based on an understanding of the same data, namely, the core sample of the Life-Style found in the client's early recollections.

Reviewing the Early Recollections for the Summaries

The therapist must identify this core sample in such a way as to display it as a model of all the other movement of the client, and with such an accuracy and lucidity (as Adler's statement introducing Part IV prescribes) as will let the person feel both understood and able to recognize his or her mistakes. This is at the heart of the psycho-clarity process.

You will remember that in Chapter 11, after the initial report and discussion of the early recollections was completed in "The Case of Janice," a second review took place. In this second review, the task of the first therapist was to remind the second therapist (whose task it would be to compose the summaries) of each early recollection in the record, with the client's age at the time of the event recollected. During this second review the early recollections that had remained unclear (as to their individual importance and meaning, or as to their place in the record) were discussed further. (For example, the Santa Claus memory and the rooftop memory required further exploration before their meanings were clear.)

To facilitate the fixing of the early recollections in mind the second therapist may write down a list of key words or phrases to provide reminders of each one. For example, in "The Case of Janice," this is the way these notes were put down in the course of the discussion:

4 - Car. Observe (listen). Safe. Good.

7 or 8 - Snake. Blunder. Energy. Fear.

8 or 9 - Basement. Water/dark/still. G-friend. Peaceful. Good.

4 or 5 - Santa. Strength/necessity. Yield.

6 or 7 - Intercourse. Dark. Sounds (uninhibited). Afraid.

8 - Thanksgiving. Fa takes pic with G-friend. Pretty. Good.

9 - Halloween. Ghost. Hidden/free. Good.

9 - Roof/between boys. Woman below. "Hanging on..."

Factors to Consider in Composing "The Pattern of Basic Convictions"

Working directly with Janice's early recollections, we can illustrate a method for forming this summary by studying the data with reference to three major factors: *Sequence, similarity,* and *symmetry.*

Sequence means the arrangement of the entire set of early recollections, and the relationship of each to the ones before and after it in the series.

Similarity means a repetition of (or a variation upon) ideas or themes in various early recollections. An example is the idea of concealment appearing in various forms in Janice's stories.

Symmetry means correspondence between two early recollections as they balance one another, or are juxtaposed as if to represent two sides of an issue. For example, if one early recollection addresses the relationship between the client and women, and another between the client and men, we have symmetrical early recollections which should be reflected in the summary by: "Men are.... Women are...." Likewise, one memory may tell what happens when I act on my own initiative, and another what happens when others lead the way or require things of me. One may illustrate life as it should be (or, as it could be if only...), and another life as it is, perhaps in a contrast of paradise and paradise lost.

We can now examine Janice's early recollections with respect to these three factors of sequence, similarity, and symmetry. We do this in an informal conversation, with the client's participation as part of the process.

Sequence

To identify sequence, make a precis of each recollection, moving from one to the next. Here is a list of titles for Janice's recollections, followed by a series of numbered paragraphs showing how the second therapist recapitulated the discussion of each recollection (see Chapter 11) in identifying the sequence:

Car
Snake
Basement
Santa Claus
Intercourse
Thanksgiving
Halloween
Roof

1. We go from the car, where I am hidden in the dark, an observer, where others are in charge, and where all is contained and safe, to

2. being on my own, still in the dark, and blundering, and letting loose an energy that is uninhibited, and associated with the masculine (it belongs to my brother), and it's frightening, to

3. the basement, again dark, again hidden, where I'm with my girlfriend, contemplating the containment and peace of the pool of water, possibly associated with the feminine, to

4. a world ruled by a man who is larger than life, who is in charge, and who can force me to do something I don't want to do, and even though I struggle I finally have to yield, and when I do yield it's all right, and he promises to bring me presents, whatever I want, to

5. a picture of how this works between a grown woman and a man, where it's dark, where she is hidden, and she is struggling, but he's bigger and stronger and on top, and where these strange noises express an untamed energy, and it's frightening, to

6. being on the lawn on Thanksgiving, again with my girlfriend, looking pretty, contained in our dress-up clothes, and being admired in the open light of day by the man, from afar, and I am happy to be admired by him, and to pose for him, to

7. being hidden from everyone in my ghost costume, enjoying the dark, even though I know and they know that I am here, enjoying the charade we're carrying out, to

8. being hidden again, this time in a perilous situation, though I know that even if I let go and fall from the roof I won't be too badly hurt, and it's just that I don't want to, I don't want to give up my position as one of the kids and take my place down among the women and have to do what they do, and I know that I can't hold on forever, but I'd rather pretend for as long as I can, even though they know and I know that it's a game.

Similarity

The next task is to identify similarities, such as common themes and the repetition or restatement of ideas. Here is the list of memories again, with our notes for each item. Question marks in parentheses (?) indicate hypotheses in formation:

Car: Containment. Dark. Hidden. Concealed. Observer.

Snake: Dark. Snake hidden, concealed until I release it. Energies are uncontained. Masculinity = "uncontainable" "indomitable" (?)

Basement: Containment. Dark. Observer. "Below stairs," in the world of women(?) (I'm there with my girlfriend.) Femininity = "contained" "subdued" (?)

Santa Claus: Daylight. "Upstairs" in the department store, in the man's world. Can struggle, but must yield. Then, promise of reward (?)

Intercourse: Dark. Mother hidden, struggling. Uninhibited sounds = uncontained energies (?)

Thanksgiving: Daylight. Man's world. He admires, we pose.

He's at a distance. I'm with my girlfriend. There is a woman's world and a man's world (?)

Halloween: Dark. Hidden. Concealed. Observer. Awareness of its being a game. No winners or losers; only participants.

Roof: Daylight. Hidden, up in the man's world. Concealed. Again, an observer. Again, aware of its being a game. If I "fall" the important thing is not that I'd be hurt; it's only that I want to hold on and hide for as long as I can before I "settle" for/ "settle down" to (?) my place as a woman.

Symmetry

With sequence and similarity in mind, the next step is to look for symmetry, that is, those juxtaposed stories that illustrate the antithetical frame of reference. In Janice's case, we found the following:

Containment vs. Absence of limits or form ("wildness"). The car and pool memories, and the snake and intercourse memories provide this.

Hidden vs. Exposed. I can be hidden by taking my place apart, in the child's position (car); below, in the woman's world (basement); by my secret actions in the dark (snake); and by my disguising myself so that no one knows whether I'm a man or a woman (ghost). Either that, or I am exposed in the daylight of the man's world, where my subordination and weakness can be seen (submitting to Santa Claus, posing for the photo).

The man's world vs. The woman's world. The women are below, along for the ride, objects of masculine admiration and desire, and receive presents in exchange for submission (sex), constraint (ornamentation), and service (laundry). The men are above, in charge, wildly exciting, unyielding, frightening, and (if the woman gives in) benign.

The game of life vs. Engagement with life. It's exciting to stay in hiding (car), to keep myself in the dark (basement), and even to make believe that nobody knows what I'm up to (Halloween). Anything else threatens to expose me, a pretender (roof) or a blunderer (snake), as posing (Thanksgiving).

Dictating "The Pattern of Basic Convictions"

Now, on the basis of the original review and interpretations, the second review, and an examination of the entire set of early recollections with reference to sequence, similarity, and symmetry, we are ready to dictate a summary of Janice's basic convictions. Notice that this summary is a first person singular statement, as if Janice herself were speaking. It is dictated in her presence by the second therapist to the first therapist.

The Case of Janice

ER SUMMARY: THE PATTERN OF BASIC CONVICTIONS

I am part of things and apart from things, happy to be carried along in the stream of life, and able to observe and to listen from the security of my privacy.

When I try to act on my own, I blunder into the discovery of the energies that only men know how to handle. These energies are fascinating but frightening, because they seem so uncontrollable to me.

Feminine things are still and mysterious. We women are in on them together, without having to talk about it. It doesn't help for a woman to resist the imperatives of masculine power, however, and I know that my peace comes through yielding to it, however strange it may seem to me at first.

All the same, there is something disturbing about the inevitability of the submission that is required of a woman in her life with a man. I make a show of resistance to it, and I pretend that I can take my place as "one of the boys."

It is easier for me to be a woman with a man when he also keeps his distance and doesn't try to see beyond my appearances. I am happy that my soul is my own, and that I can keep my desires hidden from the scrutiny of others. I only wonder how much longer I can hold on to my position and maintain my pretenses, before I am discovered and exposed as a woman who has overreached and disgraced herself by trying to act like a man.

Client Reactions

After the dictation and recording of "The Pattern of Basic Convictions," the therapists ask the client for any reactions to the work. Having taken part in the entire discussion of the early recollections, and having assisted in formulating the conclusions reached, the client is usually in accord with the summary, even though the therapists may need to clarify some phrases or make some stylistic changes. Frequently the client is startled at hearing the dictation. Having one's own most fundamental and unconsciously held attitudes and convictions put into a focused and coherent statement is a powerful (and uncommon) experience of being understood. If we attain to our goal of "a real explanation...so clear that the patient knows and feels his own experience instantly" (Adler, p. 335), we may expect to see some form of the recognition reflex: Clients may respond with expressions of profound relief, sometimes in a sigh, a sucking in of the breath, an exclamation, or a free, unembarrassed flow of tears. It is wise to allow time for this. An experience this far out of the ordinary can be disorienting; the client's efforts to maintain composure, if there is no invitation to react freely, will block the ability to attend to anything else.

Factors to Consider in Composing "The Interfering Ideas"

> We want to establish the context [of the error] and make it clear to [the client]. We want to convince him to the point where he cannot take a further step without the conviction [that this is an error].... If he actually recognizes his error -- if he understands the connection and persists in his attitude despite the harmfulness involved -- we can only say that he has not understood everything.... *Really* to recognize an error and then not to modify it runs counter to human nature; it is opposed to the principle of the preservation of life.
>
> (Adler, 1963, p. 3)

After the brief exchange inviting, allowing, and responding to the client's feelings, the therapist states the final summary, called "The Interfering Ideas." This can be introduced with a comment such as, "Now let's see if we can isolate a few of the ideas that are likely to be contributing to your difficulties. Ready? Number One..."

What follows is an unusual procedure. Everyone knows how discouraging it is to be criticized, and how little we are prepared to learn from people who assault us with statements beginning, "The trouble with you is...." How then can the therapist hope to identify the client's errors in a convincing, and encouraging, way? How can we say, "Some of your ideas -- the ones that appear to be expressed in the movement of your life until now -- are mistaken"? How can we know that *we* are not mistaken when we say it? The answer lies with the client, with whom we are not engaged in an argument to discover which of us is right, but with whom we are working to find a better understanding. We are not out to gain assent to our position; we want to awaken a recognition of the errors in the client, who can then see that there is a way open to a new position.

We try to remember that the errors are in the person's movement, in his or her "step" or "attitude," to take Adler's terms from the paragraph quoted above. The ideas we are referring to here are not in the client's thoughts somewhere, conscious or unconscious (although they may be logically implied by some of those thoughts). The interfering ideas are therefore more properly understood as artifacts created by the therapist and introduced into the client's thoughts, to bring the meaning of the client's movement into clear awareness. We remind the reader of "Edward," in the first case presented in this book (Chapter 2, pp. 15-18), and our observations there about the arrangement made to safeguard self-esteem. Our argument was that the private sense, being antisocial, cannot be put directly into words and cannot be expressed clearly in language because language itself is a common creation, intended for the expression of a common sense. Private sense and language are therefore incompatible; to keep a private sense of movement from being exposed as antisocial, it must be kept unspeakable and so, also, unthinkable, in the pain and constriction of the psycho-muddle we spoke of toward the beginning of this book (p. 20).

To state the interfering ideas is, therefore, to confound the logic of the arrangement, and to speak *as if* the private sense could be stated in the common language. It is to frame statements that would have to be true (and clearly, to the common sense, cannot be) for a person's behavior to be intelligent and appropriate. Now, in the course of the psycho-clarity process, and with the client's collaboration, we have introduced these statements into our conversation in such a way as to reveal their impossibility and absurdity. Discouraged people are innocent of the implications of their quests for positions of personal superiority. In one way or another, it is as if we are confronting the client's demand that, in order for him or her to be free to fulfill a private goal of personal superiority, everyone else is required to be satisfied with inferior positions by comparison. We are speaking about the unspeakable; the unthinkable can now be thought of for what it is.

The therapist is, of course, a fellow human being, also with a schema of apperception that is not without biases. This is why it is absolutely essential for us as therapists to be aware, as much as possible, of our own recurring biases and the errors to which we are prone. Everyone who works as a therapist should have had the experience of being in therapy, and everyone who aspires to assess the life-styles of others should collaborate with someone already experienced in this work for a thorough, convincing, and detailed Life-Style Assessment of his or her own.

Furthermore, no one should work alone with a client. The intensity and intimacy of understanding that can be achieved through a successful Life-Style Assessment occasions opportunities for self-aggrandizing behavior on both sides of the transaction. Every therapist works better, more honestly, and more clearly for the client's benefit when there is a co-therapist sharing the task. Failing the availability of a co-therapist, we recommend that you seek out a senior colleague for regular case consultation.

Assuming that these conditions are met, we must still consider the theoretical question of how one error-prone human being can identify errors in the movement of another. Individual Psychology approaches this task by asking where there is a departure from *social usefulness* in the particular conviction that would have to be correct for the person's movement to make sense. Adler's concept of the *Gemeinschaftsgefühl* provides the frame of reference. As we have stated elsewhere (1984):

> This term refers to the individual's awareness of belonging to the human community and the extent of his or her sense of being a fellow being. Social interest...can be thought of as an index to successful adaptation: The more developed the social interest, the more diminished the individual's feelings of inferiority, alienation, and isolation (p. 7).

Gemeinschaftsgefühl is, therefore, not only a *feeling*; as Adler said, "it is an evaluative attitude toward life" (p. 135). Because of the importance of this concept, we will take some time here to expand upon it.

Social interest is the awareness of being one among others with an equal share of responsibility for shaping the common life. It has these characteristics:

1. It is an inherent potential of human life.

2. It is culturally and individually developed, as the capacity for speech is developed in the course of acquiring a language.

3. It is an evaluation of self, others, and the whole of life, indicating the extent of interest in the human community, its inheritance from the past, its present situation, and its survival into the future.

4. It is manifested in cooperation and in identification with others.

5. In the development of our common life it inspires participation in conformity to useful custom, with good humor; in resistance to injustice, with courage; and in rebellion against exploitation, with resolve.

6. It is therefore an index to successful adaptation.

"The Interfering Ideas" is a summary statement of convictions that fail to fit the requirements of life, but would have to be present to account for and make a client's misdirected movement intelligent -- and intelligible.

We can identify these distorted private truths as biases in the antithetical mode of apperception. These are the exaggerated and exclusive either/or ideas in a person's apperceptive schema, reflecting "the primitive attempts of the child to orient himself in the world and to safeguard himself" (Adler, p. 249).

The following list of antithetical categories (such as you may state to express the convictions necessary for a client's erroneous movement) is a small sample of the kind of thinking that life (in all its shading and ambiguity) eludes. These are not to be confused with so-called polarities or polar extremes. The client does not move as if either of the two positions were on a continuum of possibilities, but instead as if they were opposed to one another, and so to be framed: *Either* I am/people are __________, *or* I am/people are __________.

masculine - feminine
above - below
good - bad
right - wrong
perfect - worthless
indulged - victimized
heroic - cowardly
competent - blundering
safe - exposed
optimistic - negative
comfortable - wretched
accommodated - rejected
enduring - defaulting
impressive - disregarded
respected - insulted
dominant - submissive

fair - despotic
selfless - selfish
cooperative - obstructive
controlling - humiliated
uncommitted - trapped
loving - hateful
aggressive - contemptible
cynical - gullible
assertive - considerate
faultless - corrupt
managing - exploited
predictable - flighty
rational - emotional
ruthless - weak
conforming - maverick
glamorous - repulsive

In every case, no matter what form the antithetical reasoning takes, fictions relating to security, power, and superiority (often including masculinity) are attached to one side, while total, intolerable loss of these things (with femininity) is attached to the other. To be human is to be able to extend the idea of death to anything symbolic of loss of status. "I'd rather die than have to do something like that!" "He's murdering me with his sarcasm!" "She'll kill me if she finds out!" These expressions are more than hyperbole. The social embeddedness of individual life is complete; there is no life for us that does not depend on our capacity to live among others. Our status among others can therefore be experienced as a matter of ultimate significance.

Consequently, the antitheses show the ways in which the great line of life, the line of striving from below to above, is traced -- or missed -- in an endless variety of individual fictions. In enumerating the interfering ideas we are asking our clients to recognize that, in creating the unique fictions on which their styles rest, they have gone beyond what is reasonable and socially useful to exaggerations and distortions that are damaging to them as well as others. They have imposed requirements on their lives that life does not impose; they have set terms and conditions upon their readiness to live among others that the others are unable to meet.

Composing "The Interfering Ideas"

In Janice's movement, as revealed in her early recollections, we noted exaggerated ideas about the constituent characters of masculinity and femininity; about social positions above and below; about the presumed danger of being exposed; and about fears of blundering and letting loose "forces" she is unable to control.

It was our task to put these ideas into clear statements of fact, in common language from the standpoint of a common sense. To do this requires a certain artistic abstraction of the ideas from the muddle of their unarticulated place in her images. We want to show her that those images imply impossibilities, that they are in fact caricatures of the truth.

One more thing is required, if we are to succeed in this: We must, to borrow one of Adler's homelier metaphors, "besmirch a clean conscience." It is not enough to show her how she suffers as a result of her errors. She knows better than we that this is true; this is what brought her to see us. Of course she wants to be relieved of pain. What she cannot see is the place that pain plays in an arrangement she has created, and the trouble it causes for others. In every departure from the genuine requirements of cooperative social living there is an antisocial element. It is this that needs to be exposed, so that the innocence of her suffering can be replaced by a responsibility for her share in shaping our common life.

The Case of Janice

ER SUMMARY: THE INTERFERING IDEAS

1. She has an exaggerated idea about the value or the importance of keeping her thoughts and feelings hidden and private, as if she were fearful of taking responsibility for her own life.

2. Her ideas about masculine and feminine are confused with exaggerated notions about energy and passivity. Men act; women endure. Men dominate; women are subdued. Therefore, men are subject to criticism; women are free to criticize.

3. She has some idea that she is capable of acting recklessly and thereby of provoking or loosing forces, presumably masculine, beyond her control. She therefore believes that she cannot be straightforward in her dealings with men, and feels safe only when she is striking poses with them.

4. As a further consequence of her notions about masculine and feminine, she has some idea that she has succeeded in "rising above" her proper destiny as a woman by means of her professional achievements, and she has a matching apprehension that she won't be able to hang on to this position. In this way she privately transforms her accomplishments into superhuman (or at least super-feminine!) heroism.

After The Interfering Ideas have been worked out and written down in the presence of the client, we again ask for a reaction to the work. Assent to the ideas is almost always expressed; opposition to any of the conclusions is rare. Sometimes people say, "I don't get it." We have to be prepared to respond, "We may be wrong. This is only the way it looks to us on the basis of everything we've talked about so far." Unless we can find a word or phrase that is more readily recognized by the client, we ask only that he or she think it over until our next meeting, with an assurance that we have recorded nothing more than a working hypothesis for further discussion.

Conclusion to the Life-Style Assessment

With the recording of The Interfering Ideas, we complete another phase of the Life-Style Assessment. In our practice, there are three more steps: A session with one of the therapists, devoted to reviewing the typescripts of the three summaries; a review of the audiotape of the Initial Interview (which the client does alone); and a final evaluation session with both therapists.

After the summaries are typed, the client and first therapist meet to discuss them together. They first address the client's thoughts and feelings following out of the previous session (when the early recollections summaries were presented). The client is then asked to read each summary aloud, one statement at a time, pausing at any point to react (for example, by asking for explanations of ideas that are not understood, by raising questions, or by affirming recognition and agreement).

Reading the summaries aloud is an important exercise. It moves the new way of looking at things one step further from being an imposition of the therapist toward being a work wrought by the client. With each assent to the statements made in the summaries, the client is claiming the story as autobiography and acknowledging a new orientation as authentic. Each difficulty the client has in recognizing what is meant by a statement opens the way to further discussion, to reminders of what was said in earlier meetings, and to a finer and more precise focus of clarity.

During the reading and discussion the therapist makes notes of issues raised, adding them as footnotes on one of the photocopies of the transcript. The client retains the original typescripts.

As soon after this meeting as is convenient, and sometimes immediately following it, the client reviews the Initial Interview audiotape. Clients in our practice, in which all sessions are taped and available for review, expect this process as part of the Assessment. We ask them to listen to the audiotape with their life-style summaries in hand for reference, and suggest that they take notes for later discussion if they wish. They ask, "What am I supposed to get out of this?" We tell them that we cannot predict what they will get out of it, and that we have no particular expectations. We also tell them that people take different things out of the experience, and that they find it useful and encouraging. After this audiotape review is completed, one of the therapists talks over the experience briefly with the client, and confirms the appointment for the next meeting.

The audiotape review is a successful innovation in Life-Style Assessment. Clients come to their first session in the office with complaints about themselves and about life. By the time of their review of the audiotape of that session they have fully explored their histories, basic beliefs, and previous rehearsals of character. Now, with this exploration and the summaries fresh in mind, they listen to themselves telling their original story. It begins to make sense to them, as it did to us, how they came to have that problem, those difficulties. They begin to see what others did as responses to what they were doing, and they begin to see what else is open to them in their situation. This is the operation of the psycho-clarity process.

The final session of the Life-Style Assessment includes the client and both therapists. It is the time to review and consolidate learning, to critique the experience, and to make plans for future work together, if that is called for.

In the final session the client reports on further reactions to the summaries and the review of the audiotape. The first therapist presents the notes taken during the reading of the life-style summaries.

Any issues that may have come up since are discussed. (These will sometimes relate to the client's having shown the summaries to family members, who may have added information or raised new questions.)

After this discussion, the client, reminded that this is the last session in the Life-Style Assessment, is asked to reflect on and to evaluate the experience and its outcomes. Finally, in the light of this evaluation, the client and therapists weigh the options for further therapy. Sometimes, as Dreikurs observed, completion of the Life-Style Assessment brings therapy to an end (1967, p. 24):

> There are patients who are so shaken by the mere disclosure of their "arrangements," by the recognition of their accustomed goals, by the discovery of their [own] control of their future deviation and mistakes, that this experience alone furnishes the momentum for successful conclusion of the cure.

In other cases, the client elects to build upon what has been accomplished, and in this final Assessment session decides which of the two therapists to work with as the principal counselor, and which will function as consultant, attending sessions from time to time (typically, each fourth or fifth session) in order to maintain the advantages of multiple therapy.

What happens in the psycho-clarity process after this? That is a subject for another book. Whatever else that other book may have to offer, we believe that in concluding this one we can do no better than to quote Adler's way of summing the matter up:

> From the very beginning the consultant must try to make it clear that the responsibility for his cure is the patient's business.... The adviser can only point out the mistakes; it is the patient who must make the truth living (p. 336).

APPENDIX: THE INDIVIDUAL PSYCHOLOGY CLIENT WORKBOOK

TABLE OF CONTENTS

RELEASE

I hereby consent that ______________________________
Name of Practice, Partnership, Corporation
and any persons authorized by ______________________________
may make or use for any educational purpose reproductions of my voice and of any written and oral statements which I have given or furnished to the foregoing in connection with any services which I have received or will receive from the foregoing and all authorized persons thereof and I for myself, heirs, legal representatives and executors forever release and discharge the said ________________ and all persons working for or with them from any claims, demands, causes of action, whether in law or in equity, which may arise out of such use and further agree to indemnify and hold harmless the foregoing from any and all costs, expenses, liabilities and indebtedness, including reasonable attorney's fees, directly or indirectly connected therewith.

DATED this_____________ day of______________, 19___.

____
(Signature)

BILLING AGREEMENT

____

____

____

DATED this_____________ day of______________, 19___.

____
(Signature)

General Diagnosis

INITIAL INTERVIEW

The Life Situation (Items 1 - 20)

1. Date________________________ 2. Present Age__________

3. Date of Birth_________

4. Name, address, home phone; maiden name; full name of spouse:

5. Occupation, position, address, work phone; occupation of spouse:

6. Preferred phone and mailing address (home or work):

7. Marital status (age of spouse, how long married, anniversary, previous marriages of both spouses; or, current love relationship, how long, level of relationship):

8. Children (names, ages, sex; deceased children and other pregnancies; adoptions, difficulties of conception; from other marriages):

9. Level of education; military service; religion:

10. Parents (intact marriage, divorced, or separated; remarriages of parents; if parent deceased, date and cause; CL's age at time of any family disruption; parents' current life situation and state of health; other adults present in pre-adolescent household):

11. Siblings (list by first names from oldest to youngest, placing CL, deceased siblings, and Mother's other known pregnancies in their ordinal positions; using CL's age as a baseline, note the difference in years between CL and siblings; in parallel column note step-siblings and CL's age when they entered the family; note present whereabouts and occupations of all siblings):

12. When you were a child, if anything could have been different, what would you have wanted it to be?

The Life Situation (conclusion)

13. Are you currently under a physician's care? What for? (Note type of problem; if the "presenting problem" which brought CL in to see you is a physical symptom, see Item 21; note signs):

14. Are you taking medication? (purpose, name, dosage, how long, effects and side effects):

15. Date of last physical examination:

16. Name, address, and specialty of physician(s) being consulted, if any:

17. General health (energy level; appetite; sleep; exercise; level of sexual activity; use of alcohol and drugs, including "recreational drugs"; tobacco; caffeine; note physical signs):

18. Previous counseling or therapy (when, reason, type, with whom, how long, outcome):

19. Referral source:

20. Emergency contact (name, address, phone, relationship):

The Presenting Problem (Items 21 - 28)

21. What brought you in to see us? If a physical symptom, describe location, sensations, intensity, frequency.

22. When did it start? What else was going on in your life at that time?

23. Have you noticed a pattern?

24. What happens as a consequence of having this problem? Who is most affected by it?

The Presenting Problem (conclusion)

25. What have you done about it until now?

26. How do you explain this situation to yourself?

27. How would your life be different if you did not have this problem?

28. What do you expect will come out of our work together?

NOTE: If the presenting problem reveals an acute difficulty requiring immediate counseling, defer the remainder of the Initial Interview Inquiry (The Life Tasks) until a subsequent session.

The Life Tasks (Items 29 - 34)

LOVE

29. Situation. Tell me about your love relationships. (If CL lacks relationships of emotional or sexual closeness, ask: How do you account for this?)

Key prompting questions: What makes a man a "masculine" man to you? What makes a woman a "feminine" woman? How do you compare yourself to your list of associations for your own sex? Do you experience difficulty in expressing love and affection for others? Difficulty in receiving such expressions from others? What does your partner complain about in you? What do you complain about in your partner? Describe your first encounter with your partner. What was there about him or her that impressed you at that time?

30. Goals. What do you want to improve or change in this area of your life?

WORK

31. Situation. Tell me about your work. (If CL has no occupation or is currently unemployed, ask: How do you account for this? Explore interests and ambitions in this area.)

    Key prompting questions: What has been most satisfying to you in the jobs you have held? Least satisfying? What other work have you done? Why have you left those jobs? Are you aware of anything about the way you work that causes trouble for you (e.g., procrastination)? Do you feel appreciated at work? How do you evaluate your relationships with others at these levels: superiors, peers, subordinates? Members of the other sex?

32. Goals. What do you want to improve or change in this area of your life?

FRIENDSHIP AND COMMUNITY

33. Situation. Tell me about your friends and your life in the community. (If CL reports few or no connections with others, ask: How do you account for this?)

Key prompting questions: From where do you draw your friends? How many close friends do you have? How often are you together? What do you do? Do you have friends of the other sex? How do your friendships end? How much do you feel you are able to confide in your friends? What sort of impression do you think you make on people the first time they meet you? Does this impression change over time? If I were to call one of your close friends and ask, "What do you value in (CL)?", what would he or she say? What kind of connections do you have in your community?

34. Goals. What do you want to improve or change in this area of your life?

Date______________________

SUMMARY OF IMPRESSIONS DERIVED FROM THE INITIAL INTERVIEW

The second therapist (ST) dictates the Summary of Impressions Derived from the Initial Interview to the first therapist (FT) in the presence of CL at the conclusion of the review and interpretations of the Initial Interview.

Special Diagnosis

LIFE-STYLE ASSESSMENT

CL's present age________ Date________________________

Family Constellation, Part I: Parents, Other Adults, Milieu

1. Father's name____________________ Occupation____________________

   Age at CL's birth______ Age, if living______ Or, at death_______

   Yr & cause of death____________________ CL's age at death______

2. What kind of a man was your father when you were a child, up to age 10 or 11, in the pre-school and grammar school years? Consider activities, personality, health, level of education, and values (i.e., what was important to Father):

3. How did he relate to you and the other children?

   Favorite child:

   Discipline and how you felt about it:

   Expectations regarding your behavior and achievement:

4. How do you see yourself now as like Father? Unlike Father?

5. Tell me briefly about Father's background and family of origin.

6. Mother's name____________________ Occupation____________________

Age at CL's birth______ Age, if living______ Or, at death_______

Yr & cause of death____________________ CL's age at death______

7. What kind of woman was your mother when you were a child, up to age 10 or 11, in the pre-school and grammar school years? Consider activities, personality, health, level of education, and values (i.e., what was important to Mother):

8. How did she relate to you and the other children?

Favorite child:

Discipline and how you felt about it:

Expectations regarding your behavior and achievement:

9. How do you see yourself now as like Mother? Unlike Mother?

10. Tell me briefly about Mother's background and family of origin.

11. Parents' relationship. Tell me about how your parents got along with each other when you were a child. (Were they affectionate? Was one of them "the boss"? If they argued, what about? Who seemed to initiate the trouble, and what was the outcome? Did you takes sides, openly or covertly? How did you feel about the trouble? Did you feel sorry for one of them?)

12. Other significant adults. Tell me about any other adults who were important to you when you were a child. (If not already clear: Describe the character and role of any other adults living in the pre-adolescent household. Describe other adults who impressed you as a child, either positively or negatively.)

13. Family milieu. If not already clear, inquire into: Socio-economic, ethnic, religious, and cultural characteristics of the family and into the family's standards and values.

Date ______________________

Family Constellation, Part II: The Situation of the Child

Sibling Array

Using the following page, array the names of the siblings from oldest to youngest, across the page from left to right. Include CL, and any siblings deceased, or separated from the family and living in institutions or elsewhere. Also note Mother's other known pregnancies terminated by abortion, miscarriage, or still-birth, entering them in the appropriate ordinal positions. Using CL's age as baseline, note the difference in years, plus or minus, between each of them and CL. Include step-siblings, and note CL's age at the time they entered the family. Use the following items to guide the discussion with CL, placing appropriate information in the boxes on the following page.

14. What kind of children were you? Describe each of the children, beginning with yourself, with respect to personality, health, and activities.

15. Note any subgroupings among the children: Who played with whom; who fought and argued with whom; who looked after and took care of whom; who taught and guided whom.

16. Note how each of the children distinguished himself or herself from the others; for example, by taking the place of the one who was:

academic	the problem child
athletic	religious
artistic	socially successful
entrepreneurial	handicapped
the good child	sickly

17. If any of the children was handicapped or sickly, note the child's and family's attitudes toward the difficulty.

18. Which sibling were you most like? Least like? In what ways?

19. To what extent did each of the children accept, reject, or modify the family's standards and values?

20. Childhood chronology. If not already clear, note any changes in the course of CL's childhood and adolescent development experienced by CL as major events or turning points (e.g., divorce, a move to another community), and CL's age at those times.

SIBLING ARRAY

21. What were your favorite stories, TV shows, fictitious or historical characters? What was there about them that you liked?

22. Did you daydream? What about?

23. Do you remember any night dreams? Describe. How did you feel when you woke up?

24. Did you have any particular fears as a child? How did others respond?

25. Was food and eating an issue in the household? In what way?

26. What were you good at? What did you most enjoy?

27. Was there anything you did not enjoy? Anything that was particularly hard for you?

28. Did you experience difficulty in your mental or emotional development? How was this addressed in the family? In school? How did you feel about it?

29. Think back to your early years, up to age 6 or 7. What did you want to be when you grew up? What was there about that that appealed to you? How and when did this change?

Family Constellation: The Situation of the Child (conclusion)

30. Describe how you got along in the world of the neighborhood. How would you characterize your role among the children (e.g., leader, follower, jester, outsider, etc.)? Did you have friends of the other sex?

31. Describe how you got along in the world of the school. Was your role in this setting different from your role in the neighborhood? If so, in what ways, and how do you account for it? Did you have friends of the other sex? How did you get along with teachers? What were your favorite and least favorite subjects, and what was there about them that you liked or disliked?

32. Describe your bodily development in childhood, and how you felt about it. How did it compare with that of your peers? Consider height, weight, strength, speed, coordination, vision, hearing, anomalies. Did you have any special difficulties (e.g., bed wetting)?

33. Describe your sexual development, and your sexual experience and initiation. How did you learn about sex? How did you feel about the bodily changes that took place at puberty? (Females: How old were you at the menarche? Describe what happened. Did you understand what was happening? How did you feel about it?) Describe your experience as a sexual person during adolescence and young adulthood, and your evaluation of yourself at that time.

Date_______________________

SUMMARY OF THE FAMILY CONSTELLATION

ST dictates the Summary of the Family Constellation to FT in the presence of CL at the conclusion of the review and interpretations of the family material.

Summary of the Family Constellation (continued)

Date________________________

Record of the Early Recollections

Ask for CL's Early Childhood Recollections (ERs). After recording the account of the recollection, narrow its range to the moment most vividly recalled, as if in a snapshot capturing a moment in the action, and ask how CL felt at that moment.

Prompting questions: How far back can you remember? What is the first incident or moment you remember in your life? Tell me about it. How old were you at the time? What is the most vivid moment in the action of the story? How did you feel in that moment?

Note that the first ER to be recorded is to be the first incident of memory. ERs recorded after the first need not be in chronological order. After recording the first ER, ask, "What is the next thing you are able to recall from before age 9 or 10?" Or, "What comes up next from your childhood before age 9 or 10?"

---

1. Age______

Most vivid moment:

Feeling:

---

2. Age______

Most vivid moment:

Feeling:

Record of the Early Recollections (continued)

3. Age______

Most vivid moment:

Feeling:

4. Age______

Most vivid moment:

Feeling:

5. Age______

Most vivid moment:

Feeling:

6. Age______

Most vivid moment:

Feeling:

Record of the Early Recollections (conclusion)

---

7. Age_____

Most vivid moment:

Feeling:

---

8. Age_____

Most vivid moment:

Feeling:

After recording eight ERs, ask CL if there is any other recollection that is important to him or her that has not been recorded in the Life-Style Inquiry to this point. If another ER is forthcoming, record it here:

Age_____

Most vivid moment:

Feeling:

Date____________________________

ER SUMMARY: THE PATTERN OF BASIC CONVICTIONS

ST dictates the summary of the Pattern of Basic Convictions to FT in the presence of CL at the conclusion of the review and interpretations of the ERs.

Date______________________________

ER SUMMARY: THE INTERFERING IDEAS

This summary is also dictated in the presence of CL, immediately after the presentation of The Pattern of Basic Convictions.

PROGRESS NOTES

Session No.____ Summary Date __________

Session No.____ Summary Date __________

Session No.____ Summary Date __________

Date__________________________

INTERIM ASSESSMENT OR TERMINATION INTERVIEW: THE SECOND SET OF EARLY RECOLLECTIONS

Unprompted Recollections

Without reference to the original set of Early Recollections, follow the same procedure to obtain a second unprompted set.

---

1. Age______

Most vivid moment:

Feeling:

---

2. Age______

Most vivid moment:

Feeling:

---

3. Age______

Most vivid moment:

Feeling:

4. Age______

Most vivid moment:

Feeling:

5. Age______

Most vivid moment:

Feeling:

6. Age______

Most vivid moment:

Feeling:

7. Age______

Most vivid moment:

Feeling:

Unprompted Recollections (conclusion)

8. Age_____

Most vivid moment:

Feeling:

Prompted Recollections

Remind CL by a word or phrase of any stories from the original record of recollections (pages 19-21) which have not, so far, been retold in this second set. Record the current version below in the numbered space which corresponds with that of the original report.

1. Age_____

Most vivid moment:

Feeling:

2. Age_____

Most vivid moment:

Feeling:

Prompted Recollections (continued)

---

3. Age______

Most vivid moment:

Feeling:

---

4. Age______

Most vivid moment:

Feeling:

---

5. Age______

Most vivid moment:

Feeling:

---

6. Age______

Most vivid moment:

Feeling:

Prompted Recollections (conclusion)

7. Age_____

Most vivid moment:

Feeling:

8. Age_____

Most vivid moment:

Feeling:

Date______________________

SHIFTS IN THE PATTERN OF BASIC CONVICTIONS

ST dictates the summary of the Shifts in the Pattern of Basic Convictions to FT in the presence of CL at the conclusion of the review and interpretations of the Second Set of Early Recollections.

Note shifts in attitude, emphasis, and outcome revealed in each story, being attentive to any differences in the language employed by CL, in the inclusion of fresh detail, and in the feelings and impressions reported.

REFERENCES

Adler, A. *Cooperation between the sexes: Writings on women and men, love and marriage, and sexuality.* H. L. Ansbacher & R. R. Ansbacher, Eds. New York: Norton, 1982. (Originally published, 1978.)

Adler, A. *The education of children.* Chicago: Henry Regnery, 1970. (Originally published, 1930.)

Adler, A. *The Individual Psychology of Alfred Adler.* H. L. Ansbacher & R. R. Ansbacher, Eds. New York: Harper and Row, 1964. (Originally published, 1956.)

Adler, A. *The problem child.* New York: Capricorn, 1963. (Originally Published, 1930.)

Adler, A. *Superiority and social interest* (3rd Rev. ed.). H. L. Ansbacher and R. R. Ansbacher, Eds. New York: Norton, 1979. (Originally published, 1964.)

Adler, A. *What life should mean to you.* New York: Perigee, 1980. (Originally published, 1931.)

Ahlstrom, S. *A religious history of the American People.* New Haven: Yale, 1972.

Allen, T. (Producer). *Rudolf Dreikurs: Individual Psychology counseling and education* (Part I). Alexandria, VA: American Association for Counseling and Development, 1969. (Film)

Bartlett, J. *Familiar quotations* (14th Rev. ed.). E. Beck & M. Rackliffe, Eds. Boston: Little, Brown, 1968.

Baruth, L., & Eckstein, D. *Life style: Theory, practice, and research.* Dubuque, IA: Kendall-Hunt, 1981.

Belove, L. First encounters of the close kind. *Journal of Individual Psychology,* 1980, 36 (2), 191-208.

Dinkmeyer, D., Sr., Dinkmeyer, D., Jr., & Sperry, L. *Adlerian counseling and psychotherapy* (2nd ed.). Columbus, OH: Charles Merrill, 1987.

Dreikurs, R. *Psychodynamics, psychotherapy, and counseling* (Rev. ed.). Chicago: Alfred Adler Institute, 1973. (Originally published, 1967.)

Dreikurs, R. (with Vicki Soltz). *Children: The challenge.* New York: Hawthorn, 1964.

Dreikurs, R., Mosak, H. H., & Shulman, B. H. Patient-therapist relationship in multiple psychotherapy, I and II. *Psychiatric Quarterly*, 1952, 26, 219-227; 590-596. Also in R. Dreikurs (Ed.), *Group psychotherapy and group approaches*. Chicago: Alfred Adler Institute, 1960.

Eckstein, D., Baruth, L., & Mahrer, D. *Life style* (2nd ed.). Dubuque, IA: Kendall-Hunt, 1982. (Originally published, 1975.)

Eliade, M. *Cosmos and history*. New York: Harper and Row, 1959. (Originally published, 1954.)

Ellenberger, H. *The discovery of the unconscious*. New York: Basic Books/Harper Colophon, 1970.

Griffith, J. Organ jargon. *Individual Psychology: The Journal of Adlerian Theory, Research & Practice*, 1984, 40 (4), 437-444.

Griffith, J., & Powers, R. L. *An Adlerian lexicon: Fifty-nine terms associated with the Individual Psychology of Alfred Adler*. Chicago: AIAS, Ltd., 1984.

Mosak, H. H. Early recollections as a projective technique. *Journal of Projective Techniques*, 1958, 22, 302-311.

Mosak, H. H., & Shulman, B. H. *The life style inventory*. Chicago: Alfred Adler Institute, 1971.

Powers, R. L. Myth and memory. In H. H. Mosak (Ed.), *Alfred Adler: His influence on psychology today*. Park Ridge, NJ: Noyes, 1973.

Powers, R. L. Unpublished lecture presented at the Alfred Adler Institute of Chicago, 1979.

Powers, R. L., & Griffith, J. The big numbers. *Individual Psychology Reporter*, 1986, 4 (3).

Powers, R. L., & Griffith, J. Psycho-clarity. *Individual Psychology Reporter*, 1982, 1 (1).

Powers, R. L., & Griffith, J. *The Individual Psychology client workbook*. Chicago: AIAS, Ltd., 1986.

Shulman, B. H. *Contributions to Individual Psychology*. Chicago: Alfred Adler Institute, 1973.

Untermeyer, L. (Ed.), *Modern American poetry/Modern British poetry* (Combined 5th and 6th eds.). New York: Harcourt, Brace, 1942.

Winthrop, H. Scientism in psychology. *Journal of Individual Psychology*, 1959, 15, 112-120.

INDEX

D

E

ABOUT THE AUTHORS

Jane Griffith and Robert L. Powers are husband and wife, and co-authors of *An Adlerian Lexicon: Fifty-nine Terms Associated with the Individual Psychology of Alfred Adler* and *The Individual Psychology Client Workbook*.

They are founders and officers of The Americas Institute of Adlerian Studies, Ltd., a teaching, consulting, and publishing company, and are in the private practice of psychology at Adlerian Psychology Associates, P.C., Chicago, Illinois.

Robert L. Powers is a graduate of Capital University (Columbus, Ohio), Yale University, the University of Chicago, and the Alfred Adler Institute of Chicago, where he has been a professor since 1965. He is a past president of the Chicago Psychological Association and the North American Society of Adlerian Psychology, and is on the Council of the International Association of Individual Psychology.

Jane Griffith is a graduate of Hollins College (Roanoke, Virginia), the University of Maine, and the Alfred Adler Institute of Chicago. Before entering the field of professional counseling she was a teacher, college administrator, and the executive director of an educational foundation. She is the Editor of the *Individual Psychology Reporter*, the quarterly publication of AIAS, Ltd.